South Biscay

La Gironde to La Coruña

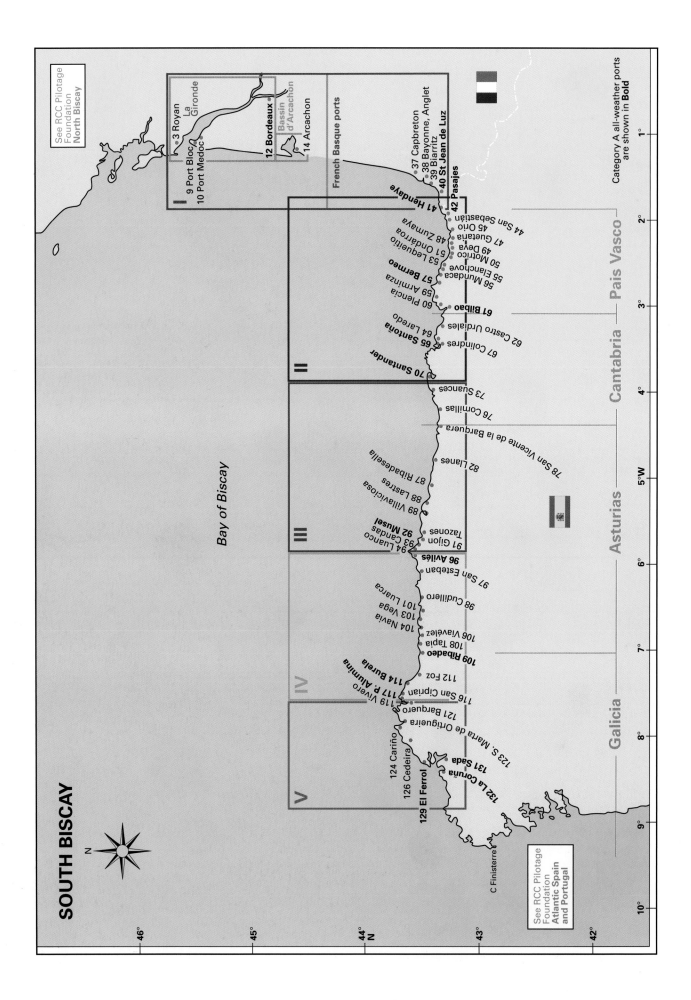

SOUTH BISCAY

Bay of Biscay

See RCC Pilotage Foundation **North Biscay**

3 Royan
La Gironde
9 Port Bloc
10 Port Medoc
12 Bordeaux
Bassin d'Arcachon
14 Arcachon

French Basque ports

37 Capbreton
38 Bayonne, Anglet
39 Biarritz
40 St Jean de Luz
42 Pasajes
41 Hendaye
44 San Sebastián
45 Orio
47 Guetaria
49 Deva
48 Zumaya
50 Motrico
51 Ondárroa
53 Lequeitio
55 Elanchove
56 Mundaca
57 Bermeo
59 Arminza
60 Plencia
61 Bilbao
62 Castro Urdiales
64 Laredo
67 Colindres
65 Santoña
70 Santander
73 Suances
76 Comillas
78 San Vicente de la Barquera
82 Llanes
87 Ribadesella
88 Lastres
89 Villaviciosa
91 Gijon
93 Candás
Tazones
92 Musel
94 Luanco
96 Avilés
97 San Esteban
98 Cudillero
101 Luarca
103 Vega
104 Navia
106 Viavélez
108 Tapia
109 Ribadeo
112 Foz
114 Burela
116 San Cipriàn
117 P. Alumina
119 Vivero
121 Barquero
123 S. Marta de Ortigueira
124 Cariño
126 Cedeira
129 El Ferrol
131 Sada
132 La Coruña
C Finisterre

Galicia · **Asturias** · **Cantabria** · **Pais Vasco**

II
III
IV
V

See RCC Pilotage Foundation **Atlantic Spain and Portugal**

Category A all-weather ports are shown in **Bold**

46° 45° 44° N 43° 42°
10° 9° 8° 7°W 6° 5°W 4° 3° 2° 1°

N

South Biscay

La Gironde to La Coruña

ROYAL CRUISING CLUB
PILOTAGE FOUNDATION

John Lawson

Imray Laurie Norie & Wilson

Published by
Imray Laurie Norie & Wilson Ltd
Wych House The Broadway St Ives
Cambridgeshire PE27 5BT England
☎ +44 (0)1480 462114
Fax +44 (0) 1480 496109
Email ilnw@imray.com
www.imray.com
2006

First edition 1971 (Adlard Coles)
Fifth edition 2000
Sixth edition 2006

ISBN 0 85288 842 2

British Library Cataloguing in Publication Data.
A catalogue record for this title is available from the British
Library.

Printed in Singapore by Star Standard Industries

CORRECTIONAL SUPPLEMENTS

This pilot book may be amended at intervals by the issue of
correctional supplements. These are published on the internet at
our web site www.imray.com and also via www.rccpf.org.uk and
may be downloaded free of charge. Printed copies are also
available on request from the publishers at the above address.
Like this pilot, supplements are selective. Navigators requiring
the latest definitive information are advised to refer to official
hydrographic office data.

CAUTION

Whilst every care has been taken to ensure that the information
contained in this book is accurate, the RCC Pilotage Foundation, the
authors and the publishers hereby formally disclaim any and all
liability for any personal injury, loss and/or damage howsoever
caused, whether by reason of any error, inaccuracy, omission or
ambiguity in relation to the contents and/or information contained
within this book. The book contains selected information and thus is
not definitive. It does not contain all known information on the
subject in hand and should not be relied on alone for navigational
use: it should only be used in conjunction with official hydrographic
data. This is particularly relevant to the plans, which should not be
used for navigation.

The RCC Pilotage Foundation, the authors and publishers believe
that the information which they have included is a useful aid to
prudent navigation, but the safety of a vessel depends ultimately on
the judgment of the skipper, who should assess all information,
published or unpublished.

WAYPOINTS

This edition of the *South Biscay* pilot includes the introduction of
waypoints. The RCC PF consider a waypoint to be a position likely
to be helpful for navigation if entered into some form of electronic
navigation system for use in conjunction with GPS. All waypoints are
given to datum WGS 84 and every effort has been made to ensure
their accuracy. Nevertheless, for each individual vessel, the standard
of onboard equipment, aerial position, datum setting, correct entry of
data and operator skill all play a part in their effectiveness. In
particular it is vital for the navigator to note the datum of the chart
in use and apply the necessary correction if plotting a GPS position
on the chart.

The attention of the navigator is drawn to the Waypoint paragraphs
on pages 6 and 53 of the text.

We emphasise that we regard waypoints as an aid to navigation for
use as the navigator decides. We hope that the waypoints in this pilot
will help ease that navigational load.

POSITIONS
Positions given in the text and on plans are intended purely as an
aid to locating the place in question on the chart.

PLANS
The plans in this guide are not to be used for navigation – they are
designed to support the text and should always be used together
with navigational charts. Every effort has been made to locate
harbour and anchorage plans adjacent to the relevant text.

All bearings are given from seaward and refer to true north. Scales
are indicated on the plans. Symbols are based on those used by the
British Admiralty – users are referred to *Symbols and
Abbreviations (N 5011)*.

Contents

Foreword *vii*
Preface *vii*

The Atlantic coast of France

Cruising on the Atlantic coast of France 1
Technical and navigational information 5

I. La Gironde to Hendaye
Pointe de la Coubre to Cabo Higuer

Planning guide 9
1–13   La Gironde *10*
14–36   Bassin d'Arcachon *28*
37–41   French Basque ports *35*

The north coast of Spain

Cruising on the north Spanish coast 46
Technical and navigational information 53

II. Pasajes to Santander
Cabo Higuer to Cabo Mayor

Planning guide 56
42–55   Pasajes to Elanchove *57*
Lequeitio to Bermeo (Cabo de Santa Catalina to
Cabo Machicaco) *76*
56–70   Mundaca to Santander (Marina del Cantabrico) *78*

III. San Pedro del Mar to Avilés
Cabo Mayor to Cabo Peñas

Planning guide 104
71–96   Ria de San Pedro del Mar to Avilés *105*

IV. San Esteban to Puerto Alumina Española
Cabo Peñas to Punta Roncadoira

Planning guide 138
97–117   San Esteban de Pravia to Puerto Alumina Española *139*

V. Portocelo to La Coruña
Punta Roncadoira to Torre de Hercules

Planning guide 165
118–132 Portocelo to La Coruña *166*

Appendix
1. List of lights *190*
2. Waypoints *195*
3. Charts *196*
4. Glossary *200*
5. Suggested yacht/crew particulars list in Spanish/English *202*

Index *203*

THE RCC PILOTAGE FOUNDATION

In 1976 an American member of the Royal Cruising Club, Dr Fred Ellis, indicated that he wished to make a gift to the Club in memory of his father, the late Robert E Ellis, of his friends Peter Pye and John Ives and as a mark of esteem for Roger Pinckney. An independent charity known as the RCC Pilotage Foundation was formed and Dr Ellis added his house to his already generous gift of money to form the Foundation's permanent endowment. The Foundation's charitable objective is 'to advance the education of the public in the science and practice of navigation', which is at present achieved through the writing and updating of pilot books covering many diffent parts of the world.

The Foundation is extremely grateful and privileged to have been given the copyrights to books written by a number of distinguished authors and yachtsmen including the late Adlard Coles, Robin Brandon and Malcolm Robson. In return the Foundation has willingly accepted the task of keeping the original books up to date and many yachtsmen and women have helped (and are helping) the Foundation fulfil this commitment. In addition to the titles donated to the Foundation, several new books have been created and developed under the auspices of the Foundation. The Foundation works in close collaboration with three publishers – Imray Laurie Norie and Wilson, Adlard Coles Nautical and On Board Publications – and in addition publishes in its own name short run guides and pilot books for areas where limited demand does not justify large print runs. Several of the Foundation's books have been translated into French, German and Italian.

The Foundation runs its own website at www.rccpf.org.uk which not only lists all the publications but also contains free downloadable pilotage information.

The overall management of the Foundation is entrusted to trustees appointed by the Royal Cruising Club, with day-to-day operations being controlled by the Director. All these appointments are unpaid. In line with its charitable status, the Foundation distributes no profits; any surpluses are used to finance new books and developments and to subsidise those covering areas of low demand.

PUBLICATIONS OF THE RCC PILOTAGE FOUNDATION

Imray
The Baltic Sea
Norway
North Brittany and the Channel Islands
Faroe, Iceland and Greenland
Isles of Scilly
The Channel Islands
North Biscay
Atlantic Islands
Atlantic Spain & Portugal
Mediterranean Spain
 Costas del Azahar,
 Dorada & Brava
Mediterranean Spain
 Costas del Sol & Blanca
Islas Baleares
Corsica and North Sardinia
North Africa
Chile

Adlard Coles Nautical
Atlantic Crossing Guide
Pacific Crossing Guide
On Board Publications
South Atlantic Circuit
Havens and Anchorages for the South American Coast
The RCC Pilotage Foundation
RCC PF Website www.rccpf.org.uk
Cruising Guide to West Africa
South Georgia
Supplements
Passage planning guides

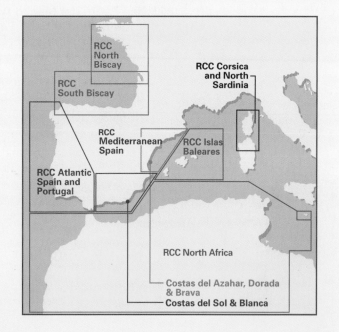

Foreword

The *South Biscay Pilot* was first published in 1971 and was one of many titles given to the Pilotage Foundation by the late Robin Brandon. In 2000, John Lawson used his considerable practical experience to build on the work of his predecessors to produce the fifth edition, and he subsequently maintained a strong hands-on interest in the region as it continued to develop.

The long coastline lying downwind of the Bay of Biscay, and subject to swell, storm and fog, may not appeal to everyone, although, with modern boats and effective weather forecasts, many more yachtsmen are now exploring the area during the summer months. I am grateful to John Lawson who, in this sixth edition of *South Biscay*, has not merely updated the information but has presented it in an easy to follow manner.

Sadly, John Lawson died shortly after clearing the proof of his book. I thank the proof readers – Tony French, Cormac McHenry, Oliver Roome and Sandy Watson – and also Ros Hogbin of the Pilotage Foundation and the team at Imray who have ensured final publication as John would have wished.

We ask that those who sail this coast will pass any updating information or photographs to Imray or to the Pilotage Foundation so we may continue to keep this book up to date via supplements.

Martin Walker
Director
RCC Pilotage Foundation
January 2006

Captain J A F Lawson RN

The RCC Pilotage Foundation has charitable status and relies on yachtsmen to give their time to help in the production of pilot books and other aids to navigation. John Lawson was ideally suited for this. His long career in the Royal Navy, followed by years as skipper of a sail training vessel and a lifetime of sailing his own boat, gave him a deep practical knowledge. His contribution matched his enthusiasm and was considerable. It included authorship of *South Biscay*, *North Brittany and the Channel Islands*, and revision of *The Atlantic Crossing Guide*. He produced an innovative series of Passage Planning Guides, which are available without charge on the RCCPF website, and he continued to pass on his expertise to current yachtsmen right up to the time of his death.

Preface

For those who have sailed these coasts before, little has changed in the French section of *South Biscay* during the five years except for the appearance of a large marina at Port Médoc near the mouth of La Gironde. There are minor changes in La Gironde up to Castets where the inland Canal Latéral de la Garonne may be entered. The Basque ports in the SE corner of the Bay of Biscay have a further addition of a marina at Hondarribia just over the Spanish border.

It is in the 330 miles along the north coast of Spain from here to La Coruña that most additions have occurred, with some 17 marinas or yacht facilities being built. While these ease the berthing problems for yachtsmen in some places, they have not been attended by further building development: the coast remains unspoilt, with hills and mountain ranges backing a rugged coastline of cliffs interspersed with rivers and estuaries rich in wild life. There are still many harbour entrances challenging enough for the most adventurous navigator.

In this edition all pilotage directions appear on the same double page as the plan of the harbour to help those navigating. Waypoints in safe water off the entrances indicate where the change from GPS navigation to pilotage may be made. Coastal waypoints show clear passages offshore along the coast. Positional plans for most harbours show the relative positions of neighbouring harbours as well as the waypoints.

John Lawson
RCC Pilotage Foundation
November 2005

Acknowledgements

Many have contributed in the last five years to the development of this book and have been thanked in the annual supplements, but particular thanks are due to Sue and Robert Evans who have continued to provide much useful information incorporated in this edition. The greatest source of information and changes has come from Peter Taylor and Robin Rundle who carried out a complete reconnaissance of the coast in the autumn of 2004, took many of the photographs that appear and did invaluable work in providing or confirming harbour soundings and local facilities. Gavin and Georgie McLaren also provided valuable hydrographic data as did David and Jill Southwood.

Patrick Roach's outstanding aerial photographs appear throughout the book and give an instant impression of all the harbours and most of the anchorages. My thanks too to Anne Hammick who has supplemented this impressive collection of aerials, as well as to John Davies for photographs and information in La Gironde and to Bob and Lynn Griffiths for last minute amendments. My thanks to the Tourist Boards of Viscaya, Cantabria, Asturias and Galicia for the reproduction of some of their material.

Bon voyage, buen viaje and safe sailing.

John Lawson
November 2005

Key to symbols used on the plans

	English	Spanish
⚓	harbour office	*capitán de puerto/capitanía*
⛽	fuel (diesel, petrol)	*gasoil, gasolina*
(25T)	travel-lift	*pórtico elevado*
⚑	yacht club	*club náutico*
⚓	anchorage	*fondeadero*
Ⓥ	vistors moorings	*amarradero, ancladero*
⌐	slipway	*varadero*

Port categories
A   Port of refuge in storms
A* Qualified storm port of refuge
B   Port accessible in gales
B* Qualified port in gale conditions
C   Entry subject to wind, tide and swell
D   Open anchorage

List of Ports

I. La Gironde to Hendaye
   Pointe de la Coubre to Cabo Higuer

 1 La Gironde approaches
     Grande Passe de l'Ouest
     Passe Sud
     La Gironde plan
     La Gironde, La Garonne, La Dordogne
 2 Bonne Anse
 3 Royan
 4 Meschers
 5 Mortagne
 6 Blaye
 7 Bourg
 8 Cavernes
 9 Port Bloc
10 Port Médoc
11 Pauillac
12 Bordeaux
13 Castets
14 Bassin d'Arcachon
15 Port d'Arcachon
16 Bélisaire
17 Port de la Vigne
18 Port de Piraillan
19 Port le Grand Piquey
20 Claouey
21 Port de Lège
22 Port d'Arès
23 Andernos-les-Bains
24 Port du Bétey
25 Port de Fontainevielle
26 Port de Tassaut
27 Port de Cassy
28 Lanton
29 Port d'Audenge
30 Port du Teich
31 Port de Mestras
32 Port de Larros
33 Port de Gujan
34 Port de Meyran
35 Port de la Hume
36 Port de la Teste
37 Capbreton
38 Bayonne and Anglet marina
39 Biarritz
40 St Jean-de-Luz, Ciboure/Larraldénia,
     Socoa and La Nivelle
41 Baie de Fontarrabie/Fuenterrabia/ Rada
     de Higuer
     Hondarribia marina
     Port Hendaye(Socoburu marina)
     Puerto Gurutzeaundi

II. Pasajes to Santander
   Cabo Higuer to Cabo Mayor

42 Pasajes
43 Río Urumea
44 San Sebastián(Donostia)
45 Río de Orio
46 Zarauz
47 Getaria
48 Zumaia
49 Deva
50 Motrico
51 Ondárroa
52 Ensenada de Saustan
53 Lequeitio
54 Río de Ea
55 Elanchove
     Lequeitio (Cabo de Santa Catalina) to
     Bermeo (Cabo Machicaco)
56 Mundaca
57 Bermeo
58 Ensenada de Bakio
59 Arminza
60 Plencia
61 Bilbao
62 Castro Urdiales
63 Río de Oriñon
64 Laredo
65 Santoña
66 Punta del Pasaje
67 Colindres
68 Río Ajo
69 Ensenada de Galizano
70 Santander

III. San Pedro del Mar to Avilés
   Cabo Mayor to Cabo Peñas

71 Río de San Pedro del Mar
72 Río de Mogro
73 Suances
74 Ensenada de Cabera
75 Ensenada de Luaña
76 Comillas
77 Ria y Ensenada de Rabia
78 San Vicente de la Barquera
79 Rio de Tina Menor
80 Rio de Tina Mayor
81 Ria de Santiuste
82 Llanes
83 Ensenada de Póo
84 Ensenada de Celorio
85 Río de Niembro
86 Playa de San Antonio del Mar
87 Ribadesella
88 Lastres
89 Ria de Villaviciosa
90 Tazones
91 Gijon (Muelles Locales)
92 Puerto de Musel
93 Candas
94 Luanco
95 Ensenada de Lumeres
96 Avilés

IV.   **San Esteban to Puerto Alumina Española**
       Cabo Peñas to Punta Roncadoira

97   San Esteban de Pravia
98   Cudillero
99   Ensenada de Artedo
100 Ensenada y Río de Canero
101 Luarca
102 Punta del Cuerno
103 Vega
104 Navia
105 Cabo de San Augustin
106 Viavélez
107 Ensenada y Río de Porcia
108 Tapia
109 Ribadeo
110 Rinlo
111 Ensenada de la Lousa
112 Foz
113 Río de Oro
114 Burela
115 Río Junco
116 San Ciprian
117 Puerto Alumina Española

V.   **Portocelo to La Coruña**
       Punta Roncadoira to Torre de Hercules

118 Portocelo
119 Viveiro
120 Isla Colleira
121 Ria del Barquero, Bares and Vicedo
122 Espasante
123 Ensenada de Santa Marta
124 Cariño
125 Santa Marta de Ortiguera
126 Cedeira
127 Punta del Frouseira
128 Cabo Prior
       Golfo Artabro
129 El Ferrol
130 Ares Marina
       Rias de Ares y Betanzos
131 Sada Marina (Fontán)
132 La Coruña

The Atlantic coast of France

Cruising on the Atlantic coast of France

The coast

The South Brittany coast changes in character from the rocky inlets and fierce tidal streams of the north to a more benign, sandy and low-lying coastline with

The flat pine-covered coast of the Landes

extensive inlets and bays to the south until Ile d'Oléron is reached. South of this for the next 140 miles lies the largely featureless and flat pine-covered coast of Les Landes, only marked by the major estuary of La Gironde in the north, the large land-locked basin of Arcachon halfway down, and the four small ports in the SE corner of the Bay, before the border with Spain is reached.

Unless proceeding up La Gironde to Bordeaux to enter the French canals, the temptation is to bypass this stretch of coast and sail direct from Ouessant to the north Spanish coast. This is a pity as the Arcachon basin is a fascinating area for the family holiday in a shoal draught or bilge keeled boat; there are excellent facilities for yachts both here, at Capbreton, Bayonne, St Jean-de-Luz and Hendaye; tidal streams are no longer significant except in the river mouths or harbour entrances, the tidal range is much reduced and there are no dangers offshore. These ports all provide interesting and pleasant diversions on the outward or inward passage to the eastern end of the Spanish north coast.

Winds

Westerly winds are most frequent in the summer months in Biscay especially in July and August. In spring, early summer and late autumn winds between N and E occur more frequently. Most summer gales are associated with depressions passing to the north with backing winds followed by a veer to the NW. The reputation of the Bay of Biscay as an area of strong gales and huge seas has not been borne out by the actual weather over the last few decades. Nevertheless muggy and thundery weather can produce unforecast severe local storms which are usually preceded by a sharp fall of the barometer.

In settled weather with high pressure holding over the area, land and sea breezes will set in which can strengthen to Force 5 or 6.

Visibility

Fog, of a thickness to reduce visibility to less than ½ mile occurs less than 1 day in 20 but visibility of less than 5 miles due to mist or haze is more frequent in the summer. Reduced visibility is only likely to be of navigational significance in La Gironde and Arcachon approaches and estuaries.

The small amount of commercial, fishing and yacht traffic (except perhaps in the two areas above) does not present the threat in low visibility that is present in the more frequented waters further north.

Currents and tidal streams

There is a N-going current 5–6 miles off the coast of ½–1 knot but this will increase after prolonged westerly gales. This starts as an E-going current along the Spanish coast turning northward to follow

The Royan to Port Bloc ferry, a familiar sight on the lower reaches of the Gironde

the coastline. A S-going countercurrent within a mile of the shore will often be found.

Tidal streams in La Gironde estuary are very strong and do not always follow the expected direction in the estuary. In the other ports, tidal streams are only of significance in the rivers and entrances and these can be strong especially on the ebb. Details are in the appropriate port sections.

Swell

A feature of this part of the coast is swell which can appear without any warning, caused by a disturbance far away in the Atlantic. The French weather forecasts for shipping include forecasts of swell (*la houle*). As the coast is relatively steep-to and there are no off-lying shallows or dangers, swell only presents a problem entering or leaving harbours. It would be unwise to enter or leave La Gironde, Arcachon, Capbreton and Bayonne if there is any swell especially on the ebb. St Jean-de-Luz and Rada de Higuer can be entered in these conditions provided the off-lying shallow patches are avoided.

The effect of swell on a spring ebb at Capbreton

Type of yacht

This stretch of coast accommodates all types of yacht, deep or shoal draught, mono or multihull. In La Gironde there is yacht or marina accommodation at the entrance, at Bordeaux and at two places in between. Yachts over about 15m length and 2.5m draught will not find an alongside berth between the ports by the entrance and Bordeaux, and would be limited to using the basins there outside neaps. Similarly, larger yachts and big multihulls may find difficulties in the Capbreton, Anglet, Ciboure and Hendaye/Fuenterrabía marinas but in the latter two there are alternative anchorages, as there is at Arcachon. For yachts of about 12m in length and 2m draught or less there are few restrictions anywhere and for shoal draught or bilge keel yachts some of the smaller ports up La Gironde and Dordogne, and the many channels, small ports and the large sheltered expanse of the Arcachon basin all provide many cruising opportunities.

Provisions

French towns and villages are well equipped with shops to meet all the normal needs and there are few that do not have a *supermarché*, however small. Groceries and meat are similarly priced to the UK but often cheaper in the frequent street markets. Milk should be bought pasteurised otherwise it will not last. *Sterilisé* is similar to 'long life'. Seafoods such as mussels, crabs, prawns and oysters are good and reasonably priced, especially if bought in a market. French bread is very good but does not keep, although a baguette may be given a new lease of life after a day by being put in the oven for a few minutes. For longer lasting bread ask for *pain complet* which is similar to a wholemeal loaf.

Water

All marinas and most yacht harbours provide water points adjacent to most berths but a hose with various end fittings is useful. Some places make a small charge for it. The quality usually conforms to the current EU standard for *eau potable* but bottled water is readily available in the supermarkets.

Fuel

The use of low tax red diesel – known as *Fuel Oil Domestique* or FOD in France – is officially permitted in yachts for use with generators or heater units provided they are supplied from a different tank to the main engine. Difficulty may be found

One of the frequent street markets which can provide the cheapest and freshest of foods

Château Lafitte Rothschild, one of the grander châteaux in the Médoc

Both banks of the Gironde are covered in vineyards. Pauillac is the best port from which to visit and sample

Telephones

Public telephones in France now take only cards and not cash. Cards may be obtained from post offices, tobacconists, newsagents and some cafés/bars. Mobile telephone coverage along the coast is good.

Money

Cash machines can be found in unexpected places and are not confined to banks. All but the smallest post office will advance euros against a Visa card. Travellers' cheques are still generally negotiable.

Formalities

It is essential that a Certificate of Registry (or for British yachts the Small Ships Registry Document) is carried on board and produced on demand to the authorities. Photocopies of these documents are not acceptable in France and a failure to produce the originals is likely to lead to a fine on the spot.

The following documents should also be carried:
- RYA Certificate of Competence, at least for the skipper
- Evidence of insurance for the yacht. This is not a legal requirement but some marinas will refuse access to an uninsured boat
- Passports for all on board. These are likely to be demanded if boarded by the customs, will be needed if returning to the UK by other means and are useful as a means of identification.

Yachts registered in an EU country arriving in French waters need not complete any formalities (and should not fly a Q flag) unless they are carrying goods which are dutiable in France or have non-EU residents onboard. In these cases entry should be made at a port where there is a customs presence and the Q flag should be flown until cleared.

French Customs operate spotter planes on the Biscay coast and the yacht is likely to be overflown and photographed. Customs officers may board at any time in French waters. On the first occasion ask for *une fiche* which will be issued if the officers are satisfied and may be used subsequently to satisfy customs before they board.

The end of masted navigation on La Gironde. Pont de Pierre, Bordeaux

convincing a supplier that this is the case for bulk deliveries but there should be no objection from the customs or supplier in securing a limited amount in cans.

Recent receipts for red diesel obtained in the UK or Channel Islands should be retained and produced if needed. A 'reasonable quantity' of such fuel carried in vessels' main tanks can be imported into France without further formality or payment of tax.

FOD, however is rarely available at marinas and only from fishing ports. Marinas supply fully taxed diesel from pumps which are now nearly all operated by a credit card which must have a chip incorporated. There are still some cards issued in the UK without chips and the reliability of some of the pump operating systems is not all that it should be. Enough cash to keep topped up with fuel should always be carried and payment made at the marina office.

Petrol is often available by pump from the marinas otherwise recourse must be made to the nearest garage.

Value Added Tax (TVA)

In general, EU yachts must be able to demonstrate that they are VAT paid in order to enjoy freedom of movement within the Union. A VAT receipt issued by the builder should satisfy French Customs and a Bill of Sale and a registration document issued in the UK may do so, particularly for an older yacht. A yacht built or first registered before the first introduction of VAT in the UK and which cannot produce a VAT receipt or an exemption may have problems. UK Customs and Excise may be able to issue acceptable documentation if they are satisfied that in fact VAT has been paid, and they should be consulted. Failure to carry the correct documentation may result in a non-negotiable demand for the tax to be paid immediately at the French rate which is currently 20.6% for yachts.

Yachts registered outside the EU, on which VAT has not been paid, may be temporarily imported into the EU tax-free. At present the time limit for free importation is for 6 months but this is likely to be increased. In the past it has been sometimes possible to obtain an extension to the permitted length of stay if a yacht has been laid up in the EU while her owners return to their home countries.

New yachts exported VAT-free from the UK and calling in France en route to non-EU destinations are a special case in which early advice should be obtained regarding the current time limits which apply to them.

Yacht clubs

There are yacht clubs and sailing schools in most French harbours; they are invariably hospitable to visitors. Assistance or advice is readily given and there are often showers available.

Fishing

Fishing activity in this area is confined to some netting in La Gironde, extensive oyster and shellfish beds in Bassin d'Arcachon and a few small boats working out of Capbreton, Bayonne and Biarritz. There are small fleets of middle water boats at St Jean-de-Luz and Gurutzeaundi.

Laying up

Facilities for hauling out and laying up are available at Royan, Port Médoc, Port d'Arcachon, Capbreton, Anglet and Hendaye which, if used, would avoid a crossing of the Bay in spring to cruise the north Spanish coast.

Inland waterways

The rules and regulations for the French inland waterways apply to those entering the Canal Latéral above Castets but not for any other waterway in this book. The minimum requirements for any vessel of less than 15 metres is that the helmsman should possess an RYA Helmsman's Overseas Certificate of Competence and that a current tax disc (*vignette*) is held. Details of the latter may be obtained from Voies Navigables de France, Rue Ludovic Boutleux, 62400 Béthune, France. The French Government Tourist Office, 178 Piccadilly, London W1V 0AL ☎ 0906 824 4123 can help further and will supply details of any closures (*chômages*).

Any boat drawing more than about 1.5m may have a problem in the summer months due to lack of water on this inland route. Enquiries should be made before lowering masts and committing to the transit.

The following references may be of further help:

Guides Vagnon (Les Editions du Plaisancier) Maps and text of waterways; English translation. From Imray

Cartes Guides Navicarte (Grafocarte) Maps. From Imray

Editions du Breil Maps. From Imray

Euroregs for Inland Waterways (Adlard Coles)

Inland Waterways of France David Edwards-May (Imray)

Waterway Routes through France. Map. Jane Cumberlidge (Imray)

Through the French Canals Bristow and Jefferson (Adlard Coles).

There is a continuing interest in the past in Charente Maritime. Here a medieval play is being performed in the lovely old village of Mornac near Royan

The accompanying medieval band

Search and Rescue

The Centres Régionaux Opérationels de Surveillance et de la Sauvetage (CROSS) are Maritime Rescue Co-ordination Centres (MRCC). The area from Pointe de la Coubre to the Spanish border is in the CROSS Etel area. There are remote and linked sites at Chassiron (N end of Ile d'Oléron), Soulac (Pointe de Grave), Cap Ferret (Arcachon), Contis (halfway between Cap Ferret and Biarritz) and at Biarritz. CROSS Etel will respond to COSPAS/SARSAT emergency transmissions from EPIRBs, specialises in medical advice and is fully integrated into the DSC VHF and MF network. In an emergency CROSS Etel will respond either to a DSC activation on Ch 70 or Ch 16 or on MF. Details of the weather reports and navigational warnings broadcast from CROSS Etel and its remote stations are shown below.

Some harbourmasters require a form to be completed showing 'where from' and 'where bound'. This is passed to CROSS Etel who should be informed as soon as possible if plans change, otherwise a search may be started.

Royan lifeboat

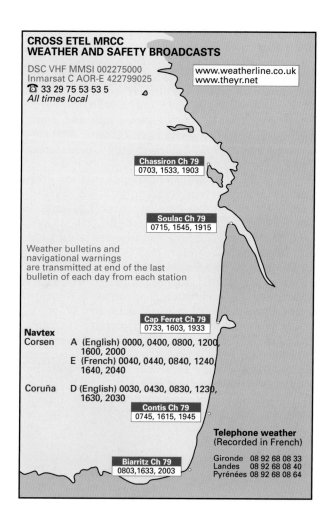

CROSS ETEL MRCC
WEATHER AND SAFETY BROADCASTS

DSC VHF MMSI 002275000
Inmarsat C AOR-E 422799025
☎ 33 29 75 53 53 5
All times local

www.weatherline.co.uk
www.theyr.net

Chassiron Ch 79
0703, 1533, 1903

Soulac Ch 79
0715, 1545, 1915

Weather bulletins and navigational warnings are transmitted at end of the last bulletin of each day from each station

Cap Ferret Ch 79
0733, 1603, 1933

Navtex
Corsen   A (English) 0000, 0400, 0800, 1200, 1600, 2000
         E (French) 0040, 0440, 0840, 1240, 1640, 2040

Coruña   D (English) 0030, 0430, 0830, 1230, 1630, 2030

Contis Ch 79
0745, 1615, 1945

Telephone weather
(Recorded in French)

Gironde   08 92 68 08 33
Landes   08 92 68 08 40
Pyrénées 08 92 68 08 64

Biarritz Ch 79
0803, 1633, 2003

Technical and navigational information

Chart datum

Chart datum is fixed at a level below which the sea level will not fall in normal circumstances, but it may do so under extreme meteorological conditions.

Predicted heights of the tides have been taken from Admiralty *Tide Tables Vol 2* and are related to chart datum and to time of HW and LW at Pointe de Grave (PdG) for each port. Simple interpolation from these times and heights using the 1/12th Rule, the relevant tidal diagram or one of the many electronic systems available can work out the tidal height at any specific time. The datum of the French charts, if used, is the same as the Admiralty (BA) charts and the calculation for tidal heights similar.

Horizontal chart datum – satellite-derived positions

Positions derived from satellite systems such as GPS are usually expressed in terms of World Geodetic System 1984 (WGS 84). Admiralty and French charts in this area are in a mixture of WGS 84 and European Datum 1950 (ED 50). If in the latter, they all show a correction to be applied when using positions aligned to WGS 84. In this area these corrections are in the order of 120m in latitude and 100m in longitude. DGPS is transmitted from Cap Ferret (44°38´.77N 1°14´.84W). Range 97M.

Caution should be exercised if using pre-metric BA or old French charts which do not show any correction and where there may be significant discrepancies between the latitude and longitude on the chart and that shown by GPS set to any datum.

Heights

On BA charts this is above MHWS and applies to the air clearance under bridges or overhead obstructions. On French charts it is above MTL.

Bearings

Bearings are given in degrees True from seaward. The magnetic variation is at present (2005) 1½°W in the north of the area to 2½°W in the south. Magnetic bearings in compass points are sometimes given in the text to indicate a general direction.

Positions

The latitude and longitude given under Location for each port are NOT waypoints. They indicate the general position of the port.

Waypoints

There are two types of waypoint shown in this pilot:

Coastal waypoints These indicate a clear track offshore along the coast. The track between adjacent waypoints carries at least 2m to a width of 400m unless the space between them on the list in Appendix 2 is marked with -----. Nevertheless, the waypoints and the tracks between them must be plotted and checked on an up-to-date chart before being used for navigation. Coastal waypoints are shown on the plans at the beginning of each part.

Arrival waypoints For individual ports or anchorages. They are placed at a safe distance from the destination at a point roughly where pilotage will take over from GPS navigation. Arrival waypoints are shown on the plan for each port or anchorage.

In a few instances an arrival waypoint may also serve as a coastal waypoint.

The waypoints given for La Gironde estuary S of Blaye are for planning purposes only.

Cordouan lighthouse in La Gironde estuary which is exceptionally well lit

Lights

The main characteristics of all lights and light buoys together with their fog signals are shown on individual plans.

A list of all lights and their full characteristics are shown in Appendix 1.

The same convention is followed as in Admiralty *List of Lights Vol D*.

This section of the French coast is covered by light numbers 1289 to 1454.6.

Charts

BA, SHOM and Imray charts for the area are shown in Appendix 3. They are also shown in the text for each section and port. BA charts may be obtained from Imray or other Admiralty chart agents and are corrected up to the date of purchase. They can be kept corrected free of charge from the internet on www.nmwebsearch.com They may also be kept corrected from the weekly Admiralty *Notices to Mariners,* available free from chart agents.

ARCS electronic raster charts have the same numbers as the paper charts. There are no SC editions in this area and BA ENC charts are unlikely to be used by yachts.

French charts may be obtained through Imray, Norie, Laurie and Wilson Ltd, Wych House, The Broadway, St Ives, Cambridgeshire, PE27 5BT ☎ 01480 462114 *Fax* 01480 496109 *Email* ilnw@imray.com but it takes some time and it may be quicker to order direct from Librairie Maritime Outremer Le Yacht, 55 Avenue de la Grand-Armée, 75116, Paris, France ☎ 01 45 00 17 99 *Fax* 01 45 00 10 02 *email* le.yacht@wanadoo.fr or from authorised agents in principal ports. Some chandlers hold a limited number of local charts. The latter do not keep them corrected after receipt. French charts with the suffix P are printed on waterproof paper and folded like a map for small craft.

The French also produce the Navicarte series of charts to a scale of 1:50,000 with large-scale inserts specifically for yachtsmen. These may be obtained either through Imray, Norie, Laurie and Wilson or direct from Librairie Maritime Outremer Le Yacht.

In general BA charts give an excellent coverage of the area and are increasingly convergent in coverage, scales, datums and styles with French charts but using slightly different symbols. It is noted in the text where a French chart has a greater coverage or larger scale than the BA equivalent. For this section this only applies to the upper reaches of the Dordogne and the Arcachon Basin.

Imray chart C42 covers the area and has inserts of some of the ports.

US charts cover the area on a small scale, with large-scale coverage only of La Gironde and Bayonne.

Harbour and anchorage plans

The harbour and anchorage plans are drawn to illustrate the pilotage directions and are not to be used directly for navigation. While the details are relatively exact the plans are not necessarily tied to latitude and longitude. Each plan will, however, show the arrival waypoint or indicate its position relative to the plan. The scale for each plan is shown in metres, or occasionally in miles.

Radio services

There are no coastal radio stations except those which are part of the CROSS Etel Search and Rescue network and there are no radio beacons except aero radiobeacons.

Port radio stations

(These frequencies are repeated in the individual port sections.)

La Gironde	Ch 12 and 16 for 24 hours; radar control on Ch 12
Bonne Anse	Ch 09 occasional
Royan	Ch 09 during working hours
Blaye	Ch 12 during working hours
Pauillac	Ch 12 during working hours
Bordeaux	Ch 12 and 16 for 24 hours; Ch 09 marina during working hours
Arcachon	Ch 09 for 24 hours
Capbreton	Ch 09 during working hours
Bayonne	Ch 12 for 24 hours
Anglet	Ch 12 during working hours.
St Jean-de-Luz	Ch 09 and 16 during working hours
Hendaye	Ch 09 for 24 hours

Firing Ranges

Firing danger areas exist from Pointe de la Négarde in the north to Capbreton in the south (see plan). They extend up to 35 miles offshore but it is usually safe to proceed along the safe zone up to 3 miles offshore. However there may be restrictions to this off Mimizan. The ranges are managed by Centre d'Essais des Landes (CEL). They keep watch on Ch 06 and Ch 10 (although the latter is mainly for fishermen) and will give permission to cross the zone if it is safe to do so. CEL ☎ 05 58 82 22 42/3.

Daily information on range use is broadcast following the Met bulletins on Ch 79 at the following local times:

Cap Ferret	0733	1933
Contis	0745	1945
Biarritz	0803	2003

The same information is held by the harbourmaster at Arcachon: Ch 09 or ☎ 05 56 22 36 75.

Gunfire warnings are also broadcast on Ch 16:

Mon–Thurs	0815	1615
Fri	0815	1030

The range is patrolled by a range craft when firings take place.

The most frequently used sector is 31A, the least used is the northern portion. It is unlikely that there will be any restrictions from Friday pm to Sunday pm or that entry to Arcachon will be hindered.

Bibliography

Admiralty Sailing Directions *Bay of Biscay Pilot* NP22
Admiralty *Tide Tables* Vol 2 NP 202
Admiralty *List of Lights* Vol NP 77
Admiralty *Maritime Communications* NP 289
Cruising Association Almanac
Reeds Oki *Nautical Almanac*
Bloc Marine *Votre Livre de Bord – Manche/Atlantique*

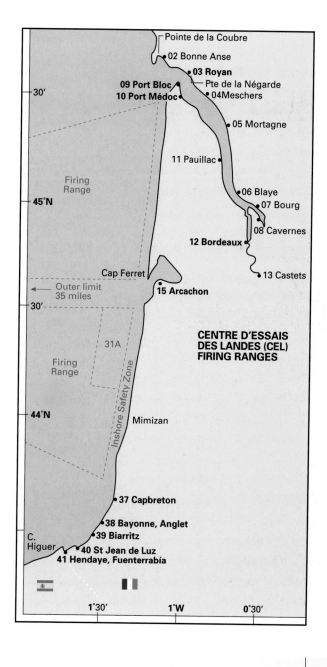

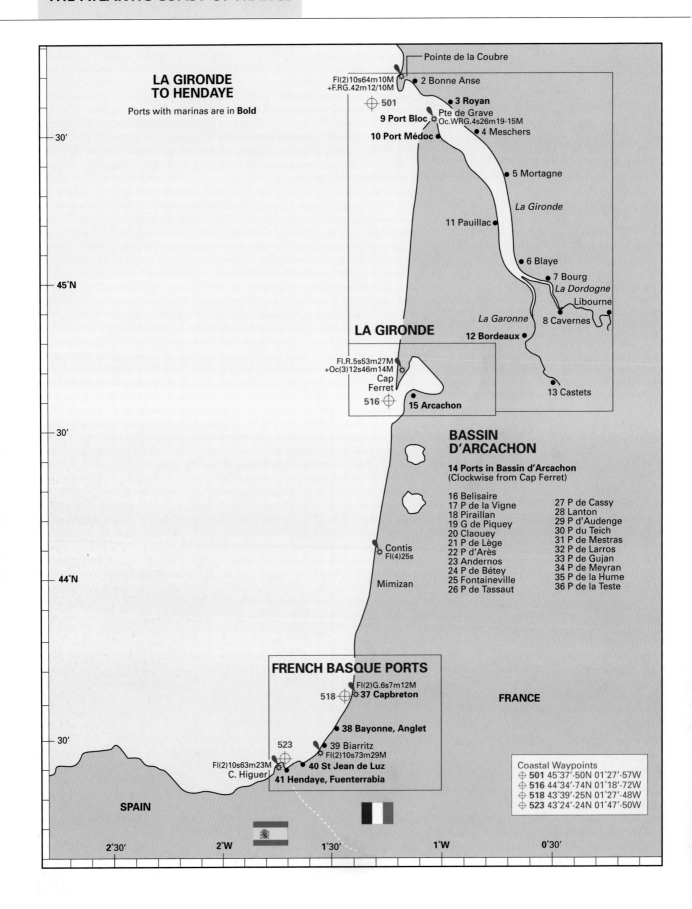

LA GIRONDE TO HENDAYE

Ports with marinas are in **Bold**

Pointe de la Coubre

Fl(2)10s64m10M +F.RG.42m12/10M

⊕ 501

2 Bonne Anse

3 Royan

Pte de Grave Oc.WRG.4s26m19-15M

9 Port Bloc

10 Port Médoc

4 Meschers

5 Mortagne

La Gironde

11 Pauillac

6 Blaye

7 Bourg

La Dordogne

Libourne

8 Cavernes

La Garonne

12 Bordeaux

13 Castets

LA GIRONDE

Fl.R.5s53m27M +Oc(3)12s46m14M

Cap Ferret

516 ⊕

15 Arcachon

BASSIN D'ARCACHON

14 Ports in Bassin d'Arcachon
(Clockwise from Cap Ferret)

16 Belisaire
17 P de la Vigne
18 Piraillan
19 G de Piquey
20 Claouey
21 P de Lège
22 P d'Arès
23 Andernos
24 P de Bétey
25 Fontaineville
26 P de Tassaut

27 P de Cassy
28 Lanton
29 P d'Audenge
30 P du Teich
31 P de Mestras
32 P de Larros
33 P de Gujan
34 P de Meyran
35 P de la Hume
36 P de la Teste

Contis Fl(4)25s

Mimizan

FRENCH BASQUE PORTS

Fl(2)G.6s7m12M

518 ⊕ **37 Capbreton**

FRANCE

38 Bayonne, Anglet

523

39 Biarritz Fl(2)10s73m29M

Fl(2)10s63m23M
C. Higuer

40 St Jean de Luz

41 Hendaye, Fuenterrabia

SPAIN

Coastal Waypoints
⊕ **501** 45°37'·50N 01°27'·57W
⊕ **516** 44°34'·74N 01°18'·72W
⊕ **518** 43°39'·25N 01°27'·48W
⊕ **523** 43°24'·24N 01°47'·50W

I. La Gironde to Hendaye
Pointe de la Coubre to Cabo Higuer

This coast stretches for 150 miles from the somewhat forbidding entrance to La Gironde in the north to the small ports in the SE corner of the Bay and the border with Spain. Halfway between lies the shallow inland sea of Bassin d'Arcachon with its oysters and many small harbours.

The shore is uniformly flat and sandy and is backed by miles of pine forests. It is hard to believe that just beyond them lies one of the most fertile and productive of France's wine growing regions.

A firing range stretches to seaward for most of the coastline. Details of this may be found in *Technical and navigational information* above.

Planning Guide
Distances between ports in nautical miles
Ports with marinas in **bold** type

		Gironde entrance	Arcachon entrance	Capbreton	Bayonne Anglet	Biarritz	St Jean-de-Luz	Font/Higuer/Gurutz
B*	**Gironde entrance**		64	124	132	135	142	147
C	Arcachon entrance	64		60	68	71	78	83
C	Capbreton	124	60		8	11	18	23
B*	**Bayonne Anglet**	132	68	8		3	10	15
D	Biarritz	135	71	11	3		7	12
A*	**St Jean-de-Luz**	142	76	18	10	7		5
A	Font/Higuer/Socoburu/ Hond/Gurutz	147	83	23	15	12	5	

Lighthouse

Pointe de Grave looking WSW.

Pointe de Grave lighthouse which marks the W side of the entrance to La Gironde. It is also from here that the tidal standard is taken for these French ports and also the ports along the north Spanish coast to La Coruña

La Gironde

1 La Gironde approaches and estuary

Cat B*

This extensive estuary leads to the city of Bordeaux and to the large rivers of La Garonne and La Dordogne. Above Bordeaux the Canal Latéral de la Garonne and the Canal du Midi can be entered and may be used by craft smaller than 30m long, 5.25m wide, 1.6m deep and 3m high

Location
45°38'N 01°28'W (BXA buoy)

Shelter
Very good in Royan and Port Médoc

Depth restrictions
11m minimum on leading lines
1.7m in Royan approach
3m in Port Médoc approach

Night entry
As by day. the approaches are extremely well lit

Tidal information

	Time differences			Height differences (m)			
	HW	LW		MHWS	MHWN	MLWN	MLWS
Pointe de Grave (PdG)							
0000	0600	0500	1200				
and	and	and	and	5.4	4.4	2.1	1.0
1200	1800	1700	2400				
Pauillac							
+0100	+0100	+0135	+0205	+0.1	0.0	−1.0	−0.5
Bourg							
+0135	+0145	+0305	+0305	−0.2	−0.3	−1.3	−0.7
Bordeaux							
+0200	+0225	+0330	+0405	−0.1	−0.2	−1.7	−1.0
Libourne							
+0250	+0305	+0525	+0540	−0.7	−0.9	−2.0	−0.4

Warnings
The tidal streams are very strong and do not always follow the line of the estuary in the mouth; constant checks are required to avoid being set off the intended track. Overfalls are severe and dangerous (5m). Do not attempt to enter the estuary in strong winds from the SW through W to N if there is any swell or on the ebb tide. If in doubt, stand off. Particular care is needed between Nos. 2A, 3, 4 and 5 entrance buoys where the channel is narrow and shoals quickly on either side. Only use the south channel in fine weather, good visibility and favourable tidal conditions. Keep to the main channel unless indicated otherwise as there are a number of wrecks outside it.

The sandbanks change their positions and depths during the winter storms and an up-to-date chart (BA 3058 or SHOM 7425) should be used and the latest *Notices to Mariners* consulted.

Wind effect on tidal level
Winds between S and NNW raise the water level up to 1m and advance the time of HW by up to 15 minutes. Winds from the N through E to S decrease the level by up to 0.3m and retard the time of HW by up to 15 minutes.

Tidal streams
The following is a simplification based on the times at Pointe de Grave.

kns	Flood begins	Spring rate kns	Ebb begins	Spring rate
BXA buoy	−0430	2.6	+0100	3.3
Off Royan	−0445	3.8	+0045	3.8
Off Mortagne	−0415	2.8	+0145	3.8
Pauillac	−0315	2.8	+0215	3.8
Bordeaux	−0115	2.8	+0315	3.8
Libourne	+0045	3.8	+0410	4.7

After Bordeaux there is no noticeable flood but the downward stream is significantly lessened.

Kilometre marks
They are on both banks and show the distance from Bordeaux (Pont de Pierre) and appear on all the charts. On the Dordogne they run from Libourne (0km) to Bourg (40km) and then revert to the Garonne distances.

Weather
On Ch 79
From Chassiron at 0703, 1533, 1903 LT in French

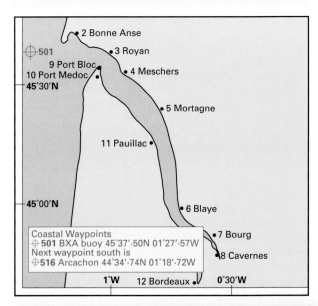

Coastal Waypoints
⊕ 501 BXA buoy 45°37'·50N 01°27'·57W
Next waypoint south is
⊕ 516 Arcachon 44°34'·74N 01°18'·72W

Pointe de la Coubre lighthouse and coastguard tower looking NE

From Soulac at 0715, 1545, 1915 LT in French
Navtex from Corsen (A) (English) and (E) (French)
☎ 08 92 68 08 33 (recorded in French)

Charts
BA 3057 (50), 3058 (25), 3068, 3069 (various)
SHOM 7070 (167), 7426 (52), 7425 (25), 7427 (various)
Imray C41, C42 (large-scale)

Radio
Port Control Bordeaux to BXA Ch 16 and 12 (24 hrs)
Radar guidance on Ch 12 on request
Gironde tide height Ch 17 (every 5 minutes)

Royan Marina Ch 09 (working hours)
Port Médoc Ch 09 (tentative)
Pauillac Marina Ch 09 (working hours)

Telephone
Royan Marina ☎ 05 46 38 72 22
Port Médoc ☎ 05 5609 69 75
Pauillac Marina ☎ 05 56 59 01 58
Bordeaux HM ☎ 05 56 90 59 34
Bordeaux No. 2 basin ☎ 05 56 90 59 57

Lifeboat
An all-weather lifeboat is maintained at Royan

La Palmyre leading line

The huge estuary has little scenic appeal. Looking S towards
La Dordogne/La Garonne junction in the distance with
Pauillac on the right

The 120 miles of coast from Pointe de Grave to Capbreton
looks like this the whole way except for the Arcachon
entrance

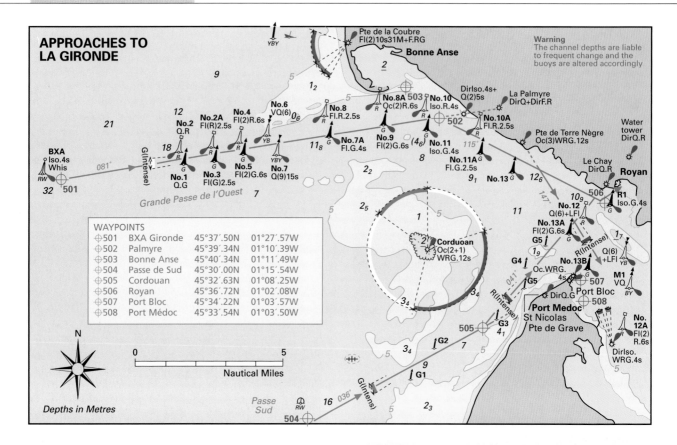

APPROACHES TO LA GIRONDE

Warning
The channel depths are liable to frequent change and the buoys are altered accordingly

WAYPOINTS			
⊕501	BXA Gironde	45°37′.50N	01°27′.57W
⊕502	Palmyre	45°39′.34N	01°10′.39W
⊕503	Bonne Anse	45°40′.34N	01°11′.49W
⊕504	Passe de Sud	45°30′.00N	01°15′.54W
⊕505	Cordouan	45°32′.63N	01°08′.25W
⊕506	Royan	45°36′.72N	01°02′.08W
⊕507	Port Bloc	45°34′.22N	01°03′.57W
⊕508	Port Médoc	45°33′.54N	01°03′.50W

Nautical Miles

Depths in Metres

PILOTAGE

BXA buoy to Royan and Port Médoc

From BXA buoy and ⊕501 to R1 buoy and ⊕506 off Royan is 20M.

Grande Passe de l'Ouest

Approach from north

By day

Warning

It is essential to keep at least 5M off the coast in the later approach to ⊕501 to avoid the dangerous shoal of Banc de la Mauvaise. The corner should not be cut and landfall should be made at ⊕501 and the BXA buoy (Iso.4s; ball topmark on RW buoy with Racon and whistle).

By night

The same warning applies as for by day. The lights are Pointe de la Coubre (Fl(2)10s+F.RG). The northerly red sector covers Banc de la Mauvaise), BXA buoy (Iso.4s7M) from which the directional and intensified La Palmyre leading lights should be visible (Front DirIso.4s20M, Rear DirQ.27M). As for the day approach, do not cut the corner and make the landfall at ⊕501 and the BXA buoy.

From south

By day

An approach to ⊕501 and the BXA buoy on a track of 000° and outside the 20m line will clear all dangers. Do not be tempted to cut a corner through

BXA buoy at the W end of Grande Passe de l'Ouest

La Passe Sud unless the three conditions for its safe use are realised (See Passe Sud, Entrance below).

By night

As for by day. The lights of Pointe de Grave (Oc.WRG.4s19M) of which only the W will be visible in passing except for the very narrow directional G sector, and Cordouan (Oc(2+1) WRG.12s) will assist.

Entrance

By day

From ⊕501 and the BXA buoy (RW) make good a track of 081° towards ⊕502 until the entrance buoys or the Palmyre leading line can be picked out.

Proceed down this line keeping between the buoys until between No. 7 and No. 9 buoys (both SHM) the channel and leading line may be safely left, turning short of ⊕502 to a track of about 110° to leave Nos. 11 and 11A buoys (both SHM) to port.

Pass No. 13 buoy (NCM) close on either side. To proceed to Royan continue on a track of 115° towards ⊕506 and R1 green conical buoy. Short of this buoy and at the ⊕ turn sharply to port to 035° up the Royan entrance channel.

To proceed to Port Médoc or upriver, from No. 13 buoy make 147° on the stern transit of Pointe de Terre-Nègre/La Palmyre lighthouses of 327° leaving Nos. 13A and 13B (SHMs) to starboard. At No. 13B course may either be shaped for Port Médoc entrance and ⊕508, or continue upriver making about 140° to pick up the many subsequent lateral buoys.

By night
At ⊕501 and BXA buoy (Iso.4s) bring La Palmyre leading lights (Front DirIso.4s Rear DirQ) into line on 081° and enter the channel between Nos. 1 and 2 buoys (Q.G and Q.R) towards ⊕502. After No. 7 buoy (Q(9)15s) the leading line and channel buoys diverge; for preference follow the latter until No. 9 buoy (Fl(2)G.6s) is abeam to port when turn to a track of about 110° towards ⊕506 to leave No. 11 (Iso.G.4s) and No. 11A (Fl.G.2.5s) to port.

Pass No. 13 buoy (Q) close on either side. To proceed to Royan continue on a track of 115° towards ⊕506 and R1 buoy (Iso.G.4s). Short of this buoy and at the ⊕ turn sharply to port to 035° towards the jetty ends at Royan (Fl(2)R10s, Fl(3)R.12s).

To proceed to Port Médoc or upriver, from No. 13 buoy (Q) make 147° on a stern transit of Pointe de Terre-Nègre (Oc(3)R on the transit) and La Palmyre (DirF.R on the transit) of 327° leaving Nos. 13A (Fl(2)G.6s) and 13B (Q.G) to starboard. At No. 13B proceed as for *By day* above.

Passe Sud (or Passe de Grave)

⊕504 to Royan/Port Médoc and La Gironde
From ⊕504 it is 9M to Pointe de Grave and 11M to Royan and ⊕506.

Approach

From north
There is no advantage to be gained or reason to use this pass when approaching from the north.

From south
Make for ⊕504 and the RW whistle buoy with a ball topmark by day; by night align the front DirQG with the rear Oc.4s to proceed up the line of 063°.

Entrance

By day
Warning
The minimum depth in the pass is 5m but this may vary. Entry should only be made in the absence of swell, the last quarter of the flood and good visibility.

Navigate to the SE red and white whistle buoy with a ball topmark ⊕504 and align the St Nicolas (white tower) and Pointe de Grave (white tower with black corners and top) lighthouses on 063°. Proceed up this line towards ⊕505 leaving G1 SHM and G2 PHM on either side. On reaching ⊕505 and before G3 SHM, turn on to 041° and align Le Chay (white tower, red top) and St Pierre (red water tower) just to the left of Royan church on this bearing. On reaching G4 PHM borrow to starboard to avoid Platin de Grave (1.9m). Cross the estuary, passing No. 13A SHM and No. 12 PHM on either side to R1 green SHM (which must be left to starboard on this approach) and ⊕506 whence it is 041° to Royan.

If going to Port Médoc or up river, leave the line in the vicinity of G4 buoy to round Pointe de Grave which, except for a 1.1m patch just to the W, is steep-to all the way round.

By night
The same *Warning* applies as by day but additionally all the buoys to Pointe de Grave are unlit. Make sure there is sufficient light to see them in time for avoidance.

Navigate to ⊕504 and align St Nicolas (DirQ.G) and Pointe de Grave (Oc.4s on this bearing) on 063° and proceed. At ⊕505 alter to 041° with Le Chay (DirQ.R) in transit with St Pierre (DirQ.R). Keep to starboard of this line after G4 buoy to avoid Platin de Grave (1.9m) and continue across the estuary leaving No. 13A (Fl(2)G.5s) and No. 12 (Fl(2)R.6s) buoys on either side, to ⊕506 and R1 buoy (Iso.G.4s) which must be left to starboard.

If going to Port Médoc or upriver, act as by day. There is a Q. NCM immediately to the N of Pointe de Grave.

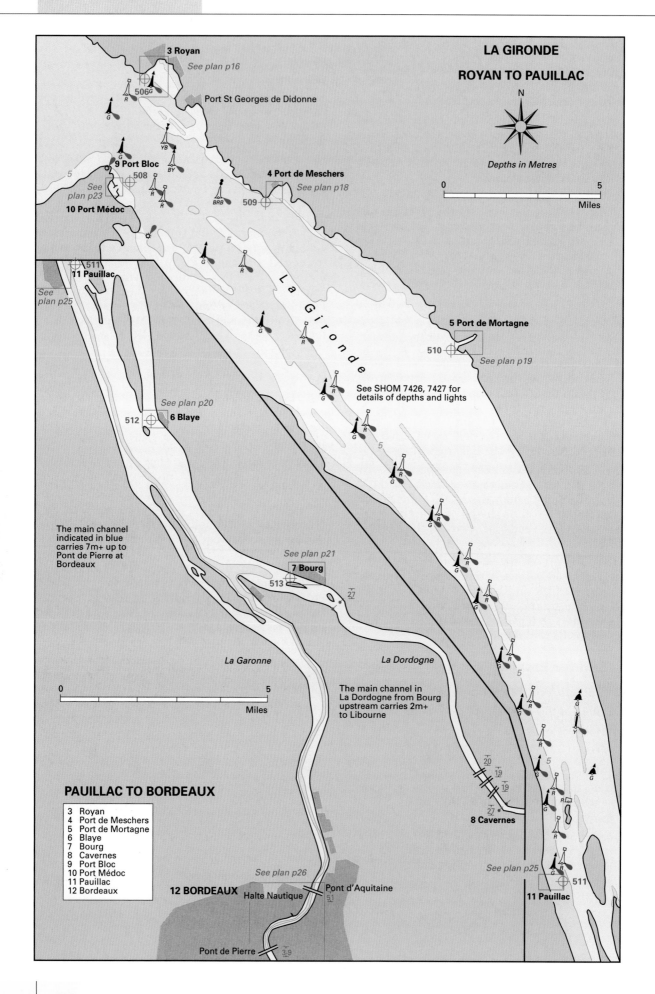

LA GIRONDE

ROYAN TO PAUILLAC

N

Depths in Metres

0   5

Miles

3 Royan

See plan p16

506 G
R

Port St Georges de Didonne

G

9 Port Bloc

YB

BY

508

4 Port de Meschers

See plan p18

BRB   509

10 Port Médoc

511

11 Pauillac

See plan p25

G

R

5 Port de Mortagne

510

See plan p19

G

See SHOM 7426, 7427 for
details of depths and lights

L a   G i r o n d e

512   **6 Blaye**

See plan p20

The main channel
indicated in blue
carries 7m+ up to
Pont de Pierre at
Bordeaux

7 Bourg

513

See plan p21

27

G

R

La Garonne

La Dordogne

0   5

Miles

The main channel in
La Dordogne from Bourg
upstream carries 2m+
to Libourne

20
19
19

27

8 Cavernes

G

R

V

G

PAUILLAC TO BORDEAUX

3	Royan
4	Port de Meschers
5	Port de Mortagne
6	Blaye
7	Bourg
8	Cavernes
9	Port Bloc
10	Port Médoc
11	Pauillac
12	Bordeaux

See plan p26

12 BORDEAUX

Halte Nautique

Pont d'Aquitaine

5.1

See plan p25

511

11 Pauillac

Pont de Pierre

3.9

2–13 Harbours on La Gironde, La Garonne and La Dordogne

Many of the smaller harbours dry out leaving a bottom of liquid mud, some have lock gates and some have pontoons along the bank in reasonably deep water. All will be crowded with local boats and, except in the marinas at Royan, Port Médoc, Pauillac and possibly Halte Nautique at Bordeaux, finding a berth for a deep draught boat will be uncertain. Port Bloc is a busy ferry port and does not welcome yachts.

All the harbours have roads and most have nearby villages. The smaller harbours should be entered between half flood and HW.

BA charts 3068 and 3069 or SHOM 7426 and 7427 are essential for navigating these waters.

Masted navigation ceases at Pont de Pierre at Bordeaux on La Garonne, and just above Cavernes on La Dordogne at another low bridge. There is a small marina on the outskirts of Bordeaux above the bridges at Bègles before the locks into the Canal Latéral de la Garonne are reached at Castets 40 miles above Bordeaux.

WAYPOINTS			
⊕501	BXA Gironde	45°37′.50N	01°27′.57W
⊕502	Palmyre	45°39′.34N	01°10′.39W
⊕503	Bonne Anse	45°40′.34N	01°11′.49W
⊕504	Passe de Sud	45°30′.00N	01°15′.54W
⊕505	Cordouan	45°32′.63N	01°08′.25W
⊕506	Royan	45°36′.72N	01°02′.08W
⊕507	Port Bloc	45°34′.22N	01°03′.57W
⊕508	Port Médoc	45°33′.54N	01°03′.50W
⊕509	Meschers	45°33′.10N	00°56′.48W
⊕510	Mortagne	45°28′.20N	00°48′.99W
⊕511	Pauillac	45°11′.90N	00°44′.20W
⊕512	Blaye	45°07′.50N	00°40′.10W
1⊕513	Bourg	45°02′.19N	00°33′.50W
1⊕514	Cavernes	44°56′.20N	00°26′.50W
1⊕515	Bordeaux (Pont de Pierre)	44°50′.00N	00°34′.70W

1. Planning purposes only

Bonne Anse looking NE near LW

2 Bonne Anse

111km mark

Small shallow marina in a wooded area near the mouth of the estuary

Location
45°42′.00N 01°12′.00W

Shelter
Good except in SW winds at HW

Depth restrictions
Dries 1.8m on approach
1–1.5m in marina

Night entry
Not lit

Tidal information
HW as for PdG

Mean height of tide (m)

MHWS	MHWN	MLWN	MLWS
5.1	4.2	2.1	1.0

Tidal streams
Flood begins
HW PdG –0440
Ebb begins
HW PdG +0050

Berthing
On pontoons

Facilities
All, except fuel from garage

Charts
Inadequate, but BA 3057 (50), 3058 (25)
SHOM 7425 (25) 7426 (52)
Imray C41, C42

Radio
Ch 09 (working hours)

Telephone
☎ 05 46 22 44 31

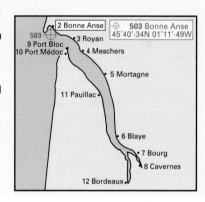

PILOTAGE

Approach and entrance

From the vicinity of No. 10 buoy make good a northerly track in the last quarter of the flood to pick out the channel which runs close along the NE shore (see photograph which shows this clearly). Care should be taken to keep to the SW of the three groyne ends. This channel is sometimes buoyed in the season.

In the bay there are a number of oyster beds marked with the ubiquitous stakes which should be avoided; the bottom is flattish sand and mud.

The entrance is very narrow, marked by two spindly posts with sharp turn-in. There are crowded pontoons in the harbour in 1 to 1.5m with the deepest water on the ones on the SW side.

Anchorage

Anchorage may be found in 1m to the W of the entrance.

Ashore in Bonne Anse

The marina is close to the holiday village of La Palmyre with some shops and with excellent beaches and unspoilt pinewoods close by.

3 Royan

100km mark

Handy marina near the mouth of the estuary with access in all weathers

Location
45°37'.00N 01°02'.00W

Shelter
Good in the marina

Warning
There are the remains of a wreck with 3m over it 200m E of R1 buoy

Depth restrictions
1.7m in entrance channel (reported less in 2004)
2.5m in marina

Night entry
Well lit

Tidal information
HW as for PdG

Mean height of tide (m)

MHWS	MHWN	MLWN	MLWS
5.1	4.2	2.1	1.0

Tidal stream
Flood begins HW–0445
Ebb begins HW+0045

Berthing
Alongside pontoon on N side of central spur

Facilities
All; 26-tonne lift, 1.5-tonne crane

Charts
BA 3057 (50), 3068
SHOM 7425 (25), 7426 (52)

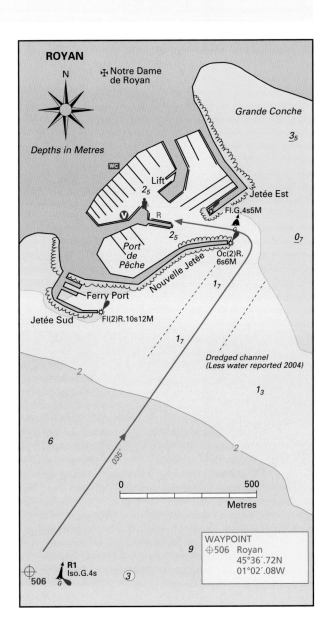

Weather
Soulac Ch 79 at 0715, 1545,1915
☎ 08 92 68 08 33

Radio10

Marina Ch 09
Gironde Control Ch 12

Telephone
Marina ☎ 05 46 38 72 22

Holiday resort and ferry port with large marina

A fashionable French resort before the Second World War, Royan was flattened by the British in 1945 and has risen from the ruins around the church of Notre Dame de Royan, of interesting modern design in dark grey stone.

The marina is large, with an obliging staff always ready to cater for visitors.

PILOTAGE

Approaches

From NW

See 1 *La Gironde approaches and estuary* for entrance.

From SE

In view of the wrecks in the channel N of Banc de St Georges it would be prudent to pass S of the latter and the SCM (Q(6)+LFl.15s), altering towards the harbour entrance when Jetée Sud head bears 025° and leave R1 buoy (Iso.G.4s) to starboard.

Entrance

By day or night

From ⊕506 and 100m to the W of R1 buoy (Iso.G.4s) make good a track of 035° towards Nouvelle Jetée head (Oc(2)R.6s). Less water than the charted 1.7m has been reported in this channel. Round Nouvelle Jetée head having regard for anyone leaving. A small SH buoy is sometimes in position to the NE of the jetée head and should be left to starboard. The reception berth is on the N side of the central spur below the harbour office.

Ferry port · Church · Reception · Entrance

Royan looking NW

Berthing

The normal visitors' berth is alongside a pontoon running along the N side of the central spur behind the harbour office; doubling up is sometimes necessary. A RIB will often meet incoming yachts outside and direct to a berth.

Formalities

The harbour office should be visited on arrival to fill in a form and pay for the berth. The customs office is in the SW corner of the harbour.

The memorial to the Cockleshell Heroes on the shore at St Georges de Didonée 1.5 miles from Royan, opened on the 50th anniversary of Operation Frankton in 1992

History

In December 1942 a daring operation by the Royal Marines code-named Operation Frankton was launched to disrupt the shipping using the docks in Bordeaux, which had been successfully breaking the Allied blockade.

On a moonless night, five armed canoes known as cockles left their launch submarine HMS *Tuna* near the Cordouan light for the 60-mile journey in four stages upriver to Bordeaux; only two reached the docks. Limpet mines were successfully laid and exploded on five merchant ships and a patrol vessel, all of which settled on the bottom.

The two canoes escaped downriver and the four marines landed on the east bank where they split up to return to the UK with the help of the Resistance. Two were caught and shot by the Germans; the only two survivors of the original ten, Major Hasler and Marine Sparks, were back in England in April.

Ashore in Royan

There are all the facilities of a major marina and this is the least troublesome place to demast before the canals.

There are some shops and restaurants in the marina but many more in the town where there is also a covered market. The beaches (locally *conches*) are excellent, clean and well patronised.

Otherwise not many tourist attractions.

4 Meschers

89km mark

Small muddy harbour with locked basin

Location
45°33'.00N 00°57'.00W

Shelter
Good in basins

Warning
Strong cross set on approach

Depth restrictions
Dries 1.5m in approach
Dries 1.5–2m in outer basin
Sill dries 2m
2m in inner basin

Night entry
Leading line lit

Tidal information
HW and LW as for PdG

Mean height of tide (m)

MHWS	MHWN	MLWN	MLWS
5.1	4.2	2.1	1.0

Tidal streams
Flood begins HW–0440
Ebb begins HW+0100

Berthing
On pontoon ends if vacant

Facilities
Water, electricity, showers, ice, launderette, chandlers; fuel and shops in village.

Charts
Inadequate for harbour but
BA 3057 (50), 3058
SHOM 7426 (50)
Imray C 41, C42

Telephone
☎ 05 46 02 56 89

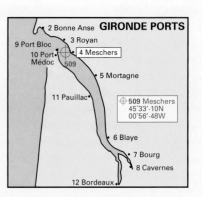

GIRONDE PORTS

2 Bonne Anse
9 Port Bloc
3 Royan
10 Port Médoc
4 Meschers
509
5 Mortagne
11 Pauillac
⊕ **509** Meschers
45°33'·10N
00°56'·48W
6 Blaye
7 Bourg
8 Cavernes
12 Bordeaux

PILOTAGE

Approach

Identify the entrance from ⊕509 or from Talmont church 2M to the SE close to the shore at the extremity of the same bay. The best time to enter is between HW–0200 and HW.

Entrance

Align the two blue posts (F lights at night) on 352° and hold this line exactly between the port and starboard posts marking the outer end of the channel. There is a further PHM mark to the E of these two posts which is left to starboard on the approach. The W side of the approach channel is marked with withies. There will be a strong cross stream at any time other than HW slack until within the inner channel.

Meschers looking NW

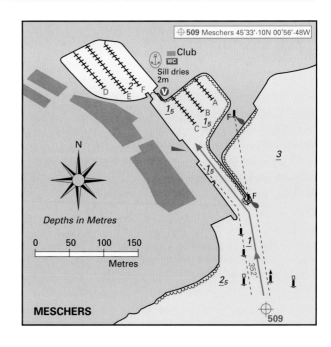

⊕ **509** Meschers 45°33'·10N 00°56'·48W

Club
WC
Sill dries 2m
V
N
Depths in Metres
0   50   100   150
Metres
MESCHERS
509

Berthing

If able to dry out, find a berth on the ends of A, B or C pontoons in the outer basin or on the NE side just outside the lock.

The lock opens HW ±0400 hours and the sill dries 2m. There is reported to be 2m in the basin. Berth alongside end of pontoons E or F.

Anchorage

Outside to the E of the beacons in mud sounding in as far as possible out of the stream.

Ashore in Meschers

Small restaurant and several shops.

5 Mortagne

75km mark

Attractive town and small harbour with a locked basin

Location
45°28'.00N 00°48'.00W

Shelter
Good

Warning
Strong cross set on approach

Depth restrictions
1.5–2m in approach
2m in outer basin
Up to 4m inside lock

Night entry
Not lit

Tidal information
HW PdG +0018
LW PdG +0030

Mean height of tide (m)

MHWS	MHWN	MLWN	MLWS
5.3	4.3	1.7	0.5

Tidal streams HW (PdG)
Flood begins HW –0415
Ebb begins HW +0145

Berthing
On pontoons in both basins

Facilities
All, but no travel-lift; fuel from the garage

Charts
None of the harbour
BA 3068
SHOM 7427 (various)
Imray C41, C42

Weather
Soulac Ch 79 at 0715, 1545, 1915
☎ 08 92 68 08 33

Radio
Ch 09 from HW–0100 to HW+0100

Telephone
☎ 05 46 90 63 15

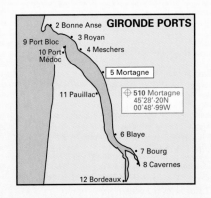

PILOTAGE

Approach

There is a minimum of 4m in the approach to ⊕510 off the entrance to the approach channel whence the village of Mortagne can be seen on the hill above. Alternatively make good a track of 050° from main channel buoy No. 22 until the entrance marks can be identified.

Entrance

The entrance marks are a destroyed port-hand beacon replaced by a W cardinal buoy, a port-hand main channel buoy (left to starboard on entering)

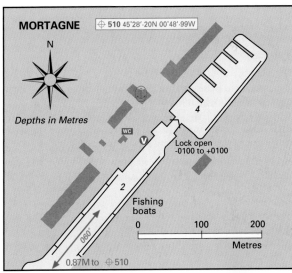

and port and starboard markers. Pass between the latter on a track of about 060°. The dredged channel is almost straight for 0.65M to the harbour entrance and marked by the occasional stake.

Berthing

On pontoon on the NW side before the lock where it probably dries. On pontoons inside the lock in up to 4m.

Anchorage

To the SE of the entrance as far in as depth allows, in mud. Quite exposed except from the E.

Ashore in Mortagne

Restaurants and shops in an attractive old town running up the hill. There is also a small boatyard.

Mortagne looking NNE

6 Blaye

37km mark

Historic town providing a fine-weather stop with good shopping

Location
45°07'.00N 00°40'.00W

Shelter
Uncomfortable in SW winds

Depth restrictions
None at moorings or pontoon; harbour dries

Night entry
Q(3)R.5s at N entrance to harbour

Tidal information
HW PdG +0140
LW PdG +0305

Mean height of tide (m)

MHWS	MHWN	MLWN	MLWS
5.2	4.1	0.8	0.3

Tidal stream (HW PdG)
Flood begins HW–0315
Ebb begins HW+0315

Berthing
A pontoon (max 12m) is placed to N of harbour below citadel; 3 mooring buoys off the town.

Facilities
An active YC otherwise minor except for shops; fuel from garage.

Chart
BA 3068
SHOM 7427 (various)

Weather
Soulac Ch 79 at 0715,1545, 1915
☎ 08 92 68 08 33

Radio
Ch 12 with Bordeaux port

Telephone
Bordeaux
☎ 05 56 31 58 64

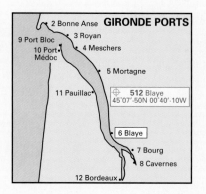

GIRONDE PORTS

2 Bonne Anse
9 Port Bloc
3 Royan
10 Port Médoc
4 Meschers
5 Mortagne
11 Pauillac
512 Blaye 45°07'·50N 00°40'·10W
6 Blaye
7 Bourg
8 Cavernes
12 Bordeaux

PILOTAGE

Approach

With a 2m draught, SHOM chart 7427 is essential to approach Braye other than just before HW. With this available the channel to the E of Iles Patiras, Bouchard and Nouvelle can be used. Otherwise leave the main channel at Nos. 51 and 52 buoys, make good a track of 125° and leave the S end of Ile Nouvelle 500m to port to head for ⊕512 or for the visitors' pontoon in front of the citadel.

Berthing

There is little shelter from the W off Blaye and the ebb can run at up to 3.5 knots; it will be distinctly uncomfortable in these conditions on the small pontoon and probably not much better at the moorings.

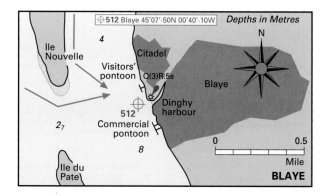

512 Blaye 45°07'·50N 00°40'·10W *Depths in Metres*
Ile Nouvelle
Citadel
Visitors' pontoon Q(3)R.5s
Blaye
Dinghy harbour
512
Commercial pontoon
Ile du Pate
0   0.5
Mile
BLAYE

Ashore in Blaye

An important town with a small drying harbour only suitable for dinghies. The conspicuous and historic citadel is of much interest. There is a good range of restaurants and small shops.

Visitors' Pontoon   *Citadel*   *Entrance*   *Commercial pontoon*

Blaye looking NE

7 Bourg

25/40km marks

Attractive and historic town with a pontoon berth and some facilities ashore

Location
45°02'.00N 00°33'.00W

Shelter
Poor in W winds

Warning
Strong W winds and ebb streams make the pontoon untenable. Drying wreck to W of pontoon

Depth restrictions
1.7m on approach.
3m+ at pontoon

Night entry
Unlit except Fl.R.4s at old dock entrance

Tidal information
HW PdG +0145

LW PdG +0300

Mean height of tide (m)

MHWS	MHWN	MLWN	MLWS
5.1	4.0	0.6	0.1

Tidal streams (HW PdG)
Flood begins HW −0200
Ebb begins HW+0315

Berthing
Visitors' berths (max 12m) on W pontoon, no doubling up

Facilities
Water on pontoon, fuel from garage; shops nearby

Chart
BA 3068, 3069 (various)
SHOM 7427 (various)

Weather
Soulac Ch 79 at 0715, 1545, 1915
☎ 08 92 68 08 33

Radio
Bordeaux Port Control on Ch 12 in emergency

Telephone
Yacht Club ☎ 05 57 68 31 72

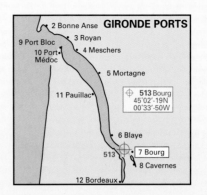

I. LA GIRONDE TO HENDAYE

PILOTAGE

Approaches

From downstream leave La Gironde by No. 52 buoy (WC) and head to port to enter La Dordogne, leaving Bec d'Ambés and its refineries to starboard. Avoid the conspicuous drying wreck just to the W of the visitors' berths which are at the W end of the long pontoon.

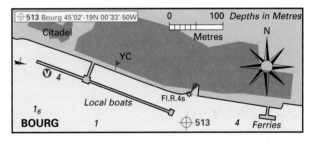

Berthing

Doubling up on the pontoons is not allowed but yachts berth on the inside where there appears to be plenty of water. If both sides are full there are no alternatives and anchoring off is not a happy option except at neaps and in fine weather.

Ashore in Bourg

An attractive old fortified town on La Dordogne just above the junction with La Garonne. Good restaurants and shops; there are two yacht clubs and a large heated swimming pool with showers near the pontoon. The citadel is worth a visit.

Bourg looking N

8 Cavernes

Tidal information
HW PdG +0230
HW PdG +0520

Tidal streams (HW PdG)
Flood begins HW +0015
Ebb begins HW +0400

Mean height of tide (m)
MHWS	MHWN	MLWN	MLWS
4.7	3.5	0.1	0.6

Chart
SHOM 7427 is the only chart to show this part of the river

GIRONDE PORTS

- 2 Bonne Anse
- 9 Port Bloc
- 3 Royan
- 10 Port Médoc
- 4 Meschers
- 5 Mortagne
- ⊕ **514** Cavernes 45°56'·20N 00°26'·50W
- 11 Pauillac
- 6 Blaye
- 7 Bourg
- 514
- 8 Cavernes
- 12 Bordeaux

Cavernes is a small village on the S bank 16km above Bourg on La Dordogne. The river is buoyed occasionally but not lit. The depth in the channel is generally over 2m. The river is crossed by three electricity cables just above Bourg (27m) and three road bridges (least height 19m) just below Cavernes.

It is a further 24km to Fronsac and Libourne but access is now not possible to masted craft due to a new low bridge between Fronsac and Cavernes.

The kilometre distances start at Libourne. Above this La Dordogne is tidal for 14 miles and navigable for 40 miles.

PILOTAGE

Approach
The passage is easy with or without SHOM chart 7427. Keep to the outside of the bends and follow the lateral buoyage. Cavernes is on the S bank on a left-hand bend just after the last bridge of three.

Berthing
There is a 5-berth pontoon off the village in 2m; water on the quay but nothing else.

Just above Cavernes on the opposite bank is a pontoon with water and electricity off the village of Asques, but there are no shops, restaurants or other facilities there.

Ashore at Cavernes
There is a restaurant but no shops. The nearest shop is at Loubés 1M to the S.

Minor harbours from Royan to Bordeaux

Port St Georges de Didonne 96km
Port de Talmont 85km
Port des Monards 80km
Port de St Sevrin d'Uzet 78km
Port Maubert 70km
Port de Conac 62km
Port de Vitrezay 60km
Port du Petit Vitrezay 59km
Port des Callognes 56km
Port des Portes Neuves 54km
Port de Freneau 50km

With the exception of the first, all these ports are muddy holes or river entrances which dry with few if any facilities. Some are marked on the approach with beacons and sometimes lights. Deep draught yachts are unlikely to want to use them and others only in an emergency and if the tide serves.

9 Port Bloc

⊕**507** 45°34'.22N 01°03'.57W

Visiting yachts are not wanted or welcomed here and it is unlikely that there will be a vacant berth. In an emergency call on Ch 09 before going in and keep clear of the ferries entering and leaving.

Looking upstream from Bordeaux. The first bridge is Pont de Pierre, with three beyond

10 Port Médoc

94km mark

Huge new marina with most facilities which is still developing

Location
45°34'.00N 01°04'.00W

Shelter
Excellent in marina

Warning
Strong cross-stream at entrance

Depth restrictions
3m at entrance
2m+ over all marina

Night entry
Pier ends expected to be lit

Tidal information
HW same as PdG

Mean height of tide (m)

MHWS	MHWN	MLWN	MLWS
5.4	4.4	2.1	1.0

Tidal stream (HW PdG)
Flood begins HW –0445
Ebb begins HW +0115

Berthing
At fingers on pontoons

Facilities
All in the marina. Shops some distance although some expected in marina.

Charts
No large-scale of marina
BA 3057 (50), 3068
SHOM 7426 (52)
Imray C41, C42

Weather
Soulac Ch 79 at 0715, 1545 and 1915
☎ 08 92 68 08 33

Radio
Probably Ch 09

Telephone
☎ 05 56 09 69 75
Taxi 05 56 09 60 47

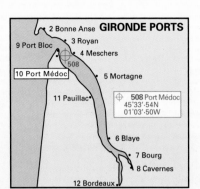

PILOTAGE

Approach and entrance

Directions for the approach using Passe de l'Ouest or Passe Sud may be found in *1 La Gironde approaches and estuary* above. From No. 13b buoy (Q.G) or between it and the steep-to Pointe de Grave (Oc.G.4s) leave Port Bloc (Fl.G.4s and Iso.G.4s) to starboard and identify Port Médoc entrance ½M to the S or make for ⊕508.

Enter on a track of about 250° allowing for a strong cross set until inside the breakwaters. The reception and fuel berth is immediately to starboard inside.

Berthing

On fingers on pontoons. 25m maximum. The berths on the outer breakwater are in 3m, the rest in 2m+. There is a pontoon for multihulls on the south wall.

Ashore in Port Médoc

The marina occupies an unpromising position between the ferry port of Port Bloc and the oil terminal of Verdon. While all the usual marina facilities are expected shortly, shops and restaurants may take longer and a taxi will be needed for serious provisioning from Soulac or further.

Port Médoc looking N

I. LA GIRONDE TO HENDAYE

11 Pauillac

47km mark

Useful halfway stop in good wine country

Location
45°12'.00N 00°45'.00W

Shelter
Good in marina but the stream sweeps through it

Warning
Only enter or leave near slack water

Depth restrictions
Entrance 1m–
2m+ in marina

Night entry
Lit but not recommended

Tidal information
HW PdG +0100
LW PdG +0150

Mean height of tide (m)

MHWS	MHWN	MLWN	MLWS
5.5	4.4	1.1	0.5

Tidal stream (HW PdG)
Flood begins –0315
Ebb begins +0215

Berthing
At the first two pontoons inside the entrance

Facilities
All, but no lift and craneage only to 1 tonne

Charts
No large-scale of marina
BA3068 (various)
SHOM 7427 (various)
Imray C41, C42

Weather
Soulac Ch 79 at 0715, 1545 and 1915
☎ 08 92 68 08 33

Radio
Ch 09 (working hours)

Telephone
☎ 05 56 59 12 16
Taxi ☎ 05 56 59 14 67

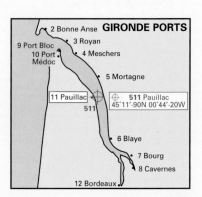

GIRONDE PORTS
2 Bonne Anse
3 Royan
9 Port Bloc
10 Port Médoc
4 Meschers
5 Mortagne
11 Pauillac
511
511 Pauillac
45°11'·90N 00°44'·20W
6 Blaye
7 Bourg
8 Cavernes
12 Bordeaux

PILOTAGE

Approaches

From north

Pauillac and ⊕511 are 1.5M south of the conspicuous oil refinery at Trompeloup. The main channel can be left at Nos. 43 and 44 buoys (Fl(2)G.6s and Fl(2)R.6s) and the outer harbour wall (Fl.G.4s and Q.G) headed for.

From south

Leave the main channel at Nos. 45 and 46 buoys (Iso.G.4s and Fl.R.2.5s) and head for the entrance.

Entrance

Entry and departure should only be attempted near slack water. The shuttering on the sides of the marina does not extend to the bottom and the stream flows through it. It is worth anchoring outside until the right moment.

Harbourmaster Crane Visitors' berth Entrance

Pauillac looking NE

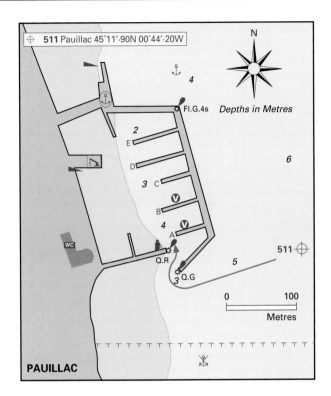

There is reputed to be 3m in the entrance which has a very sharp turn round the E breakwater head, but the mud shoals rapidly and less may be found. Keep close to the E breakwater head (Q.G) entering or leaving. There is reasonable light inside the marina but a night entry is not recommended unless it has been done before in daylight.

Berthing

The first two pontoons (A and B) ahead on entering are for visitors in depths up to 4m. They have fingers and haul-off lines.

Anchoring

Anchoring is prohibited for up to 500m south of the harbour due to cables. Either go beyond or anchor to the north off the slip to wait the tide.

A waiting buoy is sometimes placed off the entrance.

Mast stepping and unstepping

There is a 1-tonne crane on the end of the jetty in the NW corner of the harbour. Yachts with shallow draught may be able to berth out of the stream on the north or south sides of the jetty at any state of the tide but deep-draught yachts will only be able to safely carry this out near HW slack lying alongside the outer end.

The harbourmaster and staff are helpful and obliging and sometimes no charge, or only a nominal one, is made for this service. A *pourboire* is always appreciated.

Ashore in Pauillac

A useful yacht harbour halfway between Bordeaux and the sea in the centre of a famous wine growing region. Lifting or stepping masts is possible but only in safety near slack high water. There is no travel-lift but otherwise all the usual facilities including convenient shopping. The management is welcoming and friendly. English yachts have wintered afloat here.

La Maison du Tourisme et du Vin de Médoc near the marina can arrange vineyard tours.

Travel

Rail and bus services to Bordeaux (50km) and Merignac airport with internal and some international flights.

The drying crane jetty looking S

Pauillac to Bordeaux

Approach

It is 47km between the two, and there should be no difficulty in navigating this wide and well marked and lit estuary with the use of the BA or SHOM charts and benefiting from the flood and ebb streams. Poor visibility in the area is infrequent.

The ebb increases in strength upriver and with much rain up-country can exceed 5 knots, with the addition of a lot of debris including whole trees. Anchoring above Bec d'Ambès is not recommended and there are no safe or convenient stopping places for a yacht en route.

There is much commercial traffic in the river. Large ships unable to keep to the starboard side of the channel display a black ball forward and a red light by night and should be given right of way.

Lights

There are many lights and lit buoys marking the main channel up to Pont de Pierre at Bordeaux which are shown on the charts. In general white lights are leading marks, green are starboard hand and red port hand buoys or marks inbound.

12 Bordeaux

Large industrial city in the centre of a famous wine growing region

Location
44°53'.00N 00°32'.00W

Shelter
Good except for the strong streams

Warning
The ebb runs at up to 5 knots, the flood at up to 3 knots. Much debris comes down on the ebb.

Depth restrictions
6m+ in channel
3m at Lormont pontoons
2.5m at Bègles pontoons

Night movement
Not recommended

Tidal information
HW PdG +0215
LW PdG +0345

Mean height of tide (m)

MHWS	MHWN	MLWN	MLWS
5.3	4.2	0.4	0.0

Tidal stream (HW PdG)
Flood begins –0115
Ebb begins +0315

Berthing
Pontoons at Halte Nautique close to Pont d'Aquitaine
No. 2 basin in city
Bègles marina above Pont de Pierre

Facilities
Crane and water only at Halte Nautique. Water and chandler in No. 2 basin; fuel from garage. Minor facilities at Bègles.

Charts
BA 3069 (various)
SHOM 7427 (various)

Radio
Port Control Ch12 (24 hrs)

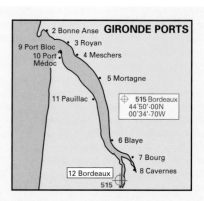

Telephone
Control ☎ 05 56 90 59 34
Lock gate ☎ 05 56 90 59 57

Berthing

It is not recommended that yachts berth on the walls on the W bank in the city which are high, rough and subject to strong streams.

Halte Nautique Just above and under Pont d'Aquitaine (clearance 51m) are three pontoons. On the W bank just above the bridge there is a small marina which is private and visitors are liable to be sent away. The pontoon above the bridge on the E side is for fishermen; the pontoon under the bridge may have a berth but the depths are not known. All pontoons have locked gates so a call ahead to Lormont YC ☎ 05 56 31 50 10 is essential. They all have small cranes but it would be most unwise to rely on them to demast. This can only be done with certainty in Bordeaux in the basins with a hired mobile crane.

Nos 1 and 2 basins (Lock 20m wide, 4m deep)
The lock only opens at HW. Entry must be requested 1½ hours beforehand (½ hour on leaving) on Ch 12 or ☎ 05 56 90 59 57. There is a waiting pontoon outside.

Halte Nautique upstream of Pont d'Aquitaine. The three pontoons on the right are private; the one above the bridge pillar on the E bank is for fishermen; a berth may be found on the pontoon just out of picture to the left

Pass through No. 1 basin and select a berth as convenient in No. 2. The NW corner near the chandler is probably the best option.

Ashore in Bordeaux

Bordeaux is a large and pleasant city in the centre of a renowned wine growing region. It is also a busy port and industrial centre and the passing yachtsman

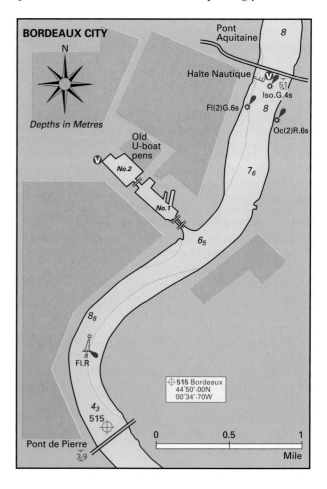

Bordeaux basins looking SE towards the locks

usually only sees the latter aspects. Both berths at Halte Nautique near Lormont and the basins have modest restaurants within walking distance but a taxi is needed for serious shopping or to see the city. There are many old and interesting buildings, churches, ruins and museums some dating from Roman times and the English occupation (1152–1453). Tours can be arranged through Syndicat d'Initiative, Allé de Tourney, 1 cours de 30 juillet who will supply maps and directions.

Travel

International airport at Merignac, bus and rail connections in all directions.

British Consul

At 353, boulevard du Président Wilson, 33200 Bordeaux. ☎ 05 57 22 21 10.

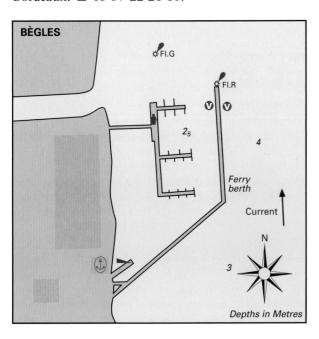

BÈGLES

Fl.G

Fl.R

Ⓥ Ⓥ

2₅

4

Ferry berth

Current

N

3

Depths in Metres

Bordeaux to Castets

A 40-mile trip through pleasant countryside

Masted navigation ceases at Pont de Pierre where the headroom is 3.9m.

The many narrow arches of this bridge obstruct the flow on the flood and the ebb, causing an appreciable fall of water through the bridge and many violent eddies on the downstream side. These difficulties are only surmountable with a very powerful engine and normally the bridge must be passed with the current. Use one of the arches marked by a white disc but not if there is a No Entry sign on it. This tidal barrier means that when coming downstream it is unlikely that the opening times of the lock to Nos. 1 and 2 basins (shuts at HW) can be met. However, it is always worth a call on Ch 12 in plenty of time if entry looks a possibility.

The flood stream becomes negligible above the bridge and only causes a stand or diminution of the river flow.

There are three bridges above Pont de Pierre, all with greater headroom and larger arches.

There is a small marina on the W bank at Bègles above the third bridge and some 5M from Bordeaux.

Bègles

A small marina with 80 berths in 2.5m and arrangements for transients who are expected to berth on the outer pontoon. This is in the full flow of the current and any debris coming down, so it is worth trying to get a berth inside.

Water and electricity on the pontoons; fuel berth and a few social facilities; shopping centre nearby.

Bègles is reasonably close to Merignac airport and is a possibility for changing crew.

Radio Ch 09 (weekday working hours).

13 Castets

The first, largest and deepest lock of the Canal Latéral de la Garonne is here about 50km from Bordeaux. Approximately 1M short of the lock are some unmarked rocks which boats drawing 1.5m will hit before HW–0200. They are shown in the *Guide Vagnon* in a diagrammatic way but even if this is held it would be wise to wait downstream at Langon until HW–0100 or later before proceeding. The locks will not open until just before HW anyway.

Approaching from downstream the right-hand lock is the one in use. There are vertical bars to secure warps to but they are widely spaced. Once through the lock, a narrow lake leads to the second lock with a 3.3m rise and warping bars. Both locks have keepers and open during working hours at HW. There is a shady, wooden quay on the S bank just through the second lock.

Bassin d'Arcachon

14 Bassin d'Arcachon

Cat C

Extensive shallow basin with a large marina and many small harbours
No waypoints are given for ports inside the Bassin d'Arcachon

Location
44°35'.00N 01°18'.00W

Shelter
Good inside Cap Ferret, none in approaches

Warning
Dangerous entrance. See below

Depth restrictions
3.9m in North Channel
1.7m in South Channel
3–1.5m in marina
Much of basin dries

Night entry
Not lit

Tidal information
HW PdG

Cap Ferret	HW	+0010
	LW	+0005
Marina	HW	+0020
	LW	+0005

Mean height of tide (m)

MHWS	MHWN	MLWN	MLWS
4.1	3.3	1.3	0.5

Tidal streams (HW PdG)
At entrance
Flood begins –0520
Ebb begins –0045

Berthing
On pontoons in large marina

Facilities
Extensive at Marina and in Arcachon town

Charts
BA 2664 (200), 2750 (49)
SHOM 6766 (49)
Local (see below)

Weather
Cap Ferret Ch 79 at 0733, 1603 and 1933
☎ 08 92 68 08 33

Radio
Marina Ch 09 (working hours)
Call *Cap Ferret* Ch13/16 for conditions at entrance

Telephone
Marina ☎ 05 56 22 36 75
Cap Ferret ☎ 05 56 60 60 03

Lifeboat
A lifeboat is stationed at La Vigne inside the entrance on the E side of Cap Ferret peninsula

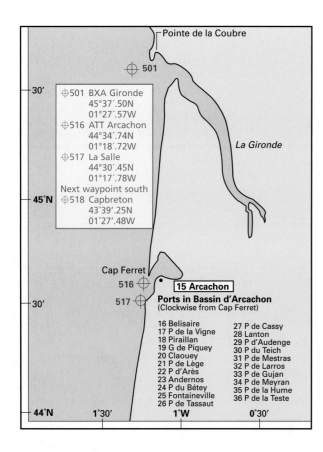

Warning

The entrance channels are re-marked each year as they change in the winter storms but they may change after re-marking. Only enter between HW–0300 and HW+0100 and with less than 1m swell. Good visibility is also important as the buoys are far apart and unlike most French harbours there are no leading marks.

In the last 15 years the South Channel has silted and the North Channel deepened to a least depth of 3.9m to become the major channel.

There is an air-to-air, air-to-sea and land-to-sea firing range on both sides of the entrance (see *Technical and navigational information* above for details). It is unlikely that entry to Arcachon will be prevented by its activities but there may be some restriction from or to the south.

In the basin green seaweed and pine needles may block engine filters.

Local charts

There are two local charts on a larger scale than SHOM 6766, produced by Feret et Fils from drawings by Jean-Marie Bouchet and available in local bookshops.

PILOTAGE

Approaches

From north

A featureless coast extends from the mouth of La Gironde along which the beacon at Pointe de la Négarde, Hourtin lighthouse, the beacon at La Grigne and Cap Ferret lighthouse are conspicuous. Do not cut the corner if entering Arcachon; head for the ATT ARC outer buoy and ⊕516 before turning in. The huge sand dune of Pyla (103m) is located 2M SE of Cap Ferret and is a conspicuous feature.

From south

From Capbreton a similar featureless coast stretches for 60M along which the Contis lighthouse, Bicarosse beacon and the firing range buildings stand out (see *Technical and navigational information* above for details). There is a 3M lane

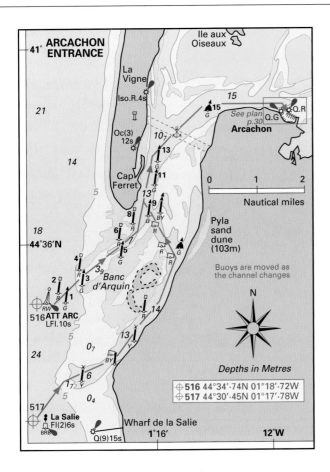

Entrance

By North Channel

It is advisable to enter from the vicinity of ⊕516 and the ATT ARC approach buoy (red buoy with ball top, white stripes, LFl.10s) during the last quarter or half of the flood. Follow the channel marked by a series of unlit red or green pillar buoys. The bar between Nos. 4 and 5 buoys has a least depth of 3.9m. The channel leads NE turning N towards Cap Ferret in the later stages. In any sea or swell there will be breakers on the sands on either side. Entry should not be attempted with a swell of more than 1m or on the ebb.

Once under the lee of Cap Ferret follow the channel round to the E for the final 5M past the piers and town of Arcachon to the marina. Older charts show a series of dangerous wrecks in this channel which have now been cleared to a least depth of 5m.

The entrance to the marina is marked by a large stone anchor on the port-hand side of the entrance and Q.R and Q.G lights.

By South Channel

This channel has silted considerably and should be treated with caution. The same caution as above about swell should be observed. Least depth on the bar to the NNE of La Salie buoy (Two black balls on BRB buoy, Fl(2)6s) was 1.7m but once inside it deepens quickly.

From ⊕517 or La Salie buoy make good a track of 035° over the bar to leave the first yellow buoy with × topmark to starboard. The channel is thereafter marked by red can buoys usually with square topmark to port, yellow or green pillar buoys usually with × topmark to starboard. There is the

between the shore and the range area. The 20m line provides a good danger limit from the shore which should be watched carefully when approaching the extended Arcachon shoals and ⊕517 if entering by the South Channel.

Arcachon entrance looking N towards Cap Ferret

North Channel

South Channel

occasional cardinal buoy. When Pyla Dune is reached, turn NNW towards Cap Ferret lighthouse to join the North Channel; then proceed as above.

At night

Not recommended unless there is a good moon and it has been done before by daylight.

15 Port d'Arcachon

Large modern marina with all facilities close to town centre

PILOTAGE

Entrance

It is 50m wide and leads in on 180°. Keep to the starboard hand on entry by the wavebreaker as there is a 1.5m patch by the fuel berth on the E side of the entrance. If this depth is no problem, go to the fuel berth to arrange a berth, or to pontoon A.

Berthing

Try to negotiate a berth in the SW corner, which shortens the walk to town considerably. Most berths are in 3m.

Anchorage

In 2m or more outside clear of moorings and the entrance.

Ashore in and around Arcachon

A large modern seaside town with good shops, many restaurants and a casino with many beaches close by. The whole of the Bassin has been given over to the cultivation of oysters and shellfish since Roman times, and this is still the main industry.

Facilities

Everything expected in a large modern marina. The travel-lift (45-tonne), cranes (20-tonne), slips and workshops are in the SE corner. Yacht club at SE end of N arm.

Inner entrance looking S

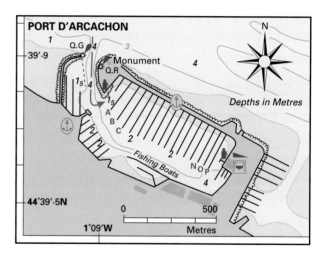

Leisure

Europe's largest sand dune at Pyla by the entrance has a magnificent view from the top (103m) and a good beach at its foot. It is popular with hang gliders. Banc d'Arquin between the two entrance channels used to be a nature reserve but is often inundated or modified by the sea. Temporary buildings are put there in the season to illustrate the work of the reserve and ferries run there from Arcachon and Pyla. A visit to the Roman ruins can be rewarding. Devotees of Bernard Cornwell will recognise much of the area from *Sharpe's Siege*.

Travel

Good rail and bus services. The nearest major airport is at Merignac, Bordeaux (70km) but there are active grass airfields at Arcachon and Andernos.

Arcachon Marina looking S

16–36 Small harbours around Bassin d'Arcachon

Many small harbours have been constructed round the sides of the basin in the easily worked sandy soil for the use of local boats and those who tend the shellfish beds. Although leisure craft have infiltrated many of the harbours, some are private and there is no room for visitors. A few retain some water behind sills but most dry to soft mud and are not suitable for deep draught boats without legs.

SHOM chart 6766, BA chart 2750 or the two large-scale charts available locally are essential to explore further than the main channels.

Brief details of these harbours are given below.

Warnings

Keep clear of the oyster beds which are marked with posts, particularly between HW+0300 and HW–0300.

Green seaweed and pine needles may clog filters and logs.

PILOTAGE

The main channels usually have enough depth for small yachts even at springs (1–5m). The bottom is soft and sandy mud; the water is clear and the bottom can be seen. The channels are marked by beacons at all junctions and bear a letter and number as shown on SHOM 6766. The banks of the channels are marked by stakes at the 0m line.

It is advisable to explore on a rising tide and allow plenty of time to visit several harbours in search of a berth. Streams in the larger channels can reach 6 knots at springs.

Islands

Ile aux Oiseaux in the centre of the Bassin is ¾M long and 3m high and this and a smaller island nearby are the only islands of significance.

16 Bélisaire

Not a port but a long pier used by car ferries from Arcachon. There is a large area for moorings to the S of it and a good anchorage about 100m off the coast open to the SE and S. There is a small village and shops nearby and a large water tower 600m S and 400m inland from the pier to which runs a pipe from Pyla on the opposite shore; anchoring is prohibited on either side of this pipe. The moorings extend S close to the shore to the spit running N from the E side of Cap Ferret.

I. LA GIRONDE TO HENDAYE

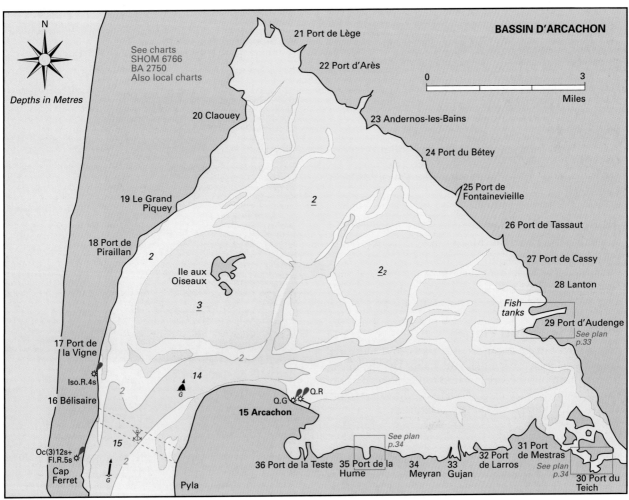

17 Port de la Vigne

A medium-sized private yacht harbour with 270 berths on two pontoons; also two quays with pontoons. Only very short visits are allowed (i.e. to fuel), max. length 8.5m but there are moorings and an anchorage to the S in up to 5m close to the beach. Red and green buoys and stakes mark the entrance and there is an Iso.R.4s light on the S of the entrance; 1m is reported in the entrance and inside. A partial barrier on the starboard hand breaks up any swell. There is a harbourmaster and a variety of facilities including fuel and water, restaurants and shops close to the harbour.

An all-weather lifeboat is moored off the entrance.

Port de la Vigne looking W near HW

Warning

A bank with least depth of 0.8m lies 200m offshore for some distance N and S of the entrance. An approach from Bélisaire Pier keeping 100m offshore will avoid it.

18 Port de Piraillan

A small drying harbour for oyster and fishing boats with a large area of moorings and space for anchorage to the E. The harbour is in the form of a square with quays and quayed islands in the middle. The surrounding area is covered with pines.

19 Port le Grand Piquey

Not a port but an excellent anchorage and mooring area with a pier for landing and a slip. Depths up to 5m offshore but the streams in the channel run at up to 2½ knots. Boatyard, mechanic, chandlery and shops in the village. Good fish restaurant.

20 Claouey

Not a harbour but a popular launching site with an anchorage and a large area of moorings which dry. Approach from S via beacons C1, C0 and B0. There

is a large slip, *club nautique*, WCs, showers, boatyard, chandlery and shops in the village. Surrounded by pine trees.

21 Port de Lège

A small drying harbour for work boats. The approach is northwards from beacon B1; note that the last two miles are through a nature reserve and there is a fish farm to the E of the entrance. Entry is only possible at HW and there are two quays which dry out on soft mud. Water available and a shop nearby.

22 Port d'Arès

More a landing place than a yacht harbour, approached from beacon C8. It has a brick quay with firm sand alongside it. There is a water point on the quay and the *club nautique* has WCs and showers. There is a boatyard, mechanic and chandlery. Open to winds from the S sector.

23 Andernos-les-Bains

A large harbour with 160 berths exclusively for fishing and oyster boats but there are drying moorings outside the harbour. Turn N into the channel at beacon D14. In the harbour there are waterpoints on the quays, a slip, mechanic, chandlery and shops nearby. The harbour and area outside is exposed to the SW especially at HW.

There is a 300m pier between Andernos and Port du Bétey.

There is small airfield to the N of Andernos for light aircraft.

Andernos-les-Bains looking SE

24 Port du Bétey

A small drying harbour entered from beacon D14 with a buoyed channel and 150 places for yachts and workboats. Yachts secure alongside quays or bows

Bétey looking NE

Cassy looking NE

to the wall. Drying moorings outside but uncomfortable in a SW wind. Facilities include water points, fuel nearby, two WCs and showers, a slip and shops at Andernos-les-Bains.

25 Port de Fontainevieille

A medium-sized drying yacht harbour entered via beacons E6 and E7 turning to port just before E8 out of the Tassaut channel. It has 200 berths for yachts in a basin with pontoons. There is 1m in the entrance channel at half tide. Drying moorings outside the harbour. Facilities include water on the pontoons, pumped fuel, slip, restaurant, *club nautique* and a harbourmaster.

Port de Fontainevieille looking NNE 2 hours after LW

26 Port de Tassaut

A very small attractive harbour used by oyster boats. Enter via beacons E6, E7 and E8. The harbour dries and has 180 berths, a slip, water points and a landing place. There is a harbourmaster and a *club nautique*. Fuel nearby. Restaurants and shops in nearby village. There is a sailing school and moorings outside the entrance. A submerged wall to starboard on entry is marked by stakes.

27 Port de Cassy

An attractive medium-sized harbour with a few oyster boats. There is a winding entrance channel entered by beacon F3; a water tower to the N of the harbour helps identification. Quays and pontoons in three basins provide 225 berths (3 for visitors). The harbour dries on mud and sand and legs are obligatory if not of shallow draught. There are WCs, showers, water, a slip and crane plus a *club nautique* and shops in the village.

28 Lanton

Not a harbour but an area with fish farms and an estuary which would be suitable for further development.

29 Port d'Audenge

A medium-sized yacht and workboat harbour which has recently been enlarged. Workboats use the centre basin. For yachts there are 130 berths in the Nouveau Bassin (New Harbour) and 85 berths in the Ancien Port (Old Harbour). Maximum length 10m.

Entrance down a long channel marked by beacons G4, G6 and G8 and stakes towards a tall, grey water tower. Enter at HW–0200 to HW+0200. The harbour dries at LW, soft sand and mud.

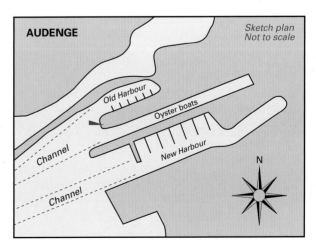

AUDENGE — *Sketch plan Not to scale*

I. LA GIRONDE TO HENDAYE

There is a harbourmaster, water and electricity, two WCs and showers, fuel in the village, two fish restaurants and the usual shops in the large village of Audenge.

30 Port du Teich

A small drying harbour for yachts in the River L'Eyre on the S bank. Approach from the vicinity of K15 beacon. The entrance channel is buoyed and marked by perches further in. Max 12m. Normal supplies from the village of Le Teich. Good fish restaurant.

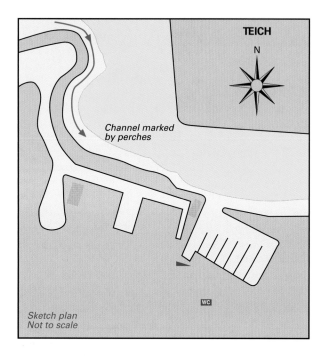

31, 32 and 33 Ports de Mestras, Larros and Gujan

Three medium-sized harbours side-by-side for fishermen and oyster farmers, with picturesque cottages lining the harbour walls. They all dry out at low water. Usual supplies from the large village of Gujan-Mestras. Larros has a large cross on its breakwater head. There is a local boat builder.

Worth a visit, but an empty berth is unlikely to be found. There is a good fish restaurant at Gujan.

The complex of Mestras, Larros and Gujan looking S

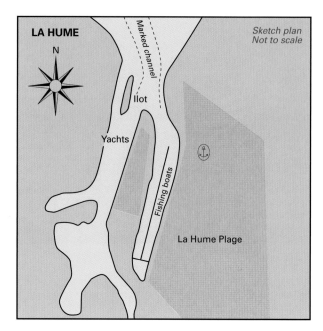

34 Port de Meyran

A small harbour with drying berths each side used by oyster and fishing boats. Leave the main channel at beacon K5.

35 Port de la Hume

A medium-sized harbour for yachts, oyster and fishing boats. Leave the main channel at beacon K3, entrance channel marked by stakes and yellow buoys. It has quays and pontoons, a slip and a large restaurant specialising in fish dishes.

36 Port de la Teste

One of the larger harbours tucked behind Port d'Arcachon with a long and winding entrance channel from K1 beacon. Most of the berths are private and all dry to soft mud. Fuel nearby and a good fish restaurant. Shops in La Teste village.

Port de la Teste looking S

French Basque Ports

37 Capbreton

Cat C

Holiday resort with large marina but shallow entrance

Location
43°39'.00N 01°26'.00W

Shelter
Good once inside

Warning
See right

Depth restrictions
Min 1.5m in entrance
Max 2.40m in marina

Night entry
Lit but no leading lights

Tidal information
HW PdG –0035
LW PdG –0035

Mean height of tide (m)

MHWS	MHWN	MLWN	MLWS
4.2	3.3	1.7	0.7

Tidal stream
Up to 3kns ebb in entrance
1kn or less inside

Berthing
On pontoons
Max length 23m

Facilities
All, but a good walk to the shops

Charts
No large-scale
BA 1102 (200)
SHOM 6786 (130)
Imray C17

Weather
Ch 79 at 0745, 1615, 1945 from Contis
Ch 79 at 0803, 1633, 2003 from Biarritz
☎ 08 92 68 08 40

Radio
Ch 09 (working hours)

Telephone
Marina ☎ 05 58 72 21 23

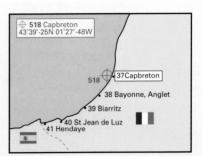

Warning
Le Fosse (or Le Gouf) de Capbreton, a deep submarine valley rising from 1300m, runs at right angles to the coast and ends 2M offshore. Confused and breaking seas will be found here in heavy weather especially around the edges. Avoid it in these conditions.

PILOTAGE

Approaches

From north

A straight and featureless coastline with only Contis lighthouse breaking the monotony until the houses of Capbreton appear and the lighthouse at the end of the N breakwater can be identified. ⊕518 is off the entrance.

From south

A similar featureless coastline from Bayonne northwards to ⊕518 when the breakwaters can be identified.

By night

The lights at Contis and Bayonne will assist and the 20m contour line provides a danger limit from the shore which is hazard-free in both directions. Otherwise it is GPS navigation in deep water.

Entrance

This can be attempted at any time under fair conditions when draught permits (least depth 1.5m) but in any sea or swell only between HW–0200 and HW+0100. Do not enter if the waves break right across although they will usually be breaking at the sides.

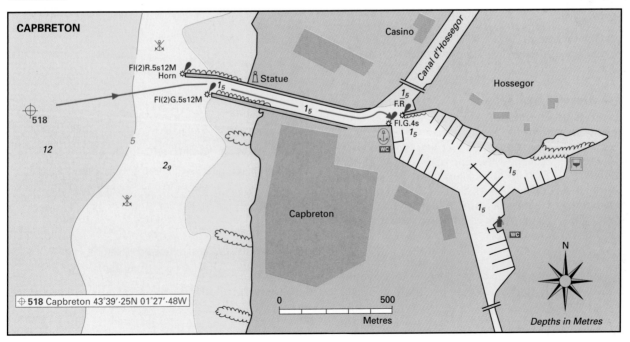

Capbreton marina looking ESE

The south breakwater has an underwater extension at its end for 30m which is awash at half tide.

At any time other than slack water be prepared for a cross set in or out of Canal d'Hossegor when entering the marina.

There are two stone heads with beacons (F.R and Fl(4)G.12s) at the marina entrance.

Anchorage and moorings

None, and anchorage is prohibited outside on either side of the entrance.

Berthing

Maximum length 23m. On pontoons with fingers. The marina is dredged to 1.5m but most of the outer part carries 2m. 60 visitors' berths.

Ashore in Capbreton

Capbreton is devoted primarily to the 'better class' holidaymaker and to the yachtsman. There are only a few, small local fishing boats. There is an excellent yacht club with showers, bar and restaurant and adequate shops in Hossegor and Capbreton, although a good walk away. There is a casino and fine bathing beaches close by. A dinghy trip up the Canal d'Hossegor (more a lake than a canal) and Lac Martin may amuse.

Travel

Bus service in all directions; rail from Bayonne; airfield (mostly internal flights but some packages) at Biarritz (25km).

Capbreton entrance looking ENE 2 hours after HW

Formalities

Customs available if required.

Repairs

30-tonne travel-lift, 1.5-tonne crane; small boatyard; sailmaker.

38 Bayonne and Anglet Marina

Cat B*

Historical town and commercial port with large marina accessible in most weathers

Location
43°32'.00N 01°32'.00W

Shelter
Good in Anglet

Warning
Give way to merchant ships in entrance and channel. Only attempt entrance from HW–0400 to HW+0100 in any sea or swell

Depth restrictions
8.3m in entrance
2.5m in marina
5.3m in harbour channel

Night entry
Well lit plus leading lights

Tidal information
HW PdG –0032
LW PdG –0032

Mean height of tide (m)
MHWS	MHWN	MLWN	MLWS
4.2	3.3	1.7	0.7

Tidal streams (HW PdG)
Flood begins –0550
Ebb begins +0100
Flood up to 4kns, ebb up to 5kns

Berthing
On pontoons in Anglet.
Possible alongside berth upriver

Facilities
All in Anglet; shops nearby

Charts
BA 3640 (10), 1102 (200)
SHOM 6557 (50), 6558 (50)
Imray C17

Weather
From Biarritz on Ch 79 at 0803, 1633 and 2003
☎ 08 92 68 08 40
Navtex A or D

Radio
Port Control Ch 12 and 16
Anglet Ch 09 (working hours)

Telephone
Marina ☎ 05 59 63 05 45
Port ☎ 05 59 50 31 50
Customs ☎ 05 59 59 08 29

Ashore in Bayonne

Four miles of estuary lead to the attractive old city. Most of the commerce and industry is concentrated on the N and E banks of the river at Boucau below the first bridge. The next bridge just below the cathedral is lower and restricts further navigation for another 40 miles to Pony to small craft.

A taxi or bus will be needed to reach the city from Anglet but it is worth the trip to see the 13th-century cathedral, Roman remains, two museums and the citadel. There are also good beaches to the north and south but sometimes heavy surf.

Anglet marina is well appointed and has all usual facilities including a 13-tonne travel-lift, crane and a welcoming yacht club. There are shops and restaurants within easy walking distance.

History

The harbour and town were created by the Romans around 100 BC and many Roman remains including the foundations of Le Vieux Château can still be seen. Gascony (which includes Bayonne) became an English province in 1150 AD and the English held it for 300 prosperous years. However, with their departure and the loss of trade with Britain, the river silted up and the town fell on hard times. The river was eventually dredged in the 18th century and the town prospered again with a free port and a large fishing fleet.

L'Adour River looking SW to the marina at Anglet

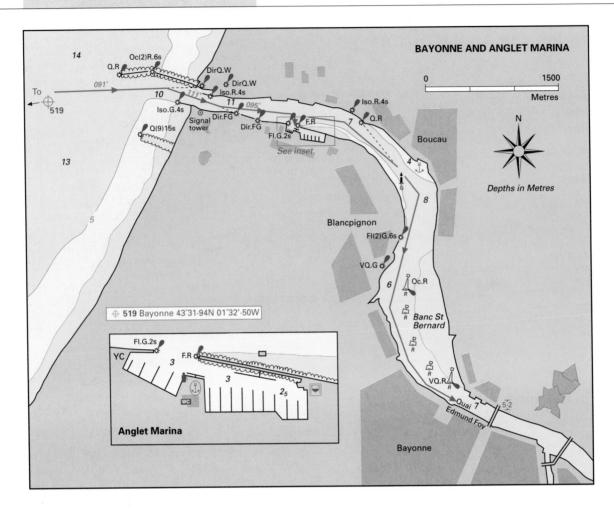

BAYONNE AND ANGLET MARINA

⊕ 519 Bayonne 43°31·94N 01°32′·50W

Anglet Marina

PILOTAGE

Approaches

From N

Head for ⊕519, the landfall buoy is about ¾M NNW of it. The N breakwater end is conspicuous as are the warehouses and silos at Boucau.

From S

The low coastline is broken by the rocky outcrop of Pointe St Martin and its lighthouse in front of Biarritz town. Head for ⊕519 and the breakwater end and buildings at Boucau will be identified.

By night

The lights of Pointe St Martin, Capbreton and the landfall buoy (LFl.10s) will assist until the well lit entrance is identified.

Entrance

By day and night

From ⊕519 align the first set of leading marks on 091° (both white pylons, red tops and Q.W intense on line) and proceed on this line to leave the outer breakwater end 100m to port (Q.R). Before reaching the inner breakwater heads pick up the next leading line on 111° (front white hut, green band DirF.G, rear white tower green bands DirF.G) and pass through the inner entrance on this line. The inner entrance ends are lit by Iso.R and Iso.G both 4s.

When the conspicuous port signal tower is abeam to starboard alter to about 095° to proceed up the centre of the channel. The entrance to the marina is marked on its W side by a white pylon, green top Fl.G.2s. The stream sets strongly across this entrance except for HW and LW slack. It is hardly necessary to stick to the next two leading lines if proceeding further upriver. Remain in the centre of the channel until Pointe de Blancpignon is passed, then favour the W bank and observe the lateral buoyage.

Berthing

In marina Up to 18m, dredged to 2.5m on pontoons with fingers. 60 visitors' berths. Reception at right angles to entrance and fine on the port bow on entry; this is also the fuel berth; office is adjacent.

Upriver Berths near the city centre are now cut off by a bridge with 5.2m clearance. Just before this on the S bank Quai Edmund Foy may provide a temporary berth but the face is piled and is for commercial use. Foreign yachts will be chased away from the small naval base jetty on the W bank opposite Banc St Bernard.

Anchorage

It is possible to anchor out of the main fairway in 2–4m, mud and sand but the streams run strongly especially on the ebb. Much debris comes down if the river is in spate. The anchorage shown off Boucau has good holding but is very noisy.

39 Biarritz

Cat D

Still a fashionable watering-place but to the yachtsman only an open anchorage and tiny boat harbour not usable in any swell. A visit is only worthwhile in fair and settled weather

The town lies 3½ miles S of Bayonne and 7 miles to the NNE of St Jean-de-Luz.

Tidal information, charts and weather

As for Bayonne.

Warning

The Plateau de St Jean-de-Luz lies between 1½ and 4 miles offshore with a minimum depth of 10m. The sea breaks over some of the rocky shallows in heavy weather or swell and should be avoided.

Depth restrictions

There is up to 1m in the approach to the tiny harbour which dries to 0.8m in the two basins; the third basin has a sill; the entrance is about 6m wide with a very sharp turn in to port. A dinghy can be left here.

Anchorage

As indicated on the plan in about 3m, adequate holding.

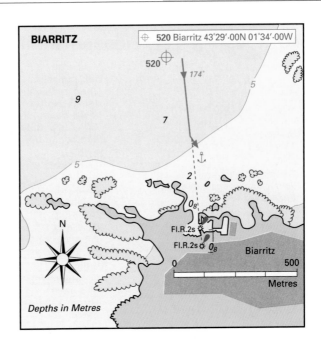

Ashore in Biarritz

The town has many better class restaurants, shops, casinos and places of amusement, most within reasonable walking distance of the harbour. Excellent beaches with supporting infrastructure. There are no facilities specifically for yachtsmen.

Travel

Medium-sized airport. Bus and rail connections in all directions.

Biarritz harbour looking SSE

Entrance

I. LA GIRONDE TO HENDAYE

40 St Jean-de-Luz, Ciboure/Larraldénia, Socoa and La Nivelle

Cat A*

Large bay with seaside resorts and a small marina

Location
43°24'.00N 01°41'.00W

Shelter
Good Ciboure/Larraldénia and Socoa; anchorage exposed in northerlies

Warning
A number of off-lying banks break in heavy weather. In these conditions only the leading lines from ⊕521 should be used

Depth restrictions
Ciboure 1m on approach
Socoa Dries
La Nivelle bridge height 1.9m

Night entry
Well lit leading lines

Tidal information
HW PdG –0042
LW PdG –0037

Mean height of tide (m)

MHWS	MHWN	MLWN	MLWS
4.3	3.3	1.7	0.6

Tidal streams
The flood enters by the east entrance, the ebb exits by the west, ½ and 1 knot respectively.
Flood begins HW PdG –0600
Ebb begins HW PdG 0000

Berthing
Larraldénia Pontoons and 8 visitors' berths
Socoa Moorings afloat and drying
La Nivelle Only for less than 8m and lowering mast

Anchoring
Off Socoa or SE corner clear of obstructions

Facilities
Larraldénia Water, electricity and fuel plus others
Socoa Water by hand, fuel at HW, plus others
Good shops at both places

Charts
BA 3640 (10),1102 (200)
SHOM 6558 (5)
Imray C17

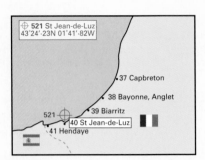

Weather
Biarritz Ch 79 at 0803, 1633, 2003
☎ 08 92 68 08 40
Navtex A or D

Radio
Ciboure Ch 09 (working hours)

Telephone
Harbourmaster ☎ 05 59 47 26 81
Biarritz airport ☎ 05 59 43 83 83

Coastguard
There is a coastguard/signal station in a tall white tower just to the S of La Socoa lighthouse

PILOTAGE

Approaches

The directions below are given for heavy weather to avoid the shoal patches which have a least depth of 15m over them. In fine weather or little swell more direct lines may be taken.

From W

By day or night

A good offing should be maintained after Cabo Higuer to clear Les Briquets 1M off the conspicuous Pointe St Anne. Proceed then outside the Belhara Perdun shoal to pick up the Socoa/Bordagain leading

Ciboure and Larraldénia marina looking S

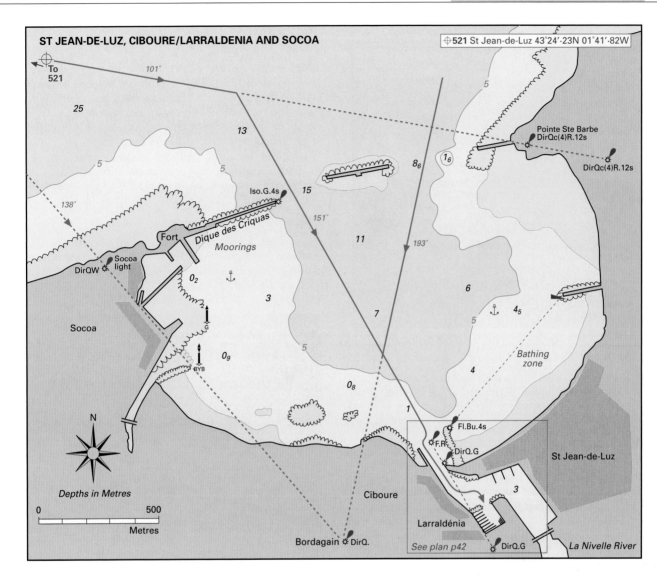

ST JEAN-DE-LUZ, CIBOURE/LARRALDENIA AND SOCOA

⊕521 St Jean-de-Luz 43°24'·23N 01°41'·82W

Depths in Metres

See plan p42

line 138° (front Q, rear DirQ) to proceed to ⊕521, thence on the Sainte-Barbe leading line 101° (front DirOc(4)R.12s, Rear DirOc(4)R.12s) transferring to the inner leading line 151° (front DirQ.G, rear DirQ.G) to pass through the W entrance. See *Appendix 1* for more details of these leading marks and lights.

From N

By day or night

Pick up the Socoa/Bordagain leading line and proceed down it to ⊕521 and thence as from W to pass through the W entrance.

From E or NE

By day

Follow the coast about 1M off and outside the 20m line inside the shoal patches until the Tour de Bordagain (tall stone tower on top of hill with trees round it) bears 193°. Keep on this bearing to pass through the E entrance. Do not cut the corner due to Les Esquilletac shoal.

By night

It would be prudent to proceed outside the shoals towards ⊕521 until the inner leading line (both Q.G) on 151° is identified and proceed down this through the W entrance.

Entrance

Ciboure Larraldénia Marina is between two rocky training walls just SW of the leading line. At night be careful not to go between the Finger Mole and the E training wall as the front leading light is well back. The entrance is dredged inside the wall-ends to 3m but it shoals to 1m outside. Delay entrance to HW if there is any swell as it can break right across. Once inside this entrance, the entrance to the marina will be fine on the port bow behind another wall running out from the W bank.

Berthing

Larraldénia Up to 16m in 3m on pontoons with fingers, 8 for visitors. In the event of the marina being full, a berth in the fishing harbour on pontoons may be possible.

Socoa Drying berths may be available in the harbour. Enquire at the yacht club.

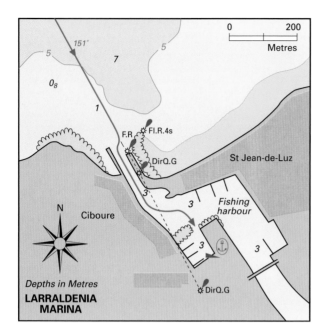

LARRALDENIA MARINA

Depths in Metres

Moorings

There are 3 visitors' moorings near the root of Digue des Criquas off Socoa in the middle of a number of private ones. Contact the YC if a private one is picked up.

Anchorages

The normal yacht anchorage is to the SW of the W entrance and to the S of the moorings. Holding is doubtful and two anchors would be wise in heavy weather. Landing can be made just inside the Socoa harbour entrance.

An alternative anchorage is in the SE corner of the bay clear of the bathing zone in 3m or more. There is a landing pier in the corner of the bay.

Ashore in St Jean-de-Luz/Socoa

St Jean-de-Luz is a lively place with many amusements including a casino to entertain the tourists, of which there are many in August. There is a chandlery and basic services here but few repair facilities. Shops and restaurants in Ciboure.

Socoa has the very friendly Yacht Club Basque with restaurant and showers and there is also a diving club for those wanting any underwater work; a good selection of shops and restaurants. Fuel can be brought by *camion* around HW to an alongside berth ☎ 05 59 26 06 98.

Travel

Good rail and bus services in all directions. An airfield at Biarritz (15km) has some European flights; international flights from Fuenterrabía (10km) are via Madrid.

Socoa looking SSW. Note distinctive striated grey cliffs below Socoa lighthouse which stretch a few miles to the west

St Jean-de-Luz looking SE

Socoa

41 Baie de Fontarrabie/Fuenterrabia/Rada de Higuer[1], Port Hendaye (Socoburu Marina)[2], Hondarribia Marina[3], Puerto Gurutzeaundi[4]

[1]Cat D

[2]Cat B* France

[3]Cat B* Spain

[4]Cat A Spain

The bay, estuary, harbours and Río Bidasoa lie between France and Spain. A large part of the bay is neutral area and the boundary between the two countries is complex (see BA chart 1181 for some details). There are two first-class marinas and plenty going on ashore

Location
43°23'.00N 01°47'.00W

Shelter
Complete in Gurutzeaundi
Complete in both marinas

Warning
River Bidasoa bar breaks in a swell and on the ebb

Depth restrictions
1m on Río Bidasoa bar
3m in Gurutzeaundi, Socoburu and Hondarribia

Night entry
Well lit but no leading lights

Tidal information
HW PdG −0040
LW PdG − 0030

Mean height of tide (m)

MHWS	MHWN	MLWN	MLWS
4.2	3.1	1.6	0.5

Tidal streams
No significance except in río entrance where ebb can reach 5 knots

Berthing
At pontoons in both marinas. See details below

Facilities
All, in both marinas

Charts
BA 1157 (25), 1102 (200)
SHOM 6558 (50), 6786 (130)
Imray C17

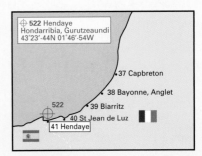

522 Hendaye
Hondarribia, Gurutzeaundi
43°23'-44N 01°46'-54W

37 Capbreton
38 Bayonne, Anglet
522
39 Biarritz
40 St Jean de Luz
41 Hendaye

Weather
Biarritz Ch 79 at 0803, 1633 and 2003 in French
Pasajes Ch 27 at 0840, 1240, 2010 in Spanish
Navtex A or D

Radio
Hendaye Ch 09 (24hrs)
Hondarribia Ch 09, 10 (24hrs)

Telephone
Socoburu ☎ 05 59 48 06 10
Hondarribia ☎ 943 64 17 11
Taxi ☎ 943 63 33 03
Airport ☎ 943 64 12 67

I. LA GIRONDE TO HENDAYE

Socoburu Marina   Runway   Hondarribia Marina

Baie de Fontarrabie looking SSE over Río Bidasoa

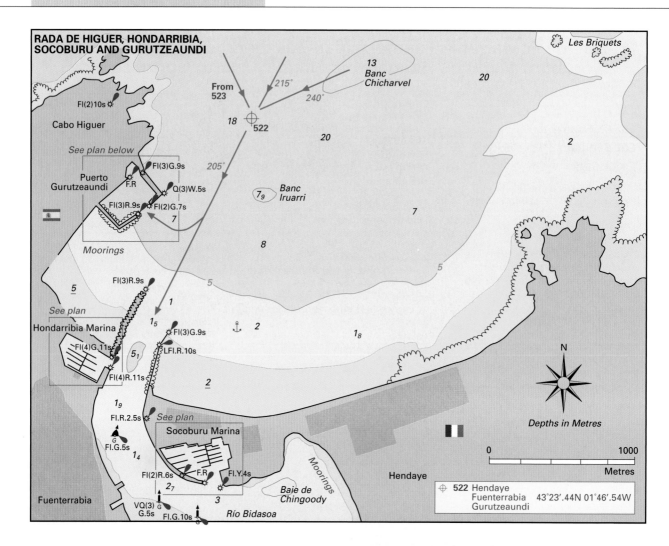

RADA DE HIGUER, HONDARRIBIA, SOCOBURU AND GURUTZEAUNDI

PILOTAGE

Approaches

From W

By day or night

Navigate to ⊕523 to the N of Cabo Higuer (Fl(2)10s23M) and thence to ⊕522 whence a track of 205° will lead between the training wall heads of the Río Bidasoa (Fl(3)G.9s5M, Fl(3)R.9s5M). This track will leave Banc Iruarri (7.9m) 200m to port and pass Puerto Gurutzeaundi to starboard. This fishing port has Q(3)5s on its E corner and the entrance is marked by Fl(3)R.9s and Fl(2)G.7s lights.

From E

By day or night

⊕522 or Cabo Higuer lighthouse (Fl(2)10s23M) should be approached on a track of 240° or less to avoid Les Briquets rocks to the NE of the bay. In heavy weather this should be reduced to 215° to avoid Banc Chicharvel (13m). Proceed as above on reaching ⊕522 and do not turn short if there is any sea or swell, to avoid Banc Iruarri (7.9m).

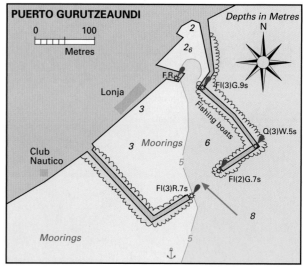

PUERTO GURUTZEAUNDI

From N

By day or night

A southerly course to ⊕522 clears all dangers and the lights of Cabo Higuer (Fl(2)10s23M) and Le Socoa lighthouse (Q.12M) assist. The houses of Hendaye above a long sandy beach stand out clearly.

Puerto Gurutzeaundi (Spain)

This fishing port may be used as a refuge in the worst weather and sea conditions if the entrance to Río Bidasoa is impassable. The entrance is straightforward from an approach course of from 280° to 350° after taking particular care to avoid Banc Iruarri. Either anchor in the outer harbour, pick up a mooring or go alongside in the inner harbour which has a least depth of 2m.

Entrances

The least depth outside the Río Bidasoa training wall ends is 1m and it deepens inside to about 5m. Do not enter if it is breaking across the entrance.

Hondarribia Marina (Spain) Turn to starboard into the marina 400m up from the W training wall end. The entrance is marked by Fl(4)R.11s and Fl(4)G.11s on prominent pylons.

Socoburu Marina (France) Continue up the río leaving a SHB (Fl.G.5s) and SH beacon (VQ(3)G.5s) to starboard, follow the marina wall round to port at about 50m off passing a Fl(2)R.6s on its elbow and turn sharply to port into the entrance (F.R and Fl.Y.4s).

Berthing

Hondarribia Marina (Spain) Reception berth is pontoon G marked by a yellow light at its end. Maximum length 16m, depths 2–3m; finger pontoons. Office is in centre of SE side.

Socoburu Marina (France) The reception pontoon is alongside the N wall almost in front of the offices. Continue turning to port inside the entrance and go up the channel between the pontoon ends and turn sharply to starboard to berth on this pontoon. Maximum length 20m, depths mostly 3m, finger pontoons.

Moorings

There are a lot of private moorings in Baie de Chingoody to the SE of Socoburu. Ask at Socoburu office before picking one up.

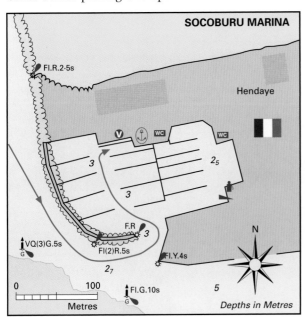

SOCOBURU MARINA

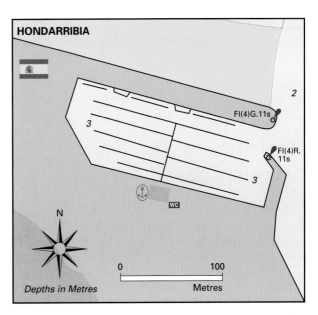

HONDARRIBIA

Anchoring

Anchorage in 2–5m mostly sand is available anywhere in the main bay clear of any moorings but will be subject to swell.

The main sheltered anchorage is in Baie de Chingoody clear of the moorings which are now extensive in the NE corner. In reaching the anchoring area leave two green beacons (VQ(3)G.5s) and LFl.G.10s) to the SW of the marina breakwater, and the end of the airport runway to starboard. Keep a careful eye open for aircraft when passing the line of the runway and anchor well clear of it.

Ashore in Hondarribia

The marina has all the facilities including a 36-tonne travel-lift and 5-tonne crane plus fuel (24 hours). Shops, *supermercados* and restaurants are 5 minutes' walk away in the attractive old town of Fuenterrabía where Charles V's castle, Guadaloupe church, Mont Jaizkibel and Castillo San Telmo are worth a visit, and a wander round the old fortifications provides a pleasant interlude.

Ashore in Hendaye

Socoburu has all the facilities of a first-class marina including a 30-tonne travel-lift, a secure laying up area and a welcoming yacht club. Hendaye is a popular family seaside resort with much activity in the season.

Travel

Locally there is a half-hourly bus service which runs between Hendaye and Fuenterrabía. Otherwise there are the usual bus services in all directions in France and Spain. The large railway station at Irun is 4km from Hondarribia and connects with the French and Spanish networks; the latter includes a slow line along the north coast to La Coruña.

The local airport at Fuenterrabía (also known as San Sebastián airport) services local flights and international flights via Madrid; Biarritz, 25km away, has the occasional charter and international flight, otherwise connects with Paris.

The North Coast of Spain

Cruising on the north Spanish coast

The coast

The north Spanish coast stretches nearly 300 miles from the French border at Hendaye in the east to Galicia with its major port of La Coruña in the west. There are nearly 70 harbours and estuaries and hundreds of anchorages for the yachtsman to enjoy on this still largely undeveloped coastline. As distance from the main conglomeration of yachts to the north increases, correspondingly fewer yachts reach this cruising area. This does not mean that the ports and harbours are deserted, as the Spanish are quick to fill up any facilities that are created with their own leisure and fishing craft, and marinas and harbours just for yachtsmen, while growing in number, are few and far between. The harbour extensions and improvements over the last two decades have not usually been accompanied by excessive shore side developments and there are many examples of improved and safer ports which still retain their unspoilt charm ashore.

The coastline is lush and green throughout the year, being well watered by the many small rivers that rise in the mountains behind. The latter are dominated near the middle part of the coast by the Picos de Europa, which is part of the main Cordillera stretching across the whole of northern Spain.

The highest peaks of the Picos remain snow-covered for most of the year and provide wonderful opportunities for walking and climbing.

The coast is not difficult navigationally. The tidal range is moderate, tidal streams and currents slight, the water is clear and there are few off-lying dangers. However, it is rocky and subject to swell which may prevent access to many of the smaller ports and rivers; ports of refuge in storm conditions are few and far between. Fog becomes more than an occasional problem in the summer months at the western end. Between the ports detailed in this pilot are hundreds of coastal anchorages of which some are included in the text. Many are deserted and beautiful but all are open to a greater or lesser extent to the swell and sudden weather changes. Spanish coastal charts of the 900 series are five times the scale of the Admiralty ones and would be a wise investment if exploring the coast outside the harbours.

History

The north coast was never settled by the Moors, who invaded the country in the 8th century, and because of this, the inhabitants of these northern provinces consider themselves different from those in other parts of Spain.

The reconquest of Spain also started from the north with a small but symbolic victory at Covodonga (nearest port Ribadesella). This resulted in the formation of the tiny Christian kingdom of

The Picos de Europa rising behind San Vicente de la Barquera

Asturias which by the 10th century had reclaimed most of Leon, Galicia and the northwest. This reconquest intensified in religious zeal and fervour with the divine aid of St James (whose remains lie in Santiago de Compostela) and by the end of the 13th century only Grenada in the south remained under tenuous Muslim authority.

The Moors were expelled or absorbed into Spain by the end of the 15th century. This coincided with Spain's time of world greatness in the 16th century, with exploration and expansion into the New World under such leaders as Magellan, Cortes and Pisarro, backed by a country increasingly united and bolstered by the religious fervour of the Roman Catholic church.

The defeat of the Armada against England started the reverse trend which was hastened by the European wars of the 18th century, the Peninsula War, when the British army drove the French from the country with the help of the *guerrilleros*, and the

The remains of St James lie behind the high altar in Santiago de Compostela cathedral and are visited by pilgrims from all over the world, many of whom walk there

growing independence of the South and North American colonies.

The 19th century was a period of increasingly political turmoil, encouraged by the wide differences between rich and poor. Spain remained neutral in the First World War and a succession of weak governments and an economy crippled by strikes led in 1936 to a military uprising under General Franco in Morocco, which quickly spread through the south and west of Spain. This was resisted by the Republican (left wing) movement in the north and east which led to the civil war, one of the bitterest and bloodiest in history. Violent reprisals were taken by both sides, populations were slaughtered and families divided. Thousands of volunteers from other countries joined the Republican International Brigades and Russia provided some help, but they were no match for Franco's Nationalists, supported by massive assistance from Fascist Italy and Nazi Germany. By 1939 the civil war was over and the 36-year dictatorship of Franco started with widespread reprisals against the Republicans, with over 2 million being put into concentration camps. Opposition to this state was led by the Basques, which in turn led to their savage repression.

The Basques are a very old race and different from the Spanish; they inhabit the coast from Bilbao to Bayonne, have their own language and some still wish to set up their own independent state. The separatist group ETA is a terrorist organisation which has bombed, kidnapped and assassinated to further its aims. A Basque courtesy flag flown from Bilbao eastwards in addition to the Spanish one is appreciated and sometimes demanded. In the west the Galicians have a more peaceful approach while still seeking more autonomy for the province. They also have a separate language and both Basque and Galician names are included in this pilot where appropriate.

The coast has been divided into four sections and brief descriptions will be found at the beginning of each. These roughly coincide with the provinces of Pais Vasco, Cantabria, Asturias and Galicia.

Basque flag

The church is the centre of all towns and villages. This is the one at Hondarribia at the eastern end of the coast

Winds

The prevailing winds are from the SW to the NW, although in midsummer the frequency of winds from the NE increases. Unless a secondary depression forms or a rare depression crosses the Bay itself, these winds are steady and of no great strength. Any winds from the SE through S to SW are squally and gusts may reach gale force as they sweep down from the mountains.

Visibility

At the eastern end of the coast, fog is rare but early morning mist in fair weather may obscure the coast until the sun clears it. The prevalence of fog increases the further west one goes, and up to four days' fog a month can be expected in the summer months. Low cloud at the western end may also obscure geographical features and the higher lighthouses.

Currents and tidal streams

The current along the coast is much influenced in the summer months by prolonged winds from the E or W sectors. Without the wind influence, currents tend to be W-flowing at the W end and E-flowing at the E end. However, tidal streams may at times override or reverse these flows and the result is usually weak and unpredictable. The flow off ports where predictions have been made is noted in the text. Tidal streams in estuaries, rias and harbour entrances can be strong, however, especially on the ebb, and will be greatly increased if the river is in spate. The latter condition can be seen some way off the entrance by the outflow of brown water. This discoloured outflow will persist for a long way and gives a good indication of the resultant current/stream along the coast.

Swell

Swell can appear on this coast without warning, having been generated by some disturbance far out in the Atlantic. The prevalent direction is from between W and N. It is dangerous when it is big enough to break over shallow water and in extreme conditions this can be as deep as 11m. All banks and patches should be avoided in swell conditions. It

Swell on the coast

Un burro, not needed on most yachts but invaluable to villagers

should be remembered that the depth of water is reduced by half the height of the swell and that the swell increases in height as the water gets shallower. A rule of thumb is to keep outside the 5m line in any swell conditions which will preclude any entry into many small harbours, and also remember that you may get in but be unable to get out if the swell increases.

Entering harbour in a swell should only be attempted on the flood and near HW. A worthwhile precaution is to heave-to outside the breakers and observe their pattern and run for at least ten minutes to allow for the occasional extra large wave. A number of harbours have narrow entrances where the swell may be breaking heavily on the training walls or breakwaters but where, provided the depth is sufficient, there will be a clear but narrow passage in between. But if in doubt, anchor out.

Type of yacht

This coast is suitable for all types of yachts with many deep ports and anchorages for the deeper-draught yacht. The opportunities for the shoal draught yacht or multihull able to take the ground are legion in the many rias and estuaries. There are many further opportunities for exploration up the rivers if the mast can be readily lowered or there is a powerful outboard for the tender; most of the rivers are navigable in delightful surroundings for some way but are cut off near the mouth by low bridges.

Special equipment for yachts
Ground tackle
- A second bower with 50m of warp and some chain, in addition to the usual light kedge
- A second anchor trip line
- A set of legs if the yacht is suitable for using them

Berthing gear
- Four large fenders in addition to the usual

complement. (Many of the harbour walls are rough with projections.)
- A fender board for rough and sometimes arched or piled jetties
- A ladder at least 2.5m long, to get ashore at LW. Jetties are often high and built-in ladders few or occupied
- Two long warps of 50m (one of which can be the extra anchor warp).

Domestic
50m of hosepipe with a variety of end connections.

Camping Gaz is readily available anywhere, usually from ironmongers (*ferreteria*), garages or campsites; otherwise take enough Calor cylinders to last the cruise.

Provisions
Supplies of fresh provisions, meat and fish are as readily available as in the UK. Specialist bread, vegetable, fish shops and butchers are still to be found but there are growing numbers of *supermercados* of all sizes which meet most requirements. Local markets still flourish and are the cheapest and often of the best quality. Bread varies from baker to baker and comes in all sizes; *un pan* is the most convenient size of a large baguette and, like the latter, can be revived by a short spell in the oven. Fish and shellfish are fresh and first class; there are many varieties of excellent cheeses and the yellow corn-fed chickens are very tasty.

Drinkable cheap wine can be found anywhere and is sold in all the *supermercados* as well as wine of a quality that will compete anywhere. The occasional *bodega* (where wine is sold from the barrel into bottles provided by the customer) can still be found. *Vino tinto* is red, *blanco* white and *rosado* rosé. Wines from Rioja are usually a safer bet than *vino*

The centre of all fishing activity. The *lonja* at Tazones.

corriente (local wine). *Vino de la casa* in a restaurant now usually comes out of a bottle rather than a cask and is usually of reasonable quality. Cider (*sidra*) is the local Asturian drink, often poured out at the table from a height to aerate it. Brandy is cheap; whiskies and gins can be found at UK-comparable prices.

Ice in blocks or chips can be obtained from any fishing port, where there will be an ice factory alongside the *lonja* – the centre of the fishing facility. This shouldn't be put in drinks but an increasing number of *supermercados* stock drinkable quality ice in bags.

Shops

Shops are usually open from 0900–1300 and 1530–2000. Markets usually open earlier and close before siesta time. Shops are closed on Sundays except for a few food shops in the forenoon, and everything closes for the local fiestas and special religious and civil holidays. The former are noted in the text for each port; the latter in the summer months are:

1 May	Independence Day
17 June	Corpus Christi (movable)
29 June	SS Peter and Paul
25 July	St James
15 Aug	Feast of the Assumption
12 Oct	Columbus Day

Fiestas

Fiestas are a feature of the Spanish way of life. They take place throughout the year but August is the most popular month for them, especially in the ports when the fishing boat crews are all home. They are usually of a religious nature and start with a church service followed by a procession, often headed by a sacred image and including many huge and fanciful

Cedeira fishmarket. Worth getting up early for

Giant figures waiting their carriers for the fiesta procession at Deva

figures; this may be followed by a procession of gaily decorated boats. Bands accompany the festivities and will also play for dancing in the main plaza in the evening until the early hours. Fireworks often open the proceedings in the morning and continue throughout the day. All shops and most services are closed. (Dates of local fiestas are noted in the ports sections of this pilot.) Dressing overall by visiting yachts is always appreciated on these occasions.

Water

Water is plentiful, safe, piped to most jetties and generally free. A charge for it is seldom made. Bottled water is readily available in the *supermercados*.

Telephones

Spanish telephones are either cash or card-operated. Cards may be obtained from newsagents, tobacconists, post offices and some bars. The mobile phone coverage is good all along the coast.

Fuel

There are two types of diesel: Gasoleo A, which is taxed and available for yachts, and Gasoleo B, which is untaxed and available for fishing boats. The days, alas, are over when supplies of Gasoleo B could be negotiated for yachts. Gasoleo A in pumps will only be found in marinas (with some exceptions), otherwise it must be carried from filling stations. It is advisable to top up whenever the opportunity offers itself on this coast as in many of the smaller ports there is no handy supply. Cash should always be paid although some of the bigger marinas will take cards.

Petrol pumps are found in the marinas, otherwise it must be carried from the nearest garage.

Engine oils (*aceites*) of the usual international brands will be found at filling stations.

Formalities

The Spanish are generally more relaxed about rules and regulations for yachts than other EU countries. However, the necessary documentation must be carried and produced on demand and if there is not a Spanish speaker on board, a completed form (Appendix 5) may save time and trouble. The following documents should be carried on board:

- Certificate of Registry, or for British yachts the Small Ships registry document (originals, not photocopies)
- RYA Certificate of Competence, at least for the skipper.
- Evidence of insurance for the yacht. The Third Party section of the document must be in Spanish and should be obtained from the insurance company before departure
- Passports for all on board. These will be needed for return to the UK by other means and are a useful means of identification. An *entrada* stamp will be needed at the point of arrival if not returning to the UK in the yacht.

Yachts registered in the EU arriving in Spanish waters need complete no formalities (and should not fly a Q flag) unless carrying goods that are dutiable in Spain or with non-EU residents on board. In these cases, and if an *entrada* stamp is required on a passport, entry should be made where there is a customs presence and the Q flag flown until cleared. Major marinas have resident customs officers.

Value Added Tax

The same rules apply as for France (see page 5) but are not so rigorously invoked. Nevertheless evidence that VAT has been paid on the yacht, or an exemption, should be carried. Consult the RYA guide on VAT if in doubt.

Yacht clubs

Many of the ports have yacht clubs which vary widely in their social standing and attitudes to visiting yachtsmen.

In some of the larger ports the clubs are concerned with yachting in name only and are purely social clubs with an elite membership. There are also some which have a dual function of encouraging yachting as well as having a large non-yachting social membership. In smaller ports are clubs concerned solely with yachting, clubs whose main concern is fishing with yachting of less importance, and finally those clubs that are only interested in fishing. In the larger fishing ports co-operative clubs for the professional fishermen will be found.

The dress requirement, expected behaviour, cost and quality of the facilities offered all vary widely between these various levels of clubs. An indication is given in the text where possible but in general the dress and social behaviour is higher than would be accepted by a comparable club in the UK. Non-members (Spanish or foreign) are not always welcomed or admitted, badly behaved or noisy children not appreciated and skimpy dress frowned upon. An approach of restrained courtesy in asking to use the club facilities is appreciated.

Fishing and fishing boats

Fishing is the most widespread industry on the coast and the major source of income outside the few industrial towns. Many ports have been developed to encourage this and the larger ports are expanding and becoming more dedicated to the industry and less suitable and welcoming to yachts – Ondárroa, San Vicente de la Barquera, Burela and Bermeo are examples. In the smaller ports where the fleets are reducing in size, some efforts are made to provide leisure and yachting facilities – such as at Foz, Luarca, Cudillero, Viviero, Ares and Ribadesella. The fishing by the larger boats is to some extent seasonal, when they are away in the early summer catching tunny but return in August to fill the major fishing harbours. Alongside berths for yachts in fishing harbours may be readily available in July but only anchorages will be free in August when the fleet is home for the fiesta season. Some harbours seem to be permanently full of small fishing boats.

The larger fishing boats are now built of steel but retain some of the pleasing lines of the old wooden boats. They are strong and powerful and can damage the lightly built modern yacht. The fishermen like to handle them with a certain dash and panache and will enter and leave harbour at speed regardless of the effect of wash.

In general the fishermen are kindly disposed towards yachts provided they are spoken to in their language, although some speak French. A berth alongside a fishing boat should always be requested rather than taken. If no one is on board, ask at the capitanía. An English speaker may sometimes be found if there is an information or tourist office (*turismo*).

At sea the larger boats fishing for tunny will have a series of lines astern and others on long rods on either side when they motor fast on a straight line.

...permanently full of small fishing boats. San Sebastián

Typical modern fishing boats at Elanchove

Work on nets in harbour is unending. Santona

Search and Rescue

There are two Maritime Rescue Co-ordination Centres (MRCC) on the north coast at Bilbao and Gijón. There are two Maritime Rescue Sub-Centres (MRSC) at Santander and La Coruña. In addition the coastal radio stations at Pasajes, Cabo Machicaco (MF only), Cabo Peñas and Navia are linked to MRCC Bilbao; Cabo Ortegal is linked to MRSC La Coruña.

All these stations and centres will respond to emergency calls on Ch 16 or to DSC activation on Ch 70. VHF emergency coverage on Ch 16 and Ch 70 and on MF is, in theory, total.

Red Cross and lifeboats

In Spain these two emergency services are amalgamated. Lifeboat stations are given in the text.

So too do Bilbao and Santander, which have the advantage of being both UK ferry ports and having city airports. The other marinas at La Coruña, Ares and Fontan/Sada may also have room and are close to an airport. Security in the marinas appears adequate but it would be worth appointing an agent, especially if there is any work to be done and as an extra security check. Other harbours that have resident yachts may be possibilities but a close scrutiny should be made as regards safety from weather and theft. It would be most unwise to leave a yacht afloat over winter where the swell can penetrate.

Harbour dues

Harbour dues are usually only charged in large commercial ports and marinas. The charges in the latter are comparable to the rest of the EU but the larger and newer the marina, the higher the charges.

Health

The usual EU reciprocal arrangements exist and Form EHIC (apply online, by phone or post) should be obtained to qualify. It is always advisable to take out holiday insurance to cover theft and the cost of transport home.

Spanish *farmacias* (chemists) can be identified by a green cross, usually lit. They are more widespread

Cedeira lifeboat

Boats fishing for sardines circle before netting and their movements are less predictable. At night all boats have strong deck lights and are unlikely to see low-powered yacht lights until close to. Inshore may be found the *lanternas*, small boats with bright lights to attract fish. In a swell these can be mistaken for navigational lights. Also inshore at night will be small boats fishing with no lights at all. All boats fishing should be given a wide berth.

Fishermen returning to harbour may be useful to show where the deepest water lies, especially in ports where the bar shifts, and they will be happy to lead visitors in.

Laying up

Gijón and Hondarribia have travel-lifts and facilities for laying up over the winter either ashore or afloat.

in rural areas than in the UK. They are well supplied with medicines but may not have the same named brands, and prescribed medicines should be taken with you. By law, one chemist in town will stay open after hours and the name and address of the duty chemist will be displayed on the others.

Travel ashore

Road, rail, ferry and air travel details will be found in the text of each port.

There are airports at Fuenterrabía (San Sebastián), Bilbao, Santander, Asturias (near Avilés), La Coruña and Santiago de Compostela. There are connecting flights from all to Madrid once or twice a day and occasional flights in the summer direct to UK from La Coruña, Santiago and Bilbao.

A rather slow railway line runs the length of the coast from Hendaye to La Coruña with many stops. The whole journey involves at least two changes and cannot be completed in one day.

The main north coast road is being expanded to motorway standard for most of its length and there are regular coach and local bus services.

Ferries

There are ferries from Santander to Plymouth (Brittany Ferries) and from Bilbao to Portsmouth (P & O) which take vehicles and mostly run twice weekly.

Technical and navigational information

Chart datum

Chart datum is fixed at a level below which the sea will not fall in normal circumstances, but it may do so under extreme meteorological conditions.

Predicted heights of tides have been taken from Admiralty *Tide Tables Vol II* and are related to chart datum and to times of HW and LW at Pointe de Grave (PdG) for most of the coast. At the W

Harbour

A typical north coast fishing village (Lastres) perched above its harbour behind the trees on the left

extremity these times are related to the times of HW and LW at La Coruña, but there is a conversion shown on page 186 to relate times at Pointe de Grave to La Coruña if needed.

Simple interpolation from these times and heights should be sufficient to work out a tidal height at any specific time. The tidal range at springs is 3.8m in the east, rather less in the west; the tidal range at neaps is 1.5m along the coast.

Horizontal chart datum – satellite-derived positions

Positions derived from satellite systems such as GPS are usually expressed in terms of World Geodetic System 1984 (WGS 84). BA and most Spanish charts in this area are in a period of change between ED 50 datum and WGS 84 and will carry a note showing the correction to be applied. Caution should be exercised if using pre-metric charts which do not show any correction and where there may be significant discrepancies between latitude and longitude on the chart and that shown by GPS set to any datum.

DGPS is transmitted from the following stations on this coast:

P. Estaca des Baves 43°47′.17N 7°41′.07W 100M
C. Finisterre 42°53′.00N 09°16′.23W 100M
C. Machicaco 43°27′.00N 02°45′.00W 100M

Heights

On BA charts this is above MHWS and applies to air clearances under bridges or overhead obstructions.

Bearings

Bearings are given in degrees True from seaward. The magnetic variation is at present (2005) 2°W at the eastern end and 4°W at the western end of the area. Compass points are sometimes used to indicate a general direction.

Positions

The latitude and longitude given under location for each port are NOT waypoints. They indicate the general position of the port.

Waypoints

There are two types of waypoint shown in this pilot:

Coastal waypoints These indicate a clear track offshore along the coast. The track between adjacent waypoints carries at least 2m to a width of 400m unless the space between them on the list in Appendix 2 is marked with -----. Nevertheless, the waypoints and the tracks between them must be plotted and checked on an up-to-date chart before being used for navigation. Coastal waypoints are shown where relevant.

Arrival waypoints For each individual port or anchorage. They are placed at a safe distance from the destination at a point roughly where pilotage will take over from GPS navigation. Arrival waypoints are shown at the head of each port or anchorage.

In a few instances an arrival waypoint may also serve as a coastal waypoint.

Lights

The full description of all lights including those of buoys where appropriate are shown in Appendix 3 and follow the convention as in Admiralty *List of Lights Vol D, NP 77*. Abbreviated details are shown on the plans and pilotage directions in each port section. This section of the Spanish coast is covered by light numbers 1452 to 1723.56.

Buoyage

Buoys are few compared to UK waters. At entrances to many estuaries are rocks which are not marked in any way.

Charts

BA and Spanish charts for the area are in Appendix 3. The SHOM coverage is patchy with few large scale-charts of ports. In general the BA charts give an adequate coverage for those who only cruise for a short time in the area. The Spanish charts in the 900 series cover the whole coast on a five times larger scale and would be worth getting if planning a longer cruise or wanting to explore the more remote bays and anchorages.

BA charts may be obtained from Imray or any other Admiralty agent and are corrected up to the date of the purchase. They can be corrected free from the website www.nmwebsearch.com or from weekly Admiralty *Notices to Mariners* obtainable from chart agents (but not post free). In addition to providing BA and Imray charts, Imray Laurie Norie and Wilson Ltd can obtain Spanish charts, but it takes a long time. It may be quicker to go direct to Instituto Hidrografico de la Marina, Plaza de San Severiano 3, 11007 Cadiz, España, ☎ 34 956 59 94 09, *Fax* 34 956 59 93 96 and pay in euros or by credit card. However, the quickest way to obtain them is direct from the Spanish chart agents which are situated at La Coruña, Pasajes, Ribadeo, Gijón, Avilés, Luarca, Santander and Bilbao. Ask at the capitanía or club náutico for the address and whereabouts.

Harbour and anchorage plans

The harbour and anchorage plans are drawn to illustrate the pilotage directions and are not to be used directly for navigation. While the details are

The beautiful Río de Mogro near Santander, suitable only for those of shallow draught

Weather forecast areas

Area Cantábrico covers the coast from the French border to Ribadeo, Area Finisterre from there westwards. These two areas extend to 45°N and to the north of these are Rochebonne to the east, Pazenn to the west.

Weather and safety broadcasts

All broadcasts in Spanish. All times local.

Station	Ch/Freq	Times	Working freq.
Pasajes	27	0840, 1240, 2010	Auto 25
Machicaco	17, 07	0703, 1303, 1903	2586
Bilbao MRCC	10, 16	0030, 0433, 0833, 1233, 1633, 2033	
Bilbao	26	0840, 1240, 2010	Auto 04
Santander MRSC	11	0245, 0645, 1045, 1455, 1845, 2245	
Santander	24	0840, 1240, 2010	
Cabo Peñas	26	0840, 1240, 2010	Auto 25
	16, 77	0703, 1303, 1903	2649
Navia	60	0840, 1240, 2010	
C Ortegal	02	0840, 1240, 2010	
Coruña MRSC	13	0005, 0405, 0805, 1205, 1605, 2005	
Coruña	26	0840, 1240, 2010	Auto 28
	16, 98	0703, 1303,1903	2806

Navtex

| Coruña | D | 0030, 0430, 0830, 1230, 1630, 2030 | |

Weather bulletins at 0830 and 2030

Ports and Marinas
Daily weather maps are usually available in marina offices and capitanías.

Internet
www.theyr.net provides actuals to 3-day forecasts
www.weatheronline.co.uk provides actuals and longer term forecasts

relatively exact the plans are not necessarily tied to latitude and longitude, nor are these always shown on the larger-scale plans. Each plan will, however, show the arrival waypoint or indicate its position relative to the plan. The scale for each plan is shown in metres or occasionally miles.

Radio services

Some of the coastal radio stations linked to the MRCC safety network also have working frequencies and these are shown in the table above.

Some of the larger ports have MF or VHF port communications and these frequencies are shown in the text, as are the marina frequencies. English speakers should not be expected on these frequencies but may be found in the bigger marinas.

There are no radio beacons now except aero radiobeacons at Cabo Mayor (Santander) and Cabo Peñas (between Gijón and Avilés)). Details in the relevant ports.

Bibliography

Admiralty *Sailing Directions, Bay of Biscay, NP22*
Admiralty *Tide Tables Vol 2, NP202*
Admiralty *List of Lights Vol D, NP77*
Admiralty *Maritime Communications, UK and Mediterranean, NP 289*
Reeds Oki *Nautical Almanac*
Votre Livre du Bord Manche-Atlantique (Bloc Marine)

II. Pasajes to Santander

Cabo Higuer to Cabo Mayor

This part of the coast, stretching for some 100 miles, is remarkable for the number of both small and large mountains close to the seaboard, increasing in height inland to a series of mountain ranges whose peaks are covered in snow until late spring.

The coastline generally is rocky and barren, with steep cliffs falling straight into the sea. There are virtually no outlying dangers. Ports and harbours are to be found in shallow breaks in the coastline and at the mouths of rivers.

The only ports of refuge in storm conditions from the N are Pasajes, Bermeo, Bilbao and Santander. There are many other small harbours that can be entered in less extreme conditions.

Industrial and shipbuilding centres are well spread out at Pasajes, Bilbao and Santander with many fishing ports between.

In the 50 miles between Bilbao in the W and Zumaia in the E there are no marinas, but several fishing harbours and open anchorages. The acceptance of foreign yachtsmen in the former is variable but usually welcoming and some prefer the hurly-burly of these harbours to the more well-ordered existence in the marinas. However, remember that the fishing ports will be crowded in August, and the newer the marina the more likely there are to be free berths.

Warnings

The coast between Cabo Machicaco and Cabo Villano, 8M further to the W, can have very steep and broken seas off it due to the uneven bottom. It is advisable to keep 2–3M off the coast when on passage.

An oil and gas pipeline runs N from Cabo Machicaco to a conspicuous rig offshore.

In strong or prolonged winds from the westerly quadrant easterly currents of up to 5 knots can set towards the French coast before turning north.

The only gas rig on the coast off Cabo Machicaco

WAYPOINTS

523	Cabo Higuer	43°24′.24N	01°47′.50W
524	P. Biosar	43°23′.00N	01°51′.60W
526	P. Mompas	43°20′.90N	01°58′.30W
530	I. de S. Anton	43°18′.94N	02°12′.00W
537	C. de Catalina	43°22′.18N	02°30′.13W
540	C. Ogoño	43°25′.33N	02°38′.38W
541	I. de Izaro	43°25′.83N	02°41′.30W
543	C. Machichaco	43°28′.33N	02°45′.18W
546	C. Villano	43°28′.71N	02°57′.00W
550	P. del Rabanal	43°24′.13N	03°12′.82W
553	P. Pescador	43°28′.73N	03°25′.57W
555	Cabo Ajo	43°31′.53N	03°35′.08W
558	Cabo Mayor	43°29′.73N	03°47′.08W

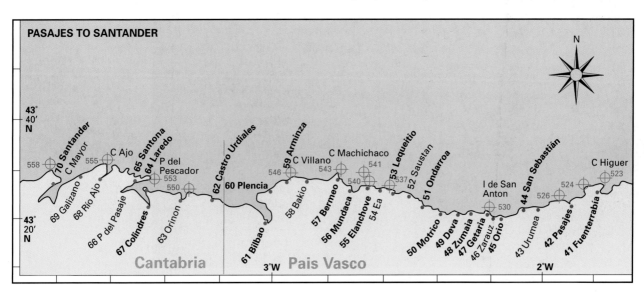

Planning Guide

Distances between ports in nautical miles
Ports with marinas in bold type

		Fuent/Higuer	Porto Moco	Pasajes	R Urumea	San Sebastián	R de Orio	Zaraaz	Guetaria	Zumaia	R de Deva	Motrico	Ondárroa	E de Saustan	Lequeitio	Ea	Elanchove	R de Mundaca	Bermeo	E de Barquio	Arminza	Plencia	Bilbao	C Urdiales	R de Oriñon	Laredo	Santoña	Colindres	R Ajo	E de Galizano	Santander
A	**Fuent/Higuer**		2	7	9	10	16	18	19	21	25	26	28	30	32	36	38	40	41	48	51	55	61	67	72	76	78	80	90	95	100
D	Porto Moco	2		5	7	8	14	16	17	19	23	24	26	28	30	34	36	38	39	46	49	53	59	65	70	74	76	78	88	93	98
A*	**Pasajes**	7	5		2	3	9	11	12	14	18	19	21	23	25	29	31	33	34	41	44	48	54	60	65	69	71	73	83	88	93
D	R Urumea	9	7	2		1	7	9	10	12	16	17	19	21	23	27	29	31	32	39	42	46	52	58	63	67	69	71	81	86	91
B*	**San Sebastián**	10	8	3	1		6	8	9	11	15	16	18	20	22	26	28	30	31	38	41	45	51	57	62	66	68	70	80	85	90
C	R de Orio	16	14	9	7	6		2	5	8	9	10	12	14	16	20	22	24	25	32	37	39	45	51	56	60	62	64	74	79	84
D	Zarauz	18	16	11	9	8	2		1	3	7	8	10	12	14	18	20	22	23	30	35	37	43	49	54	58	60	62	72	77	82
B*	**Getaría**	19	17	12	10	9	3	1		2	6	7	9	11	13	17	19	21	22	29	34	36	42	48	53	57	59	61	71	76	81
B*	**Zumaia**	21	19	14	12	11	5	3	2		4	5	7	9	11	15	17	19	20	27	32	34	40	46	51	55	57	59	69	74	79
C	R de Deva	25	23	18	16	15	9	7	6	4		1	3	5	7	11	13	15	16	23	28	30	36	42	47	51	53	55	65	70	75
C	**Motrico**	26	24	19	17	16	10	8	7	5	1		2	4	6	10	11	14	15	22	27	29	35	41	45	50	52	54	64	69	74
C	**Ondárroa**	28	26	21	19	18	12	10	9	7	3	2		2	4	8	9	12	13	20	25	27	33	39	43	48	50	52	62	67	72
D	E de Saustan	30	28	23	21	20	14	12	11	9	5	4	2		2	6	7	10	11	18	23	25	31	37	41	46	48	50	60	65	70
C	**Lequeitio**	32	30	25	23	22	16	14	13	11	7	6	4	2		4	5	8	9	16	21	23	29	35	39	44	46	48	58	63	68
D	Ea	36	34	29	27	26	20	18	17	15	11	10	8	6	4		2	5	7	13	18	20	26	32	36	41	43	45	55	60	65
C	Elanchove	38	36	31	29	28	22	20	19	17	13	11	9	7	5	2		2	4	11	13	17	23	29	33	38	40	42	52	57	62
C	R de Mundaca	40	38	33	31	30	24	22	21	19	15	14	12	10	8	5	2		2	9	12	16	22	28	32	37	39	41	51	56	61
B*	**Bermeo**	41	39	34	32	31	25	23	22	20	16	15	13	11	9	7	4	2		7	10	14	20	26	31	35	37	39	49	54	59
D	E de Bakio	48	46	41	39	38	32	30	29	27	23	22	20	18	16	13	11	9	7		3	7	13	19	24	28	30	32	42	47	52
C	Arminza	51	49	44	42	41	37	35	34	32	28	27	25	23	21	18	13	12	10	3		4	10	16	21	25	27	29	39	44	49
C	Plencia	55	53	48	46	45	39	37	36	34	30	29	27	25	23	20	17	16	14	7	4		6	12	17	21	23	25	35	39	45
A	**Bilbao**	61	59	54	52	51	45	43	42	40	36	35	33	31	29	26	23	22	20	13	10	6		6	11	15	17	19	29	33	39
A*	**C. Urdiales**	67	65	60	58	57	51	49	48	46	42	41	39	37	35	32	29	28	26	19	16	12	6		5	9	11	13	23	27	33
D	R de Oriñon	72	70	65	63	62	56	54	53	51	47	45	43	41	39	36	33	32	31	24	21	17	11	5		4	6	8	18	22	28
C	Laredo	76	74	69	67	66	60	58	57	55	51	50	48	46	44	41	38	37	35	28	25	21	15	9	4		2	4	16	20	26
A*	**Santoña**	78	76	71	69	68	62	60	59	57	53	52	50	48	46	43	40	39	37	30	27	23	17	11	6	2		2	12	16	22
C	Colindres	80	78	73	71	70	64	62	61	59	55	54	52	50	48	45	42	41	39	32	29	25	19	13	8	4	2		10	14	18
D	R Ajo	90	88	83	81	80	74	72	71	69	65	64	62	60	58	55	52	51	49	42	39	35	29	23	18	16	12	10		5	10
D	E de Galizano	95	93	88	86	85	79	77	76	74	70	69	67	65	63	60	57	56	54	47	44	39	33	27	22	20	16	14	5		5
A	**Santander**	100	98	93	91	90	84	82	81	79	75	74	72	70	68	65	62	61	59	52	49	45	39	33	28	26	22	18	10	5	

To the west it is 5 miles to R de S Pedro del Mar from Santander

Typical north Spanish coastline

42 Pasajes

Cat A*

Commercial port with impressive entrance but of little interest to yachtsmen

Location
43°20′.00N 01°55′.00W

Shelter
Inadequate for yachts except in commercial harbour

Warning
Confused seas in N winds in narrow entrance; enter at last quarter of flood

Depth restrictions
None

Night entry
As by day, well lit

Tidal information
HW PdG –0040
LW PdG –0030

Mean height of tide (m)

MHWS	MHWN	MLWN	MLWS
4.2	3.1	1.6	0.5

Tidal stream
Up to 2 knots on ebb

Berthing
Only in emergency in commercial harbour

Facilities
Few for yachts

Charts
BA 1157 (5)
Spanish 128, 945, 3911 (5)

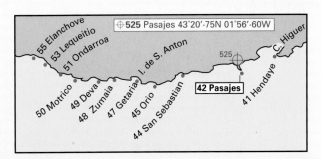

⊕ **525** Pasajes 43°20′.75N 01°56′.60W

55 Elanchove
53 Lequeitio
51 Ondarroa
50 Motrico
49 Deva
48 Zumaia
47 Getaria
I. de S. Anton
45 Orio
44 San Sebastian
42 Pasajes
525
41 Hendaye
C. Higuer

Weather
Pasajes Ch 27 at 0840, 1240, 2010
Navtex A or D

Radio
Ch 09
☎ Harbourmaster 34 943 351816

While there is very little inside to attract the yachtsman, this is the most impressive of any entrance to a harbour on the coast. It leads to two small villages on each side of Pasajes de San Pedro and Pasajes de San Juan which are quite overshadowed by the huge commercial port and industrial complex of Pasajes Ancho beyond. The two villages offer little except some restaurants of good repute, no moorings and uneasy anchorages just off a busy fairway. There is a small fair weather anchorage near the entrance but it is not much more than a lunch stop.

Nevertheless, a refuge in heavy weather when a berth in the fishing harbour in Pasajes Ancho could be sought.

Atalaya   Bancha del Este   Pasajes Ancho   La Plata lighthouse
Arando Grande   Ldg line
Bancha del Oeste

Pasajes from the N. Río Oyarzun in spate

PILOTAGE

Approaches

By day

⊕525 is in the vicinity of the safe water pillar light buoy (Mo(A)6s) situated 1¼M NNW of the entrance. There are no off-lying dangers coming from the E or W along the coast and the corner could be cut approaching from either direction to pick up the prominent leading line to seaward of the two banks (least depth 1.5m) on either side of the entrance. They are marked by two spindly metal towers at their inner ends.

By night

From ⊕525 or the safe water buoy (Mo(A)6s) pick up the three leading lights (DirOc(2)WRG.12s) 155° and stay in the narrow white sector (green to the W, red to the E). Above this light on the line are a Q and Oc.3s of 18M range.

Entrance

By day or night

Straightforward once the entrance is identified. Follow the leading line as above until Arando Grande (Fl(2)R.7s) is abaft the beam then turn to port to leave Dique de Senocoluzua (Fl(2)G.7s) and Punta de las Cruces (Fl(3)G.9s) to starboard.

Anchorages

In fine weather Ensenada de Cala Bursa is the quietest and cleanest but it is small and far from anywhere. To the NW of Ermita de Santa Ana, clear of the channel and outside the moorings in 4m mud, is handy for the best shops and restaurants but subject to wash.

The dramatic W side of the entrance
Río Urumea and San Sebastián looking SW

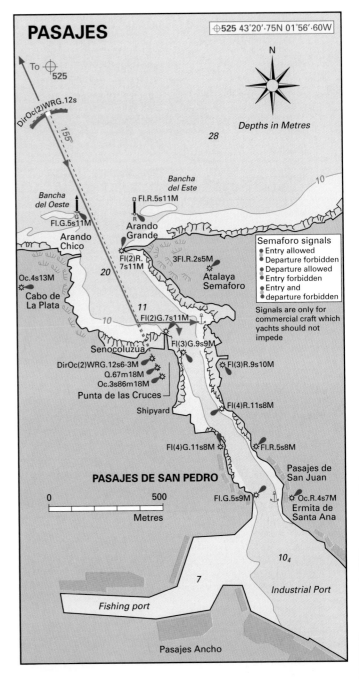

Depths in Metres

PASAJES — ⊕525 43°20'·75N 01°56'·60W

Semaforo signals
- ○ Entry allowed
- ● Departure forbidden
- ● Departure allowed
- ● Entry forbidden
- ● Entry and
- ● departure forbidden

Signals are only for commercial craft which yachts should not impede

PASAJES DE SAN PEDRO

Pasajes de San Juan

Ermita de Santa Ana

Industrial Port

Fishing port

Pasajes Ancho

Moorings

There are no visitors' moorings. Do not use the vacant moorings near the ferry which the ferry boats use at night.

Ashore in Pasajes

Facilities

Adequate food shops in both villages; good restaurants in San Juan; water on quays; fuel some distance.

Passage pilotage

Care should be taken on passage westwards from Pasajes to pass to the N of ⊕526 to avoid Bajo Pekachilla (least depth 0.2m) to the NE of Cabo Mompas.

43 Río Urumea

Cat D

Location
43°20'.00N 01°57'.00W

Care should be taken not to confuse this with the E entrance to San Sebastián when approaching from the E. Río Urumea, which dries right across the mouth, runs under three low bridges in the city of San Sebastián and thence into pleasant countryside. It is navigable by dinghy for several miles around HW.

Río Urumea and San Sebastián looking SW

44 San Sebastián (Donostia)

Cat B*

Lively holiday resort with famed beaches but with few concessions to visiting yachts

Location
43°20'.00N 02°00'.00W

Shelter
Good in harbour, fair in bay

Warning
Keep clear of La Bancha shoal outside in any swell; W entrance is not navigable

Depth restrictions
3m at harbour entrance, 1.5m+ inside

Night entry
Well lit

Tidal information
HW PdG –0050
LW PdG –0030

Mean height of tide (m)

MHWS	MHWN	MLWN	MLWS
4.2	3.2	1.6	0.6

Tidal stream
Negligible in bay; outside the flood sets E, the ebb W

Berthing
One small pontoon for visitors, otherwise fight it out with the fishermen or anchor in the bay

Facilities
Patchy, see below

Charts
BA 1157 (7.5)
Spanish 944

Weather
Pasajes Ch 27 at 0840, 1240 and 2010
Navtex A or D

Radio
Ch 09 with YC and water taxi in season
☎ RCNSS (34) 922 42 35 74

⊕ 527 San Sebastian 43°19'.80N 01°59'.96W

55 Elanchove
53 Lequeitio
51 Ondarroa
50 Motrico
49 Deva
48 Zumaia
47 Getaria
I. de S. Anton
45 Orio
527
42 Pasajes
41 Hendaye
C. Higuer

44 San Sebastian

Harbour YC

158°

Isla de Santa Clara

San Sebastián (Donostia) looking SSE

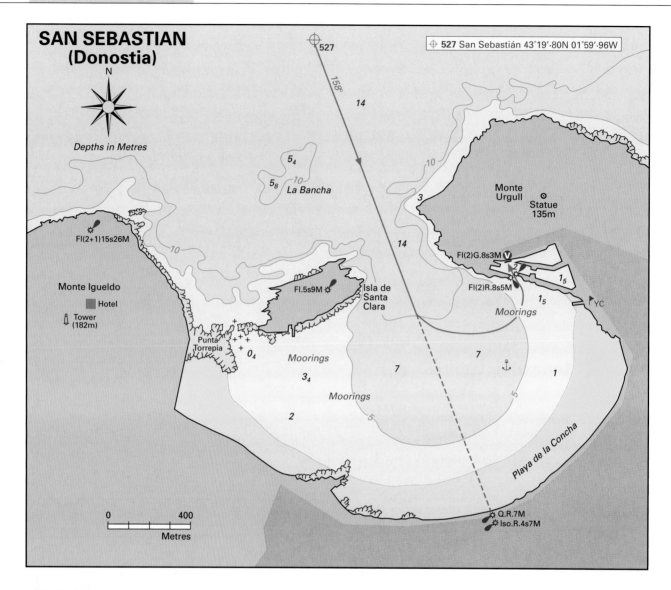

SAN SEBASTIAN
(Donostia)

N

Depths in Metres

527

158°

14

⊕ 527 San Sebastián 43°19'·80N 01°59'·96W

5₄

5₈ La Bancha

10

10

3

Monte Urgull

Statue 135m

Fl(2+1)15s26M

14

Monte Igueldo

Hotel

Tower (182m)

Fl.5s9M

Isla de Santa Clara

Fl(2)G.8s3M

Fl(2)R.8s5M

1₅

1₅

YC

Moorings

Punta Torrepia

0₄

Moorings

3₄

7

7

7

1

Moorings

2

5

5

Playa de la Concha

0   400

Metres

Q.R.7M
Iso.R.4s7M

PILOTAGE

Approaches

By day

The approaches to ⊕527 are clear and danger-free from all directions. Coming from the W, Monte Igueldo is conspicuous with a large hotel and tall tower near the summit. From the E, Monte Urgull with a huge figure of Christ on the top of it is easily identified. Once in the vicinity of the waypoint, the bay with Isla de Santa Clara in the middle and the city behind will be seen.

At night

The lights on Monte Igueldo (Fl(2+1)15s. 132m26M) and Isla de Santa Clara (Fl.5s51m9M) are readily identifiable although that of Isla de Santa Clara tends to be submerged in the city lights behind it. The statue of Christ on Monte Urgull is illuminated and very visible.

Entrance

By day

The markers of the leading line are grey posts and not conspicuous. Nevertheless from ⊕527 a track of 158° between Isla de Santa Clara and Monte Urgull can be followed with confidence as the sides of the eastern entrance are steep-to and clean. The weak tidal stream sets to the E before HW, and W after HW but this may be negated by wind-induced currents. Keep clear of La Bancha shoal (5.4m) especially in any swell. Once past Isla de Santa Clara turn to port towards the harbour entrance noting that there will be many moored boats in the bay and that it is a sharp turn to port into the narrow entrance.

By night

The leading lights are intensified on the line and easier to see than by day. Once past Isla de Santa Clara the city lights provide good background lighting and give some assistance in avoiding moorings. If going to the harbour the two lights on the breakwater ends (Fl(2)R and Fl(2)G.8s) will be reversed on the approach.

Berthing

A small pontoon is provided for visitors on the wall opposite the entrance and it will be necessary to raft up. Berthing in the N part of the harbour is not appreciated by the fishermen and the southern part is crammed with small boats. A ladder will be needed to get ashore at low water if not berthed on the pontoon.

Moorings

The Club (RCNSS) has laid additional moorings for visitors which includes a 24-hour water taxi service. Contact the Club on Ch 09 before picking up one of the many private moorings. The moorings near the clubhouse are likely to be in less than 2m.

Anchorage

Most of the suitable anchoring space has been taken up by moorings, especially to the S of Isla de Santa Clara where there is some shelter from the swell. However, an anchorage may be found as indicated on the plan or anywhere where there is a space. The bottom is sand with weed patches and not to be depended on in a blow. In the event of one from the N sector either seek shelter in the harbour or clear out. A trip line is advisable as there are a lot of old moorings scattered about the bottom of the bay.

Ashore in San Sebastián

The Real Club Nautico de San Sebastián (RCNSS) is one of the most welcoming clubs on the coast and is always ready to make visitors feel at home. It is a pity that, in spite of their efforts for visiting yachtsmen, the berthing facilities for them are so inadequate; the fishing lobby is just too strong, while geography and the reputation of La Concha as a

Visitors' pontoon looking E to fishing harbour

playa suprema makes any marina development unlikely. Serious local yachtsmen keep their boats at Hondarribia, Getaria or Zumaia.

Nevertheless, it is a lively city in a beautiful setting with traditions as a summer seat for the government and a holiday resort for royalty. Many restaurants and tapas bars, casinos and a racecourse provide entertainment.

Facilities

Water points on the quays; fuel berth for diesel only is at the outer end of the centre quay in the harbour; showers and WCs in the Club; shops and market close by; slips, and craneage up to 5 tonnes.

Leisure

La Concha and Ondarreta beaches are within easy walking distance; visits to the tops of Monte Irgueldo and Urgull give splendid views and the old town to the E is picturesque and worth a visit.

Travel

On the main train and bus services to the E and W. Nearest airport at Fuenterrabía (also known as San Sebastián) 22km and Bilbao 110km. Nearest ferry port Bilbao (to Portsmouth).

Fiestas

Several during the year but main one is Semana Grande on 15 August.

te Urgull

YC

Entrance

Harbour looking W

45 Río de Orio

Cat C

Curiosity and a sense of adventure might prompt a visit here

Location
43°18'.00N 02°08'.00W

Shelter
Good inside

Warnings
Doubtful entrance in a swell; bridge ½M inside with 17.5m clearance

Depth restrictions
Least depth 0.1m in channel, 1.5m on bar, 2.5m by town

Night entry
Lit but no ldg lts

Tidal information
HW PdG –0050
LW PdG –0030

Mean height of tide (m)

MHWS	MHWN	MLWN	MLWS
4.2	3.2	1.6	0.6

Tidal stream
Up to 4 knots on ebb

Berthing
Drying alongside berths, mooring or anchor by town

Facilities
Some but few for yachts

Charts
No large-scale
BA 1102 (200)
Spanish 944 (40)

Weather
Pasajes Ch 27 at 0840, 1240, 2010
Navtex A or D

Radio
None

Telephone
None

⊕ **528** Orio 43°18'·40N 02°07'·80W

55 Elanchove
53 Lequeitio
51 Ondarroa
50 Motrico
49 Deva
48 Zumaia
47 Getaria
I. de S. Anton
528
45 Orio
44 San Sebastian
42 Pasajes
41 Hendaye
C. Higuer

Town

Entrance

Río de Orio looking S. The dredger is leaving

PILOTAGE

Approaches

The approaches are clear and danger-free to ⊕528 from the E, W and N sectors. From here the prominent W breakwater end (Fl(4)G.11s) and the entrance to the river can be identified with the white Cruz de la Barra (illuminated) behind it. Approach the entrance on a track of about 190°.

Entrance

By day or night

The best time to enter is HW–0100 to HW, and not if the swell is breaking across. Pass the W breakwater end at 50m and keep this distance to follow the curve round, crossing over to the E bank as the first bend is approached. When Punta de la Barra is well abaft the beam, head for the centre of the centre arch and leave the Q.R on the bridge (17.5m clearance) and the Q.R beyond and to the SW of it to port. Cross to the W bank and hug this bank, which is marked by four green flashing lights on posts, until the Q.G by the boatyard is passed. Then come into the centre of the channel and head for the swing bridge.

Berthing

Alongside the town quay from drying 2.5m at the W end to a short stretch by the bridge with 1–2m. This is usually occupied by fishing boats.

Moorings

There are a few head and stern moorings in the river off the town, in 2–3m, mainly for fishing boats which could be doubled up on.

Anchorage

There may be space to anchor just below the town bridge in 2–3m or clear of the moorings lower down. A second anchor may be necessary to reduce swing.

Ashore in Orio

Facilities

There are water points on the quay; the fuel pump is only for Gasoleo B; 10-tonne crane on quay; adequate shops and a chandlery; repairs may be possible at the boatyard on the S bank.

Leisure

There are a number of unpretentious restaurants and cafés.

The local 16th-century church is of curious design. A dinghy with an engine can get 10M up the river through attractive and hilly country side.

Travel

The town is on the main E/W bus and rail routes. Nearest airports Fuenterrabía (40km) and Bilbao (95km).

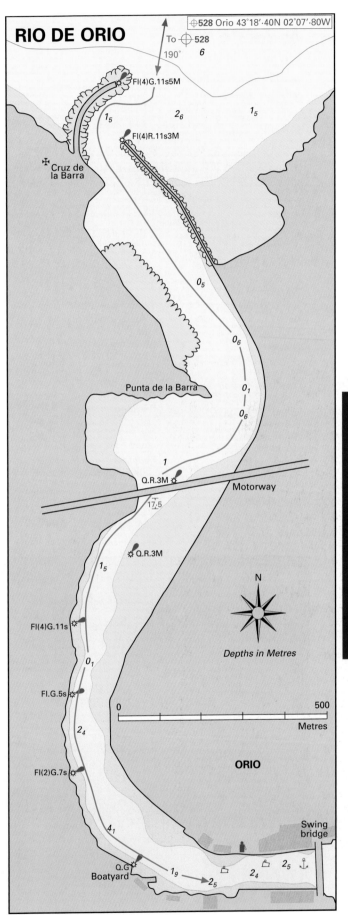

RIO DE ORIO

⊕528 Orio 43°18'·40N 02°07'·80W

To ⊕528
190°

II. PASAJES TO SANTANDER

46 Zarauz

Cat D

Anchorage and dinghy harbour only
Location
43°17'.00N 02°11'.00W

This tiny harbour at the W side of Ensenada de Zarauz dries at LW and the outer part is used as a swimming pool. The inner part is full of small boats but mooring buoys are sometimes placed off it in the summer and the harbour could be used to land in by dinghy and to visit the lively resort of Zarauz, but it is quite a walk along a busy coast road.

The harbour can be identified by its stone breakwaters under the road in front of a steep wooded cliff.

Juan Sebastián de Elacano's ship the *Victoria*, the first to circumnavigate the world in Magellan's voyage and the only survivor of a fleet of five, was built at Zarauz.

47 Getaria

Cat B*

Welcoming marina and yacht club in a busy fishing harbour
Location
43°19'.00N 02°12'.00W
Shelter
Good in harbour but uncomfortable in easterlies
Warning
Fierce gusts in harbour in W or NW gales
Depth restrictions
5.4m in entrance
4m in marina
Night entry
Well lit

Tidal information
HW PdG –0050
LW PdG –0030
Mean height of tide (m)

MHWS	MHWN	MLWN	MLWS
4.2	3.2	1.6	0.6

Tidal stream
Negligible
Berthing
On pontoons with fingers up to 12m; prior booking over 12m
Facilities
Full marina facilities

Charts
BA 1171 (Var)
Spanish 39944 (40), 3921 (10)
Imray C18
Weather
Pasajes Ch 27 at 0840, 1240 and 2010
Navtex A or D

Radio
Ch 09, 24 hours
☎ 922 58 09 59
E-mail
thage@infonegocio.com

⊕ 529 Getaria 43°18'.13N 02°11'.00W

55 Elanchove
53 Lequeitio
51 Ondarroa
50 Motrico
49 Deva
48 Zumaia
I. de S. Anton
529
45 Orio
44 San Sebastian
42 Pasajes
41 Hendaye
C. Higuer

47 Getaria

Getaria looking WSW. The marina can be seen in the centre

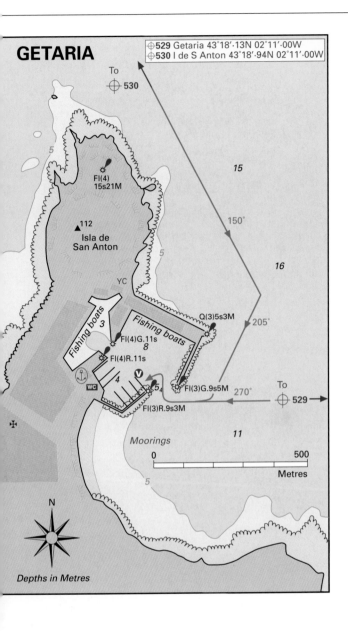

GETARIA

⊕**529** Getaria 43°18'·13N 02°11'·00W
⊕**530** I de S Anton 43°18'·94N 02°11'·00W

To
⊕ 530

Fl(4)
15s21M

▲112
Isla de
San Anton

YC

15

150°

16

205°

Fishing boats
Fishing boats
3
Q(3)5s3M
Fl(4)G.11s
8
Fl(4)R.11s
4
Fl(3)G.9s5M 270°
Fl(3)R.9s3M

To
⊕ 529

Moorings

0   500
Metres

11

5

N

Depths in Metres

PILOTAGE

Approaches

By day or night From N, E or W

All approaches to ⊕529 and 530 are clear of dangers as are the tracks from them to the harbour entrance. By day the distinctive mouse-like appearance of Isla de San Anton can be seen from afar, as can Isla de San Anton's powerful light.

Entrance

Straightforward, well marked and well lit. Turn sharp to port to the visitors' berth once inside.

Berthing

Least depth in marina is 3m on finger pontoons with only a few berths for those over 12m; 16 visitors' berths.

Moorings

None; those in the harbour are for fishing boats only, and those outside for locals.

Anchorage

Anchoring to the S of the entrance is perfectly safe and feasible but the many moorings in this area mean that you will be some distance from the entrance. See also the warning above about strong gusts in heavy weather from the W and NW.

Ashore in Getaria

A very lively little town with many cafés and restaurants and a most welcoming yacht club which is also for fishermen. The 14th-century church is well worth a visit to pay homage to the statue of Juan Sebastián de Elacano (see Zarauz above) to whom the major fiesta on 6 August is dedicated; other fiestas on 28 April and 29 June.

Facilities

All the usual marina facilities plus a chandler in the town; 32-tonne travel-lift, 5-tonne crane; many small shops and good bathing beaches close by.

Travel

The railway is some distance away but the E/W bus route is close to the town. Nearest airport Bilbao (88km) whence there is also a ferry service to Portsmouth.

Passage Getaria to Zumaia

Although only 3 miles between the two, the passage is dominated by the mouse-like Isla de San Anton at Getaria which is very much an outstanding feature of the coast. It is hardly surprising that its other name is El Ratón.

Isla de San Anton

48 Zumaia

Cat B*

Town rejuvenated by the new marina and retaining its share of industry and tourism

Location
43°19′.00N 02°15′.00W

Shelter
Very good in marina

Caution
A bar of 1.5m (but may be deeper) has been reported at the entrance and should be allowed for

Depth restrictions
3m in channel and marina
2m+ alongside town quay

Night entry
Reasonably lit but no ldg lts

Tidal information
HW PdG –0050
LW PdG –0030

Mean height of tide (m)

MHWS	MHWN	MLWN	MLWS
4.2	3.2	1.6	0.6

Tidal stream
Up to 2 knots on the ebb

Berthing
At fingers on pontoons in marina

Facilities
Usual marina facilities; shipyard; good shops

Charts
BA no large-scale
Spanish 3921 (10)
Imray C17

Weather
Pasajes Ch 27 at 0840, 1240 and 2010
Navtex A or D

Radio
Ch 09 during working hours

Telephone
Marina ☎ 943 860 938
Email
marurola@euskinet.net

⊕ **531** Zumaia 43°18′·76N 02°14′·70W

55 Elanchove
53 Lequieitio
51 Ondarroa
48 Zumaia
50 Motrico
49 Deva
47 Getaria
I. de S. Anton
45 Orio
44 San Sebastian
42 Pasajes
41 Hendaye
C. Higuer
531

Zumaia looking ENE

Town quay   Marina

PILOTAGE

Approaches

⊕531 is clear to approach from all directions and the entrance may then be closed on a track of 180° or less to avoid the rocky shoals off Punta Izustarri (½M NE of the entrance) where the sea breaks for some considerable distance off.

Entrance

See *Caution* above.

By day

Leave the W breakwater end 50m to starboard allowing for 1.5m on bar and follow the W side round at this distance or less all the way up the channel. Least depth in channel 3m. Turn to port into the marina when the entrance is open.

By night

As for by day but the visibility must be 50-100m to follow the breakwater and wall up the channel.

Berthing

On finger pontoons, the first pontoon being for visitors. Least depth in outer part of marina 3m. There are alongside berths on the Old Town wall in depths indicated on the plan but yachts are not encouraged and the pontoon is used by the ferry.

Zumaia opposite marina entrance

Moorings

None.

Anchoring

Outside to the E of the breakwaters as indicated on the plan but subject to swell.

Ashore in Zumaia

Of Roman origin, this small country town survives on a shipyard, a cement works, some coaster trade and now the marina. There are good shops and some restaurants and the museums are worth a visit. The Museo Zuloaga to the N of the marina has some El Greco and Goya paintings. The Tourist Office is just over the footbridge into the Old Town and helpful; there is a *supermercado* close to it and, for a big shop it would be worth taking a dinghy across to the ferry pontoon. The beach is relatively uncrowded by Spanish standards and can be reached by dinghy, or by ferry which also calls at the marina.

The Río Urola winds for several miles through quiet countryside and would be worth a dinghy exploration.

Facilities

The new marina has all the usual facilities including fuel and water and electricity on the pontoons; 32-tonne travel-lift and craneage; there is a yacht repair business in the marina, probably more suitable for yachts than the shipyard. There is a restaurant in the marina and more in the Old Town. While there are some shops in the New Town, the best and the *supermercado* are in the Old.

Travel

The town is very close to the railway and on the main E/W bus routes. Nearest airport Bilbao (80km) which also has a ferry link with the UK.

Fiestas

29 June San Pedron; 15 April San Telmo; 8 September Santa Maria; 29 September San Miguel.

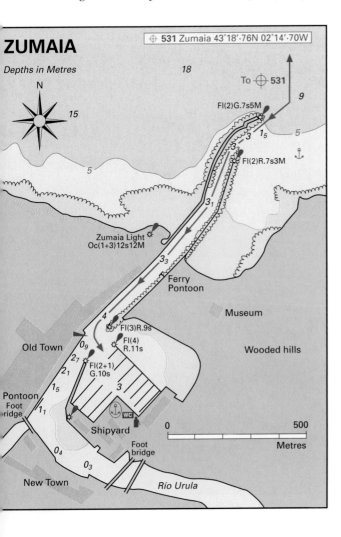

ZUMAIA

Depths in Metres

⊕ 531 Zumaia 43°18'·76N 02°14'·70W

To ⊕ 531

Fl(2)G.7s5M

Fl(2)R.7s3M

Zumaia Light
Oc(1+3)12s12M

Ferry Pontoon

Museum

Wooded hills

Old Town

Fl(3)R.9s

Fl(4) R.11s

Fl(2+1) G.10s

Pontoon Foot bridge

Shipyard

Foot bridge

New Town

Río Urula

0 — 500 Metres

II. PASAJES TO SANTANDER

49 Deva

Cat C

As a harbour it is only of marginal attraction to the passing yachtsman

Location
43°19'.00N 02°21'.00W

Shelter
Poor

Warning
Shallow bar, depth unknown

Depth restrictions
Allow for a least depth of 0.1m

Night entry
Unlit

Tidal information
HW PdG –0050
LW PdG –0030

Mean height of tide

MHWS	MHWN	MLWN	MLWS
4.2	3.2	1.6	0.6

Tidal stream
Up to 6 knots on the ebb

Berthing
Anchoring only

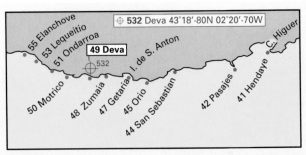

Facilities
Small country town

Charts
No large-scale
BA 1102 (200)
Spanish 3922 (10)

Weather
Pasajes Ch 27 at 0840, 1240 and 2010
Navtex A or D

No radio or telephone

PILOTAGE

Approaches

By day only

Make good a track of 210° or less from ⊕532 to avoid the end of Dique Rompeolas.

Entrance

Best between HW–0100 and HW. The bar varies in position and depth. Enter close to the W wall and follow the channel as on the plan. Note that the end of the E training wall covers.

Berthing

There is no room for deep-draught visitors in the small harbour by the bridge.

Anchorage

There is a 3m hole just below the bridge which will need some preliminary soundings to establish its position and two anchors to stay in it.

Otherwise as indicated outside.

Facilities and leisure

Fuel from garage behind railway station; good shops and restaurants; an excellent beach which is often crowded. The river winds for several miles through hilly country and might be worth a dinghy expedition.

Fiestas

15 April, 29 June, 14–24 August and 29 September.

Deva looking S from entrance

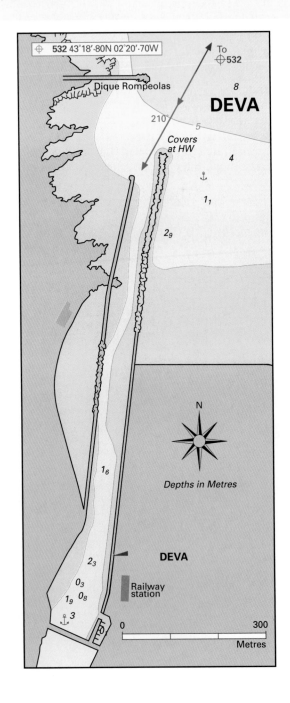

50 Motrico

Cat C

A scenically attractive town with some concessions to yachts

Location
43°19′.00N 02°23′.00W

Shelter
Good except in N–NE'lies

Depth restrictions
3–4m in most of harbour

Night entry
Well lit plus leading lights

Tidal information
HW PdG –0050
LW PdG –0030

Mean height of tide

MHWS	MHWN	MLWN	MLWS
4.3	3.2	1.6	0.6

Tidal stream
Negligible

Berthing
Alongside, mooring or anchor

Facilities
Those of a small fishing port

Charts
No large-scale
BA 1102 (200)
Spanish 3922 (10)

Weather
Pasajes Ch 27 at 0840, 1240 and 2010
Navtex A or D

Radio
None

Telephone
Cofradia ☎ 943 60 32 04

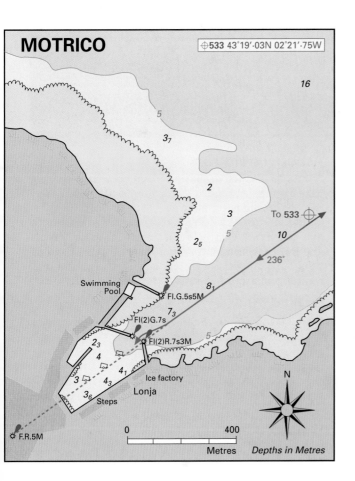

PILOTAGE

Approaches

By day

From ⊕533 pick up the leading line 236°. The front mark is the E breakwater head and the rear is a small clock tower near the top of the town on the W side of a large square, red-roofed building. There is plenty of water on either side of the line and no cross set.

By night

As for by day. The front light is Fl(2)R.7s and the rear F.R high up in the lights of the town.

Warning

Entry should not be attempted in strong NE'lies, nor is it place to be caught inside in these conditions.

Entrance

When the N breakwater (Fl.G.5s) has been passed, alter to starboard to open up the inner entrance and proceed through.

Berthing

If most of the fishing fleet is not in, berth near the steps on the S wall where there is 3–4m. A ladder may be needed at LW.

Moorings

A number of head and stern moorings in the harbour are used by the locals and fishermen but it may be possible to pick one up or double up.

Anchoring

As a last resort, anchor (with trip line) near the E end of the W breakwater and take a line to the breakwater. This might be the most comfortable option if caught inside in strong NE'lies.

Motrico looking SW

Looking SW from entrance. S quay and berths on left

Ashore in Motrico

A small, attractive Basque fishing village which hasn't quite expanded its fishing activities to the extent of Ondárroa next door nor jumped into the leisure market like Zumaia on the other side with its new marina. Nevertheless it has an unspoilt charm and most facilities and even if many of them seem to be up the hill there are enough restaurants down round the harbour to satisfy the lazy.

Facilities

Only Gasoleo B on the quay and the nearest garage is some way; water points on the S quay and plentiful ice from the factory; a 5-tonne crane on the quay and a couple of slips; there is a fisherman's type chandlery near the head of the harbour and several shops but the *supermercado* is half way up the hill.

Leisure

This is no great run ashore but there are several pleasant restaurants round the harbour, on the central spur and up the hill.

Travel

Just off the main bus and rail routes; nearest air and ferry port Bilbao (60km)

Fiestas

15 May, 22–25 July, 14 and 30 September.

51 Ondárroa

Cat B*

Orientated wholly to fishing; yachts use only exceptionally

Location
43°20'.00N 02°25'.00W

Shelter
Good inside inner harbour

Warning
Entry unwise in E'ly gales

Depth restrictions
1.5m+ over most of harbour

Night entry
Well lit but no leading lights

Tidal information
HW PdG –0050
LW PdG –0030

Mean height of tide

MHWS	MHWN	MLWN	MLWS
4.3	3.2	1.6	0.6

Tidal stream
Negligible

Berthing
None specially for yachts

Facilities
None specifically for yachts

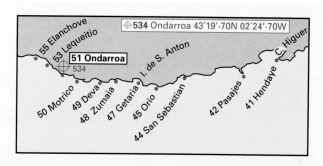

Charts
BA 1102 (200)
Spanish 3922 (10)

Weather
Pasajes Ch 27, Bilbao Ch 26

at 0840, 1240 and 2010
Radio and telephone
None

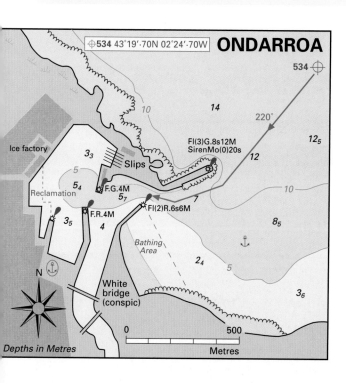

ONDARROA

Depths in Metres

Ondárroa is a major fishing port which makes no concessions to yachts. They may be accepted inside in stress of weather or when the fishing fleet is not in.

PILOTAGE

Approaches

By day or night
From ⊕534 make good a track of 220° to leave the N breakwater end (Fl(3)G.8s Racon Siren) 50m to starboard.

Entrance

Is straightforward and deep. Keep 50m or more off the N breakwater.

Berthing

The N corner of the harbour is most likely to yield a vacant alongside berth or on the E side of the E spur; otherwise double up on the fishing boats. It may be possible to anchor up the arm leading to the bridge.

Moorings

None except for small craft up the bridge arm.

Anchoring

Outside clear of the bathing area, except as above.

Ashore in Ondárroa

The town has its fair share of restaurants and tapas bars round the harbour but these are orientated more to the fishermen than the tourists. There is a unique 14th-century church and parts of the old town are of interest.

Facilities

Fuel – only Gasoleo B available in the harbour area; nearest garage on road out of town; water points on the quays; extensive boatyard facilities and slips in the harbour and up river; adequate shops.

Travel

The town is some way from the main rail and bus routes to which it has local connections. Nearest air and ferry port Bilbao (60km).

Ondárroa looking SW

II. PASAJES TO SANTANDER

52 Ensenada de Saustan

Cat D

Sheltered anchorage in case of need

⊕**535** 43°21´.34N 02°27´.08W

A bay to the W of Punta Mococoburua with a steep-to shore but a level and soft mud bottom.

Tuck as close in as weather and depths permit. Sheltered from the SE through S to NW.

53 Lequeitio

Cat C

A busy fishing harbour where yachts are welcome but it is always crowded

Location
43°22´.00N 02°30´.00W

Shelter
Good in harbour

Warning
Not on in northerly gales

Depth restrictions
2.5–4m in harbour, 5m in approaches

Night entry
Lit but no leading lights

Tidal information
HW PdG –0025
LW PdG –0035

Mean height of tide

MHWS	MHWN	MLWN	MLWS
4.3	3.2	1.6	0.6

Tidal stream
Negligible

Berthing
Occasional alongside berth in crowded harbour; anchor outside

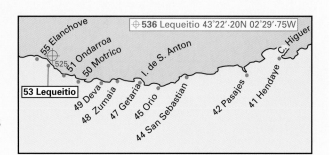

Facilities
None specifically for yachts

Charts
BA 1102 (200)
Spanish 393 (7.5)

Weather
Bilbao Ch 26 0840, 1240, 2010
Navtex A and D

Radio and telephone
None

Submerged training wall   Aislado Rock   Pontoon   Church

Lequeitio looking S

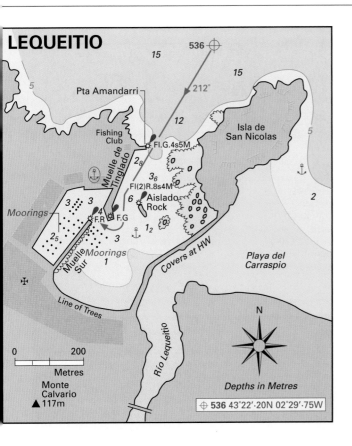

LEQUEITIO

536 ⊕
15
15
Pta Amandarri
212°
12
Fishing Club
Isla de San Nicolas
Fl.G.4s5M
Muelle de Tinglado
2₈
3₆
Fl(2)R.8s4M
6 Aislado Rock
3 3
Moorings
4
F.R F.G
1₂
2₅
3
Muelle Sur
Moorings
1
Covers at HW
Playa del Carraspio
Line of Trees
Río Lequeitio
N
0 200
Metres
Monte Calvario ▲117m
Depths in Metres
⊕ 536 43°22'·20N 02°29'·75W

PILOTAGE

Approaches

By day or night

Isla de San Nicolas with the red-roofed houses beyond is conspicuous from seaward by day. From ⊕536 identify Punta Amandarri (Fl.G.4s) and keep it just open of the end of Muelle de Tinglado (F.G) on 212°; by day the peak of Monte Calvario is almost on the same line.

Entrance

When Aislado Rock (Fl(2)R.8s) is abeam to port, alter to port to round in to the entrance to starboard, leaving all the moorings outside to port.

Berthing

The quietest berths are immediately inside on the W side of Muelle Sur where there is a pontoon, or alongside the W side of Muelle de Tinglado. Berths may be found alongside the S end of the W quay but it is very noisy with some lively restaurants and bars just across the road.

Moorings

The SW corner of the harbour is full of moorings for small boats; these, and those outside are private. There is a trot of large fishing boat moorings in the middle of the harbour which may be vacant.

Anchoring

Prohibited inside the harbour. Outside as indicated on the plan.

Ashore in Lequeitio

A picturesque and lively fishing port and holiday resort which accepts the occasional yacht. Playa de Carraspio is a popular beach particularly for surfers. A visit to the almost cathedral-sized church and the old town is of interest, and walks to the top of Monte Calvario and to Isla de San Nicolas at LW worthwhile.

Facilities

Water points on the quay, but only Gasoleo B in the port; fuel from garage behind the church; good shops and market; many restaurants and bars; slip and crane in the NE corner and boatbuilders up the river for repairs.

Travel

Buses connect with the main routes at Gernika and Deva; nearest air and ferry port Bilbao (50km).

Fiestas

29 June, 1–8 September.

54 Río de Ea

Cat D

⊕538 43°24'.00N 02°34'.78W

A narrow inlet leading to a tiny harbour and a village popular with tourists. The conspicuous red-roofed house seen on the left of the picture helps to identify it. See also photograph on page 76.

The río dries out to well below the harbour in the centre of the picture and any swell breaks here. The harbour dries 1m.

It is possible to anchor in the outer reaches in fine weather and proceed by dinghy up the río to the village which is 400m beyond the harbour. Any wind tends to blow up or down the valley but a second anchor may be needed to restrict swing.

There are some shops and restaurants which are busy at weekends; water tap at the harbour.

Ea looking SSE. See also photograph on page 76

55 Elanchove

Cat C

The epitome of a Basque village but with not much room inside the harbour

Location
43°25′.00N 02°35′.00W

Shelter
Adequate except in easterlies

Warning
Heavy gusts in bay in strong westerlies

Depth restrictions
4m in entrance; 1.5–2m inside

Night entry
Possible but little light inside

Tidal information
HW PdG −0025
LW PdG −0035

Mean height of tide (m)

MHWS	MHWN	MLWN	MLWS
4.2	3.2	1.6	0.6

Tidal stream
Negligible

Berthing
Possible but ingenuity needed

Facilities
Basic shops only

Charts
BA 1102 (200)
Spanish 393 (7.5)

Weather
Bilbao Ch 26 0840, 1240, 2010
Navtex A and D

Radio and telephone
None

⊕ 539 Elanchove 43°24′·43N 02°37′·28W   55 Elanchove

73 Suances
C. Mayor
64 Laredo
62 Castro Urdiales
60 Plencia
58 Bakio
57 Bermeo
C. Machicaco
539
70 Santander
65 Santoña
61 Bilbao
53 Lequeitio

Elanchove looking SW

PILOTAGE

Approaches

By day

The red roofs of the houses climbing up the cliff can be seen from a long way off. Approach from ⊕539 on a track of 250° clear of any dangers.

By night

As for by day. The N breakwater head light (Fl.G.3s) is the easiest to distinguish while the F.W sector of the S breakwater is lost amongst the village lights behind. It would be unwise to try to enter by night unless a previous visit has been made as there is little light inside.

Entrance

Approach the entrance on a final course of about 330° at slow speed taking care of any boat that may be leaving. Turn very sharply to port round the S breakwater head to reach the main harbour.

Berthing

The best alongside berth is on the E side of the central mole. There are ladders, plentiful bollards, a

Entrance

Elanchove looking SW

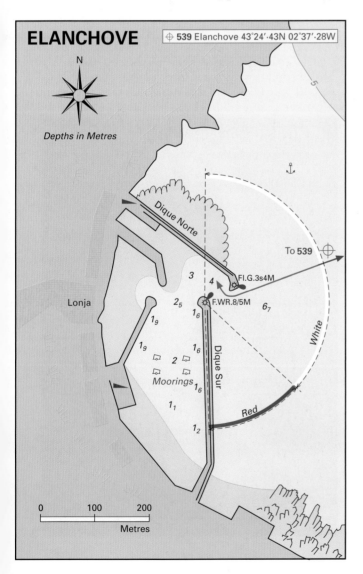

ELANCHOVE

⊕ 539 Elanchove 43°24'·43N 02°37'·28W

N

Depths in Metres

Dique Norte

To **539**

Fl.G.3s4M

Lonja

3　4

2₅　F.WR.8/5M　6₇

1₉　1₆

White

1₉　1₆

2

Dique Sur

Moorings 1₆

1₁

Red

1₂

0　100　200

Metres

---

smooth face and 1.9m alongside. However, it is popular with the fishermen and is the fish unloading berth.

The W side of Dique Sur has almost as much water but has an underwater ledge about 1m wide which dries 1.2m. A haul-off line or lines to an anchor or a buoy will be needed if securing here. The N inner breakwater has a similar obstruction.

Moorings

There is a small trot of moorings in 1–2m as indicated on the plan which is usually occupied by fishing boats and locals. It may be possible to double up here.

Anchoring

Outside as indicated in 3–4m. Beware of strong gusts in W winds. A trip line will be needed if using an anchor inside.

Ashore in Elanchove

There is little for the dilettante in this unspoilt and undeveloped village. A few small shops and simple restaurants and a steep walk up the hill for the energetic. For those staying longer, a taxi trip to Castillo Arteaga and the Basondo caves may be worthwhile.

Facilities

Minimal; a few small shops with a semi self-service store at the top of the hill; water tap at the root of the central jetty; two slips, the one in the S corner with a power winch.

Travel

The village is off the main rail and bus routes but local buses connect with them via Gernika at the top of the village. Nearest air and ferry port Bilbao (45km).

Lequeitio to Bermeo

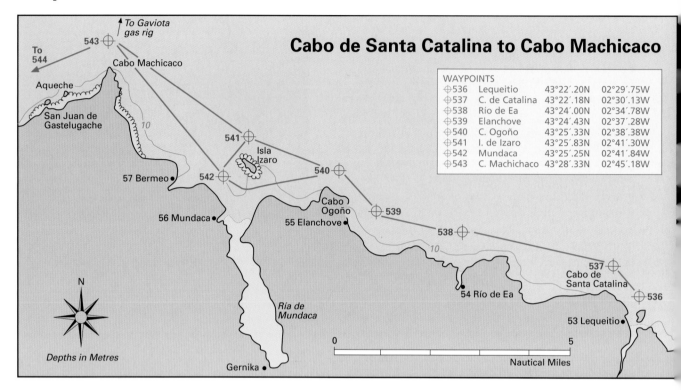

Cabo de Santa Catalina to Cabo Machicaco

WAYPOINTS			
⊕536	Lequeitio	43°22′.20N	02°29′.75W
⊕537	C. de Catalina	43°22′.18N	02°30′.13W
⊕538	Río de Ea	43°24′.00N	02°34′.78W
⊕539	Elanchove	43°24′.43N	02°37′.28W
⊕540	C. Ogoño	43°25′.33N	02°38′.38W
⊕541	I. de Izaro	43°25′.83N	02°41′.30W
⊕542	Mundaca	43°25′.25N	02°41′.84W
⊕543	C. Machichaco	43°28′.33N	02°45′.18W

Depths in Metres

0   5
Nautical Miles

From ⊕536 to ⊕543

This coastal passage of some 12 miles is of interest as it includes one of the few offlying islands along the whole coast, Isla Izaro, the tidal island of Isla de San Nicolas at Lequeitio, the tiny Río de Ea, the extensive estuary of Río de Mundaca running inland to Gernika and (at the moment) the only offshore gas rig of Gaviota off Cabo Machicaco.

From ⊕536 to ⊕540

Cabo de Santa Catalina has a conspicuous white lighthouse (Fl(1+3)20s44m17M Horn) on the cliff edge and a sawmill with stacks of timber just inland from it

The coastline between Ea and Cabo Ogoño is broken only by the small port of Elanchove. Cabo Ogoño, a reddish-coloured headland, rises to 300m.

Cabo de Santa Catalina

For details of the narrow Río de Ea see also p73

Río Mundaca entrance. Swell building up against ebb in main channel

Cabo Machicaco looking W

PILOTAGE

From ⊕540 the direct route along the coast is outside Isla Izaro via ⊕541 but there is a clean passage 400m wide carrying at least 3.4m to the S of the island if going to Mundaca or Bermeo. Spanish chart 3931 is really needed to navigate this in safety in fine weather. A track of 260°/080° passing 200m N of Piedras Otzarri, two small above-water rocks, will pass through the deepest part which shoals gradually thence towards the island.

Once through, a track of 245° on the conspicuous hermitage on Punta de Santa Catalina (no connection with the Cabo of the same name to the E) will lead towards Mundaca and the entrance to the Río Mundaca.

Entrance to Río Mundaca looking E

Río Mundaca winds for several miles S through a sandy estuary. There are 5 villages on the W bank before the historic town of Gernika is reached 7M from the sea. The first village, Pedernales, was once a thriving shipbuilding port sending out vessels of several hundreds of tons. A pleasant inland voyage but only for shallow draught boats or multihulls, on a rising tide.

Entry or exit from Río Mundaca will be dangerous if there is any swell which breaks right across the entrance, except possibly in the main channel close to Mundaca harbour

Cabo Machicaco is one of the major headlands of the whole coast and has a fearsome reputation. This is not entirely unwarranted as heavy seas extend some way seawards from the vicinity of the Cabo due to a rocky and uneven bottom. It should be passed at least 1M off and more in heavy weather.

Gernika is the spiritual capital of the Basque world and since the 10th century the assembly has met under an ancient oak tree there. The original tree has been replaced to continue as a symbol of Basque freedom and independence. The town was 80% destroyed in 1937 during the civil war by the German airforce and 1,600 killed. This dreadful act was a foretaste of much worse to come in the Second World War and is remembered in Picasso's famous painting *Guernica*, now in Madrid.

Mundaca is a small crowded harbour which almost dries out (see below). Bermeo is one of the major fishing and coaster ports on the coast but is branching into the leisure market and is establishing some yacht berths and facilities which should be valuable in what is almost an all-weather port (see below).

56 Mundaca

Cat C

Small, crowded and shallow harbour with attractive village

Location
43°25'.00N 02°42'.00W

Shelter
From the W at anchor

Warning
Strong tidal streams in river; not suitable in any swell

Depth restrictions
Most of harbour dries

Night entry
Unlit but street lights on jetties

Tidal information
HW PdG –-0035
LW PdG –0015

Mean height of tide (m)

MHWS	MHWN	MLWN	MLWS
4.6	3.7	1.6	0.6

Tidal stream
The ebb outside can exceed 3kns

Berthing
Berth inside harbour unlikely

Facilities
Adequate shops and cafés

Charts
BA 1102 (200)
Spanish 3931 (10)

Weather
Bilbao Ch 26 0840, 1240, 2010
Navtex A or D

Radio and telephone
None

PILOTAGE

Approaches

By day

From ⊕542 make good a track of 170° until Punta de la Barra is abeam when alter to 210° keeping a close eye on the depth.

See above if approaching from the E.

Entrance

Best time is HW–0100 to HW. Turn into the entrance close round the N breakwater end.

Berthing

Very unlikely there will be a mooring free in this crowded little harbour and neither inner walls on the N and S breakwaters are suitable to berth against because of steps and obstructions. A temporary berth may be found alongside another boat.

Anchoring

As indicated on the plan in 1–3m sand. The further in to the río, the stronger the streams.

Ashore in Mundaca

A delightful and unspoilt small town that has seen greater days. It is a pity that there are no provisions for visiting yachts and the anchorage outside is an uneasy one except in the finest weather.

Facilities and leisure

Water points on the quays; nearest fuel is a garage on the road out to the N; several slips and a small crane; adequate shops and several small hotels and restaurants; the old church by the harbour and the town are worth a wander round.

Travel

Rail and bus services via Gernika; nearest air and ferry port Bilbao (40km).

Fiestas

18, 25, 31 July, 10–24 August, 8 September.

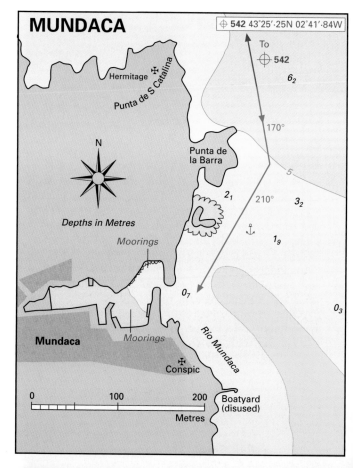

Outer harbour looking N. The pontoon on the left dries

57 Bermeo

Cat B
Principal fishing port now developing yacht facilities

Location
43°25'.00N 02°43'.00W

Shelter
Good

Depth restrictions
3–6m over most of harbour

Night entry
Well lit but no ldg lts

Tidal information
HW PdG –0035
LW PdG –0015

Mean height of tide (m)

MHWS	MHWN	MLWN	MLWS
4.6	3.7	1.6	0.6

Berthing
Alongside N wall as indicated but development in progress in the area

Facilities
Those of a small town but mainly for fishermen

Charts
BA 1102 (200)
Spanish 3931 (10)

Weather
Bilbao Ch 26 0840, 1240, 2010
Navtex A or D

Radio
VHF Ch 09

Isla Izaro   Cabo Machicaco   Río Mundaca entrance

Yacht berths and development

275°

Bermeo looking E

PILOTAGE

Approaches

By day or night

⊕542 can be approached safely from the E passing 400m to the N of Isla Izaro and in the white sector of Rosape light (Fl(2)WR.10s). See page 77 for directions to pass S of Isla Izaro by day only.

From the W or N approach the breakwater light (Fl.G.4.5s) on a track of 140° or more.

Entrance

Round the breakwater end at about 50m keeping a good look-out for any vessels leaving and make a track of about 250° to leave the Contradique end (Fl.R.3s) well to port. Turn to port to avoid the local small boat moorings and round the spur (F.G) closely to reach the yacht berths.

Berthing

Until the marina facilities are developed yachts may berth on the N wall as indicated on the plan, and also on the W side of the spur. There are some ladders but one will be needed at LW if a berth beside one is not available.

Moorings

All for fishing boats or locals.

Anchoring

Not allowed in the harbour.

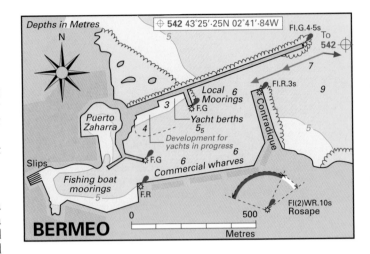

Ashore in Bermeo

The principal fishing port on this part of the coast and busy commercially with the export of steel strip, plate and timber. A development of part of the harbour for leisure was started in winter 04/05 and will eventually include all the usual yacht facilities. Part of Puerto Zaharra is to be filled in for an approach road. Until this development materialises, alongside berths for yachts are quite adequate and most facilities available if not exactly handy.

Facilities

Water points on the quay; fuel nearest garage 2km; ice from factory on quay; slips and cranes for fishing boats and chandlers; good variety of shops, market and restaurants.

Leisure

Bermeo is probably the best port from which to visit historic Gernika and there is a small train that runs from Bermeo along the Río Mundaca. Also worth a visit is the chapel at San Juan de Gastelgache on a peninsula to the W of Cabo Machicaco which is open on Saturday mornings; enquire at the Tourist Office for transport (next to the Casino at head of harbour); the Fishermens' Museum and Church of Santa Maria are of interest.

Fiestas

The best time to visit Bermeo is during one of the fiestas:

23–29 June for San Juan and San Pedro
22 July San Madalena with rowing races and visits to Isla Izaro
16 August International Folklore festival
7–29 September For Bermeo's Saints Day with many sporting events and music.

Puerto Zaharra looking N

58 Ensenada de Bakio

Cat D

⊕544 43°27'.01N 02°48'.48W

An open sandy bay 3M W of Machicaco affording some shelter from the W. Bakio is a popular resort for surfers. Anchor outside the 5m line as the surf breaks right across the bay.

A small canalised stream with a drying slip enters the bay at the W end, is much encumbered with rocks and is only suitable for dinghies at HW.

59 Arminza

Cat C
This entrance could be lethal in bad weather; little room inside

Location
43°26'.00N 02°48'.00W

Shelter
Indifferent

Warning
Not for the faint hearted; a free berth is unlikely

Depth restrictions
1m in entrance, most of rest dries

Night entry
Not recommended; unlit inside

Tidal information
HW PdG –0050
LW PdG –0030

Mean height of tide (m)

MHWS	MHWN	MLWN	MLWS
4.4	3.4	1.6	0.6

Berthing
One possible alongside berth

Facilities
Those of small village

Charts
No large-scale
BA 1102 (200)
Spanish 393 (50)

Weather
Bilbao Ch 26 0840, 1240, 2010.
Navtex A or D

Radio and telephone
None

I Possible berth

210°

Arminza looking SSW

II. PASAJES TO SANTANDER

PILOTAGE

Approach

By day

Adjust the initial track from ⊕545 to make 210° on the breakwater light which is in a grey masonry tower that is hard to pick out against the background. Best time to enter is HW–0100 to HW and not if blowing from the N or NE.

By night

Not recommended as there are no lights once inside the crowded harbour.

Entrance

Round the breakwater end at 50m and keep this distance and in the centre of the visible channel until the harbour is well open.

Berthing

The only possible alongside berth with a smooth wall and 0.3m is on the S side just beyond the blue crane. It will be tight fit to squeeze in as moorings take up most of the available space (see photo). Do not try to go alongside anywhere else as the walls are rough with a good lean on them and have rocks or a wide ledge drying at about half tide along them. A ladder will probably be needed at LW.

Moorings

Most unlikely that one will be available.

Anchoring

While certainly possible in settled weather outside, there are many rock patches and the holding uncertain. A trip line will be needed.

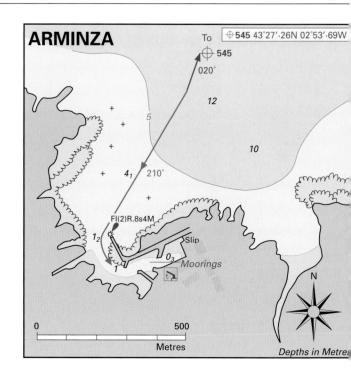

Arminza looking W. The only possible alongside berth is below the blue crane on the left

Ashore in Arminza

The village is cut off from the rest of the world amongst hills and pinewoods and has a certain charm. It is popular with sports fishermen whose boats fill the harbour and the restaurants have a following from the Bilbaons at weekends.

Facilities

Water taps on the quays; no fuel; some small shops for everyday needs and a few restaurants.

Travel

An occasional bus connects with Plencia and Bilbao, the latter being the nearest air/ferry port.

60 Plencia

Cat C

Popular seaside resort for the Bilbaons; visiting yachts anchor

Location
43°25′.00N 02°58′.00W

Shelter
Some, but little from the NW

Depth restrictions
Bar and river vary, 1m or less; inner harbour 0.5m or less

Night entry
Not advised except to anchor

Tidal information
HW PdG –0105
LW PdG –0015

Mean height of tide (m)

MHWS	MHWN	MLWN	MLWS
4.2	3.2	1.6	0.6

Berthing
Anchoring only

Facilities
Little for yachts

⊕ **547** Plencia 43°25′·23N 02°57′·58W

73 Suances
C. Mayor
70 Santander
65 Santoña
64 Laredo
62 Castro Urdiales
547
60 Plencia
58 Bakio
57 Bermeo
C. Machicaco
55 Elanchove
53 Lequeitio
61 Bilbao

Charts
No large-scale
BA 1102 (200)
Spanish 394 (5)

Weather
Bilbao Ch 26 0840, 1240, 2010
Navtex A or D

Telephone
Harbourmaster
☎ 615 77 10 16

Inner harbour

Dredger

Plencia looking SE

II. PASAJES TO SANTANDER

PILOTAGE

Approaches

By day or night

From ⊕547 make good a track of 130° on the breakwater end (Fl(2)G.7s), turning to port to anchor to the E of Punta de Astondo or in the bay. Entry into the river by night is not recommended as there are no lights once inside; but by day, round the breakwater end at 50m.

Entrance

Best time to enter HW–0100 to HW. Follow the W breakwater round at about 50m. Leave a concrete SH beacon to starboard and favour the W bank going upriver.

Berthing

A vacant berth or space in the inner harbour (0.5m over much of it) is unlikely but the harbourmaster will help if he can.

Anchoring

Below the first bend in the river to starboard is clear and there is usually 1m there but little room to swing. The river is thick with moorings above this with no room to anchor.

The alternative is to anchor to the E of Astondo where there is sometimes a mooring in the summer, or in the bay where it is all sand. Provided you have an outboard, the harbour is the best place to leave the dinghy. The watersport activities in the bay of jet skis, water-skiing and parascending cease in the evening.

Moorings

None for visitors unless the harbourmaster obliges.

Ashore in Plencia

The town is joined to Bilbao by the modern metro and Playa de Gorlitz is popular; it is crowded and noisy especially at weekends and not all of it can be avoided by anchoring in the bay; watersporters are active and the bars and cafés at the N end continue until late.

Looking upstream from the harbour

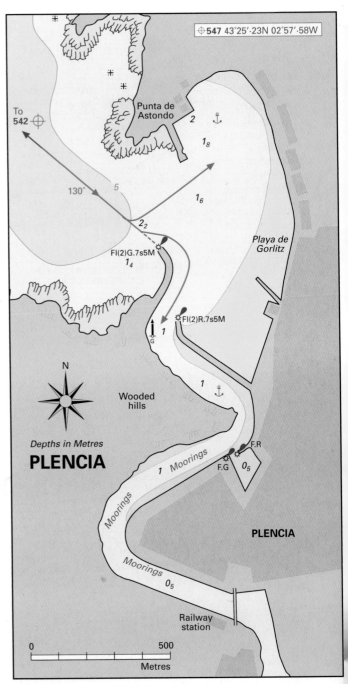

Facilities

The small harbour is in the centre of the town and most of the facilities are there. Water, diesel and petrol on the quay, plenty of shops and restaurants around it; there is a yacht club which is welcoming.

Leisure

All the joys of a seaside holiday town. If these do not appeal, the metro provides a fast and cheap way in to the city of Bilbao.

Travel

Good rail and bus services in all directions from Bilbao; airport 20km; ferry at Santurce across the bay.

Fiestas

16, 21, 22 July; 2–8 September for Sant Antolin.

61 Bilbao

Cat A

The principal Basque city and port; two excellent marinas at Las Arenas and Getxo for visitors

Location
43°24'.00N 03°02'.00W

Shelter
Excellent

Warning
The E arm of the outer breakwater is still under construction; use the main entrance and do not try a short cut over the E arm

Depth restrictions
2–3m in both marinas; deep water elsewhere

Night entry
Very well lit

Tidal information
HW PdG –0040
LW PdG –0020

Mean height of tide (m)

MHWS	MHWN	MLWN	MLWS
4.7	3.2	1.9	0.4

Tidal stream
The ebb in the river can be 3 knots

Berthing
On pontoons in either marina; many anchorages

Facilities
All of major marinas and a city

Charts
BA 1173 (12), 1174 (25)
Spanish 394A (25), 3941 (12.5)

Weather
Bilbao Ch 26 at 0840, 1240, 2010
Navtex A or D

Radio
Harbour Ch 12 and 16 (24h)
Marinas Ch 09 (working hrs)

Telephone
Harbour ☎ 944 24 14 16
Getxo ☎ 944 91 23 67
Las Arenas ☎ 944 63 76 00

PILOTAGE

Approaches

By day or night

It is some 4M in deep water from the outer entrance to the marinas at Getxo and Las Arenas. From ⊕548 cross to the in-going side of the two-way system. The E side of the entrance is a large square concrete structure marking the end of the submerged breakwater. From there proceed as indicated on the plan, keeping clear of commercial shipping. The sectored Getxo light (Oc.WR.4s) will help on the second leg.

The two chimneys near Santurce are conspicuous by day and night.

Looking N over Las Arenas and Getxo

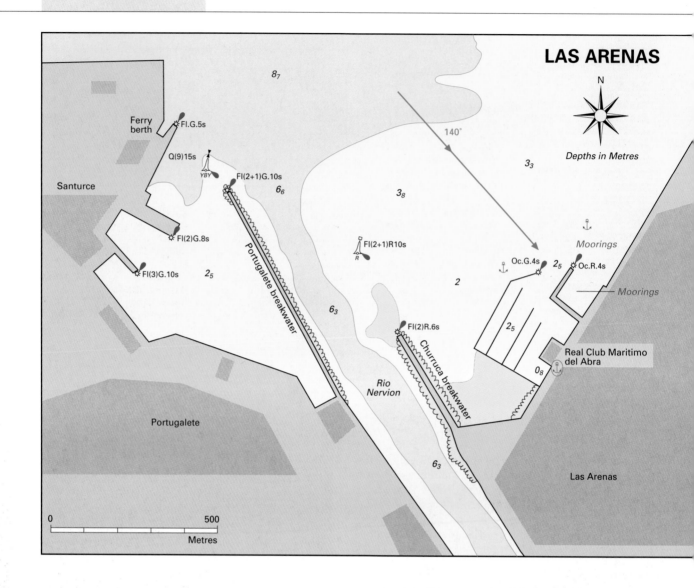

LAS ARENAS

140°

N

Depths in Metres

8_7

Ferry berth

Fl.G.5s

Q(9)15s

YBY

Fl(2+1)G.10s

6_6

Santurce

3_3

3_8

Fl(2)G.8s

Fl(2+1)R10s
R

Oc.G.4s

2_5

Oc.R.4s

Moorings

Moorings

Fl(3)G.10s

2_5

Portugalete breakwater

6_3

2

2_5

Fl(2)R.6s

Churruca breakwater

Rio Nervion

0_8

Real Club Maritimo del Abra

Portugalete

6_3

Las Arenas

0   500

Metres

Las Arenas

Entrance

By day or night

Leave the W end of the long Contradique running out from Getxo close to port (Fl.R.5s) and make good a track of about 140° for the La Arenas marina breakwater entrance (Oc.G and Oc.R.4s). At night keep a look out for unlit mooring buoys.

Berthing

A member of staff usually meets arrivals and allocates a berth but if not, take one and ask one of the berthing staff or at the Real Club del Abras. They will nearly always find a berth somewhere. There is 2–3m in the marina, shallowing in the S corner. The smaller enclosure to the NE is for local boats.

Moorings

There are a number off the marina and it may be possible to obtain one temporarily.

Up river

Las Arenas looking WSW

Anchoring

There is a good anchorage in sand and mud as indicated on the plan in 2–3m. This area is however subject to more wash from traffic than over at Getxo.

Facilities

Full facilities of a first-class marina are available; fuel 24hrs a day; water and electricity on pontoons; 35-tonne travel-lift and cranes; repair and maintenance in marina. Both yacht clubs make members of recognised YCs welcome; a reasonable standard of dress is expected in the clubhouses; Real Club Sporting is just to the S of Real Club del Abra. Both run a taxi service to the anchorage. Shops are nearby in Las Arenas and Algorta plus a good selection of restaurants. The modern and efficient metro to the City has a station 5 minutes' walk from the marina.

Getxo

Approach

By day or night

From the end of the Getxo contradique (Fl.R.5s) make good a track of about 125° to skirt the long, curving breakwater of the marina.

Entrance

Turn into the entrance between the breakwater end (Q.R) and a SHB (Q.G) and head for the E pontoon where directions to a berth will be given.

Berthing

On pontoons with fingers. There are over 800 berths and visitors are usually accommodated on the outer pontoon. Max. 18m, depths vary from 2.5–3.5m.

Moorings

There are a number off the entrance and one may be made available by the harbour office.

Anchoring

There is plenty of space to anchor in 2–3m clear of the moorings to the S of the entrance, sand and mud.

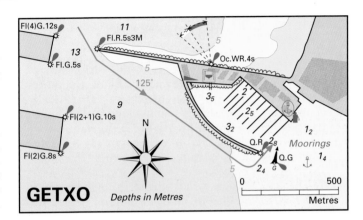

GETXO · Depths in Metres

Facilities

As a much newer marina than at Las Arenas, Getxo has rather more in the way of facilities. There is a 50 tonne travel-lift and craneage plus a good range of repair capabilities and there is no need to go outside the marina's environs to find good restaurants. The adjacent suburb of Neguri has shops of all kinds and the metro station is only ten minutes' walk. The penalty of being in a newer marina is that the charges are higher but the security is good and it would be a safe place to leave the boat.

Getxo marina looking W

The arrivals pontoon at Getxo looking S

II. PASAJES TO SANTANDER

Ashore in Bilbao

History

Bilbao was granted city rights in the 14th century and has since been the provincial capital, the most prosperous city in the province, a thriving commercial centre and a major seaport. The huge bay has been sheltered by massive breakwaters and extensions to the quays and wharves on the SW side where the work continues to expand the port facilities.

The Río Nervion winds inland through the city which is surrounded by wooded hills. This used to be the industrial centre of the city, where huge steel and iron works dealt with the ore mined in the surrounding countryside for export from the adjacent docks. This heavy industry has declined, the maritime activity moved out to Santurce and beyond and the city has become much more of a banking and financial centre with a good ration of culture thrown in.

It has a close commercial association with the UK and the assistance given to the starving city during the Spanish civil war is still remembered.

Today

A trip up the river by boat is hardly appealing. The transporter bridge at Portugalete has 45m clearance but beyond this are 5 miles of dirtily commercial docks and declining industry. There is nowhere for a yacht to secure up the river and most would prefer to make the journey by the fast and efficient new metro with stations close to Getxo and Las Arenas marinas.

For those not wanting to go as far as the city centre, the transporter bridge is within walking distance and worth a visit. The oldest (1893) of 12 left in the world, it escaped complete destruction in the civil war, was restored in 1941 and continues as a vital 24-hour car and passenger link across the river. There are lifts up the pylons and a walkway along the upper deck; a descent on the other side and a return trip on the bridge completes the circuit with some interesting views en route.

The city's main attractions are the Guggenheim Museum and the Museo de Bellas Artes, both in the same area in the NW part of the city centre and not too far from Moyua station on the metro. A combined ticket for the two places can be bought and they are a must for the culture vulture.

Other places of architectural interest and beauty are the Catedral de Santiago in the old town (Casco Viejo), Basilica de Begoña on a hill to the E of the centre but reached by a lift running from San Nicolas church near the Plaza Nueva (there is a long flight of steps), and the Museo Arqueologico, Ethnografico e Historico Vasco (the Basque Museum) near the Cathedral.

There are many other places of merit and interest but they are scattered about the city.

Restaurants, eating places, tapas bars and cafés are legion but probably the most entertaining area to seek them is in the old city (Casco Vieja).

Travel

Rail travel is not easy from Bilbao; there are four stations and three railway companies. Enquiries at a *turismo* or travel agent (see below) will probably simplify the quest.

Finding the bus stations is not much easier but there are services in both directions to San Sebastián and Santander as well as southwards.

Good motorways circle the city and go in all directions.

P&O European ferries depart for Portsmouth on Tuesdays and Saturdays at 2000.

International airport is just to the N of the city.

Useful information

Turismo Bilbao ☎ 944 16 81 68
Turismo Getxo (near marina) ☎ 944 69 38 00
Travel agents TIVE ☎ 944 23 18 62
P&O European ferry ☎ 902 02 04 61
   Fax 944 23 54 96
Car rental Avis ☎ 944 27 57 60
Europcar ☎ 944 42 49
Airport information ☎ 944 53 06 40
British Consul ☎ 944 15 76 00
Ambulance ☎ 944 41 00 81
Getxo marina ☎ 944 91 23 67
   Fax 944 91 18 18
Las Arenas marina ☎ 944 63 76 00

Portugalete transporter bridge looking seaward

62 Castro Urdiales

Cat A*
Delightful town with large but crowded harbour

Location
43°23'.00N 03°12'.00W

Shelter
Good but poor in easterlies

Warning
Indifferent holding; sand over rock

Depth restrictions
2–11m in main harbour; inner harbour dries.

Night entry
Lit but no leading lights

Tidal information
HW PdG –0100
LW PdG –0045

Mean height of tide (m)

MHWS	MHWN	MLWN	MLWS
4.0	2.9	1.5	0.4

Tidal stream
Negligible

Berthing
At anchor; alongside berth in good weather

Facilities
Those of a small town

⊕ **549** C. Urdiales 43°22'·70N 03°12'·00W

73 Suances
C. Mayor
70 Santander
65 Santoña
64 Laredo
549
62 Castro Urdiales
61 Bilbao
57 Bermeo
60 Plencia
58 Bakio
C. Machicaco
55 Elanchove
53 Lequeitio

Charts
BA 1171 (10)
Spanish 394A (10)

Weather
Bilbao Ch 26 0840, 1240 and 2010
Navtex A or D

Radio
YC and launch Ch 09

Castro Urdiales looking WNW

Yacht Club   Inner harbour   Church and castle

PILOTAGE

Approaches

By day or night

From the W, Punta Rabanal 1M to the NW with its conspicuous cemetery must be rounded before the town and harbour become visible. Castillo de Santa Ana (Fl(4)24s) and the long Rompeolas Norte (Fl.G.3s) indicate the entrance. From the E make a track of about 295° from ⊕549 to the entrance leaving Rompeolas Norte to starboard and the end of Muelle Commerciale (Q(2)R.6s) to port.

Entrance

Give the breakwater ends at least 20m clearance as there are underwater rocks.

Berthing

Alongside berths can be found along Rompeolas Norte in about 5m where there are three sets of steps but the wall is a bit rough. Only the occasional coaster uses Muelle Commerciale and a berth toward the end of this in 7m is a possibility. Both these berths are uncomfortable in any swell and a haul-off to an anchor would be needed. No room for yachts in the inner harbour.

Moorings

There are many on both sides of the harbour but none for visitors. Doubling up is not approved of but an enquiry at the YC might produce a free mooring.

Anchoring

As indicated on the plan. The bottom is sand on rock and holding should not be relied on in a blow. Anchoring in the fairway between the moorings is not allowed.

Ashore in Castro Urdiales

A pleasing and picturesque old town with a Knights Templar castle and a 14th-century church. It has an abundance of shops and restaurants, the yacht club is friendly and welcoming and there are good beaches even if crowded. A feature of the harbour is that the water is clean and clear.

Facilities

Water from the YC in cans or from a tap on Muelle Commerciale; diesel as indicated on the plan on Monday, Wednesday and Thursday in working hours but note there is 1.8m alongside by the pump; petrol from garage behind market; excellent shops nearby and a good market; boatyard in N corner of harbour, a slip and cranes; showers in the Club Náutico de Castro Urdiales who run a launch service – call them or launch *Blancona* on Ch 09.

Travel

On the main rail and bus coastal routes; nearest airports Bilbao (30km) and Santander (50km); see Bilbao above for ferry details to UK.

Fiestas

26 June, 3 August and 15 August.

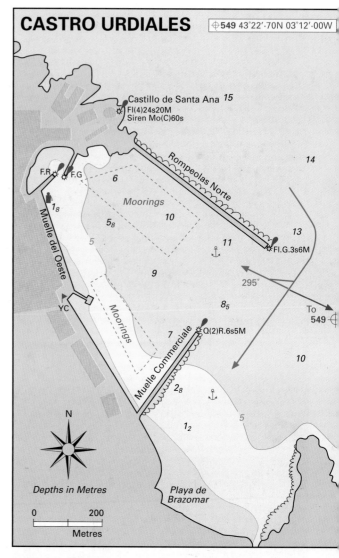

CASTRO URDIALES ⊕549 43°22'·70N 03°12'·00W

Looking NE over inner harbour towards church and castle

Leisure

One of the better eating stops along the coast – but a lot of Spaniards know this and the restaurants and the beaches, especially Playa de Brazomar, get crowded. A visit to the fine Gothic 14th-century church and Castillo de Santa Ana, and the small old quarter of the town, can be done on foot and is a pleasant way to pass the best part of a day.

63 Río de Oriñon

Cat D

Large bay sheltered from the W and a río only for shallow draught yachts and multihulls

⊕**551** 43°25´.27N 03°19´.88W

Boat harbour   Main channel hugs E shore   Oriñon village

Río de Oriñon looking SSW at LW

Anchoring

This bay gives good shelter from winds between S and W to WNW. BA chart 1102 is just about large enough scale to creep in on. The bar dries right across and the surf line is well out and it shoals gradually. Tuck close in under Cabo Cebollero as far S as depth allows.

The course of the río in the outer sands changes constantly but eventually deepens by the point on the E side where there is a 30m wide channel at half tide; this swings to the W round a sand spit marked by a low green beacon which almost covers at HW. The entrance to a wider lagoon is 100m on and there is a pool just inside with barely 1m in it but all the rest dries. Only to be attempted by shoal draughts after a recce and no swell.

On the E side of the ria, outside the bar and drying line and enclosed by rocks, is the tiny boat harbour of Islares. There are two entrances on the N and SW sides, both only 2m wide and the latter with a bridge over it. It dries approximately 1.5m inside but provides a dinghy landing on this side of the bay. There are two restaurants and a large campsite close by. Islares village is 1–2km to the E.

On the W side of the ria there are a few shops but no other facilities in a rather run down holiday village. The motorway is close and its noise obtrusive.

Channel to inner lagoon   Green beacon

Río de Oriñon. Inner entrance looking W at HW+0130

64 Laredo

Cat C

Very crowded holiday resort with a fishing harbour which largely dries. Punta del Pasaje 3M to N is better for deep-keeled yachts

Location
43°26′.00N 03°25′.00W

Shelter
Little unless dried out

Warning
Training wall to S of entrance covers at half tide

Depth restrictions
1.4m in entrance; dries over much of inner harbour

Night entry
Lit but not recommended

Tidal information
HW PdG –0025
LW PdG –0015

Mean height of tide (m)

MHWS	MHWN	MLWN	MLWS
4.7	3.2	1.8	0.3

Tidal stream
Negligible

Berthing
One possible drying berth, otherwise anchor outside

Facilities
None for yachts except shops and restaurants

Charts
BA 1102 (200),1171 (20)
Spanish 3942 (12.5)
SHOM 3542 (25)

Weather
Santander Ch 24 0840, 1240, 2010

Radio and telephone
None

Laredo looking ENE 1 hour after HW. Note most of the training wall is still covered and the fishing fleet is at sea

PILOTAGE

Approach

By day
From ⊕552 make good a track of 160° until off the breakwater ends. If approaching from the E or N, identify the N breakwater end and approach it on 170° or less to avoid El Rastrilla and its off-lyers.

By night
Not recommended as the breakwater lights will be lost in the town's lights until close to.

Entrance
Turn in to the entrance when it is open and do not overshoot as the rubble training wall will be waiting. There are rocks along the wall to seaward of the ferry berth on the N breakwater.

Berthing
The only possible alongside berth for a visitor is at the seaward end of the S quay before the crane is reached where there is 0.3 to 0.2m. The N quay is arched for part of it, and is occupied by fishing boats and the ferry.

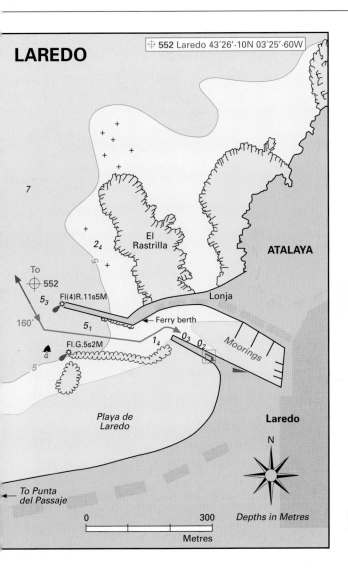

LAREDO

⊕ 552 Laredo 43°26'·10N 03°25'·60W

El Rastrilla

ATALAYA

Lonja

To ⊕ 552

5₃ Fl(4)R.11s5M

160°

5₁ Ferry berth

Fl.G.5s2M 1₄ 0₃ 0₂

G

Moorings

5

Playa de Laredo

Laredo

N

To Punta del Passaje

0   300

Metres

Depths in Metres

2₄

7

Moorings

These and pontoon berths in the harbour all dry and will be occupied by small local boats.

Anchoring

Anywhere outside clear of the entrance to the W, all sand.

Ashore in Laredo

The town's population quadruples in the summer which is some indication of its popularity as a resort. The old town by the harbour still retains its charm in spite of the rash of high-rise new buildings that has grown along the peninsula to the W. For yachtsmen it is a pleasant enough anchorage in fine weather but few concessions are made for them in the harbour where the fishing fleet has grown in size and activity.

Facilities

Water from taps on the quay; fuel from a garage in town 4 blocks SE of the end of the harbour; there is a powered slip capable of taking large fishing boats, and a 5-tonne crane; shops are concentrated in the second road back from the harbour and there is a market; there are several hotels and many restaurants.

Travel

The town is on the major E/W rail and bus routes; nearest airports Bilbao and Santander (35km). There is a scheduled bus service between Punta des Pasajes at the W end of the peninsula and Laredo.

Fiestas

26 June, 3 August, 15 August.

Leisure

The 13th-century church of La Asunción can be found at the back of the old town and a walk through the tunnel under La Atalaya to the remains of the old harbour on the other side is an experience.

Inner harbour looking E. Berth in foreground before yellow crane

65 Santoña

Cat A*

Old garrison town that has seen better days but the fishing is very active; yacht berths in the south harbour

Location
43°26'.00N 03°25'.00W

Shelter
Good

Warning
A bar lies SE of Punta de San Carlos with less than 2.3m on it; treat with caution in easterlies

Depth restrictions
As above but deep inside. Least depth 3.4m in harbour

Night entry
Adequately lit

Tidal information
HW PdG –0025
LW PdG –0015

Mean height of tide (m)

MHWS	MHWN	MLWN	MLWS
4.7	3.2	1.8	0.3

Tidal stream
Up to 3 knots on ebb in main channel at springs

Berthing
Alongside in S harbour

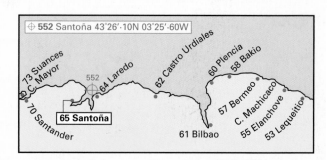

552 Santoña 43°26'·10N 03°25'·60W

Facilities
Those of a small fishing port

Charts
BA 1171 (20)
Spanish 3942 (12.5)
SHOM 3542 (25)

Weather
Santander Ch 24 0840, 1240, 2010
Navtex A or D

Radio and telephone
None

Santoña looking SE. Note sculpture between the harbours

Fishing harbour (all at sea)

Yacht harbour *Bull ring*

Moorings off Punta del Pasaje

283°

PILOTAGE

Approaches

By day or night

See *Warning* above.

The best time to enter, especially in easterlies, is the last half of the flood. From ⊕552 pick up the leading line of 283° (front Fl.2s, rear Oc(2)5s) which is not conspicuous by day and it may be easier to align the end of the second pier with the corner of the harbour (see photo). At all events keep about 300m from the N shore to avoid the shallows to the N of Punta del Pasaje.

Entrance

Come to port once past the first pier to round the shallows between the second pier and the bull ring. Round the harbour corner (F.G) and turn in to the first entrance to starboard (F.R and F.G).

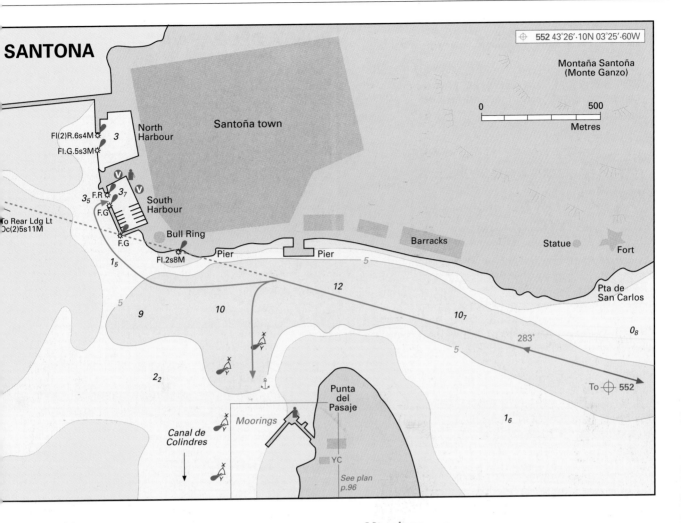

SANTONA

Fl(2)R.6s4M
Fl.G.5s3M
North Harbour
3
Santoña town

552 43°26'·10N 03°25'·60W

Montaña Santoña
(Monte Ganzo)

0   500
Metres

3_5 F.R
F.G
3_7
South Harbour

To Rear Ldg Lt
Oc(2)5s11M

F.G
Bull Ring
Fl.2s8M

1_5

Pier   Pier   5

Barracks   Statue   Fort

12

Pta de
San Carlos

5   9   10

10_7

0_8

283°

5

2_2

Canal de
Colindres

Moorings

Punta
del
Pasaje

To ⊕ 552

1_6

YC

See plan
p.96

Berthing

Berth either alongside the N wall or at the N end of the W wall between the fuel pontoon and the pontoon berths. Least depth 3.4m. The pontoons are private and should not be taken before speaking to the harbourmaster whose office is to the SE of the bull ring. The North Harbour is for fishing boats only.

Moorings

None except off Punta del Pasaje.

Anchoring

To the N or S of the moorings off Punta del Pasaje and clear of the Colindres channel. There are many anchorages in the channels of the extensive ria, sand and mud.

Ashore in Santoña

The busy fishing fleet livens up this rather faded town and there are a good selection of restaurants and shops. The area is dominated by the massive Montaña Santoña, also known as Monte Ganzo, which is worth a climb for the energetic.

Facilities

Fuel as on the plan; water taps on quay; ice factory between the harbours; adequate shops, and market 3 streets up from harbour; engineers and fisherman's chandlery.

Travel

Buses to Santander or railway 5M away; nearest air and ferry port Santander (35km).

Fiesta

Major Festival of the Sea 7 September, when it is unlikely there will be a spare berth in the harbours.

South harbour looking SSE. Yachts berth on wall by fishing boat or on E wall to the left. The entrance is off picture right

66 Punta del Pasaje

Cat A*

Welcoming and active yacht club at end of Laredo peninsula; moorings and facilities

⊕552 43°26´.10N 03°25´.60W

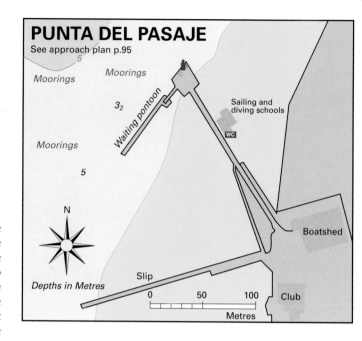

PUNTA DEL PASAJE
See approach plan p.95

PILOTAGE

Approaches

By day

From ⊕552 (see plan page 95) pick up the inconspicuous leading line 283°; if this cannot be identified align the end of the second pier with the corner of the harbour breakwater. In any event keep 300m off the N shore past the old fort on Punta de San Carlos and the barracks; turn to port when the first pier is abeam on to about 190° towards the first lit yellow buoy to the W of the moorings off the conspicuous square club building on Punta del Pasaje (see plan).

Moorings

The visitors' moorings are yellow and are in 3–6m for up to 18m long. Go alongside the fuelling berth to enquire or ask at the club after picking one up.

Anchoring

Clear of the club moorings to the N or S but do not obstruct the Colindres channel to the W of the lit yellow buoys, most of which have an X topmark.

Berthing

The pontoon running SSW from the end of the YC pier is only for temporary berthing. The fuel berth is at the end of the pier (see photograph).

Ashore in Punta del Pasaje

There is little in the immediate vicinity except the yacht club, which has more than enough facilities to satisfy the casual visitor. Payment of mooring fees entitles their use during the stay. There is a large and good restaurant, swimming pool, tennis courts, showers, laundrette and a comfortable clubhouse. There are riding stables along the road to Laredo for

those so inclined. There are repair facilities on site, fuel and water on the pontoon and a crane at the end of the pier. Shops are some distance but there are regular buses and the occasional ferry to Laredo.

It would not be practical to lay up here and unlikely that there will be room to do so.

67 Colindres

Cat A*

Small port at the end of a 3-mile channel in unattractive surroundings entirely given over to fishing; yachts are not welcome

⊕552 43°26´.10N 03° 25´.60W

Approaches

In the unlikely event of a yacht needing to go to Colindres, the Canal de Colindres is entered to the W of Punta del Pasaje. Keep to the W of the moorings marked by yellow buoys off the point. The channel running approximately 180° from there on is now marked by a number of starboard hand buoys and carries 2m; deviation from the channel will find a charted depth of 0m. See BA chart 1171 (20) or Spanish 3942.

Entrance

Turn sharply to port in to the entrance just before the two low bridges. Alternatively anchor opposite on the other side of the channel clear of moorings.

Berthing

There is a least depth of 2m along most of the quays which if not already occupied by large fishing boats may soon be.

Facilities

None for yachts; some small shops in the village.

Looking NNW along Real Club Náutico pier

Ria de Santoña
(includes Santoña, Punta del Pasaje and Colindres)

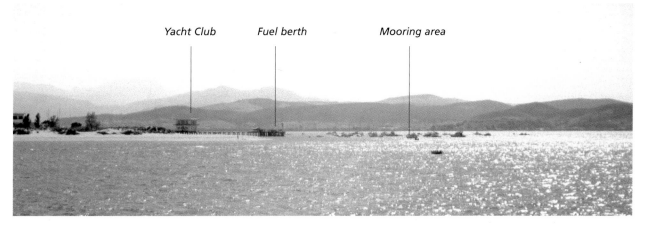

Punta del Pasaje seen across the main channel from Santoña town

Santoña leading line 283°

68 Río Ajo
Cat D

⊕**554** Río Ajo 43°31´.24N 03°34´.28W

Looking N from Colindres harbour entrance towards Montaña Santoña which dominates the area

69 Ensenada de Galizano

⊕**556** Galizano 43°29´.54N 03°41´.37W

The outer bay offers shelter from SE through S to W. Any further entry should only be attempted by shallow draught craft after a recce at LW. The bar, seen in the photo, dries right across but inside the río deepens and hugs the W shore round a steep bluff on which there are a few houses.

A small bay just to the E of Cabo Galizano which provides shelter from the W through S to E on a sandy bottom but open to the swell. Río Galizano at its eastern corner dries at its mouth. Ensenada de Galizano is much frequented at weekends in fine weather by day sailors from Santander.

70 Santander

Cat A

Large industrial, commercial and ferry port with two good marinas and all the facilities of a large city; good travel links

Location

43°29'.00N
03°46'.00W

Shelter

Excellent

Warning

In gale conditions and/or a big swell leave Isla Mouro to the W on entering

Search and rescue

A lifeboat is maintained here

Depth restrictions

0.4m to Pedreña, 9m in length
2.2m in Marina del Cantabrico

Night entry

Excellently lit

Tidal information

HW PdG –0040
LW PdG –0025

Mean height of tide

MHWS	MHWN	MLWN	MLWS
4.7	3.2	1.8	0.3

Tidal stream

Ebb rates are 3–4 knots off Punta Rabiosa, more if River Astillero is in spate

Berthing

On pontoons in either marina, anchored off YC

Facilities

All those of a major city and marinas

Charts

BA 1145 (15), 1102 (200)
Spanish 4011 (15), 401 (50)

Weather

Santander Ch 24 0840, 1240, 2010
Navtex A or D

Radio

Marina Ch 09
Santander port Ch 08, 16
Santander MRSC Ch 16, 74

Air radio beacon

Cabo Mayor MY 289.5

Telephone

Marina ☎ 942 36 92 98
Taxi ☎ 942 36 91 91
Airport ☎ 942 20 21 20
Brittany Ferries ☎ 942 36 06 11
British Consul ☎ 942 22 00 00
Yacht Club ☎ 942 27 30 13

⊕ **557** Santander 43°28'·50N 03°44'·48W

73 Suances
C. Mayor
557
70 Santander
65 Santoña
64 Laredo
62 Castro Urdiales
60 Plencia
58 Bakio
57 Bermeo
C. Machicaco
55 Elanchove
53 Lequeitio
61 Bilbao

Santander entrance looking ENE

Isla Mouro Palace La Cerda Punta Rabosa

236°

260°

YC and Darsena de Molnedo

Brittany Ferry

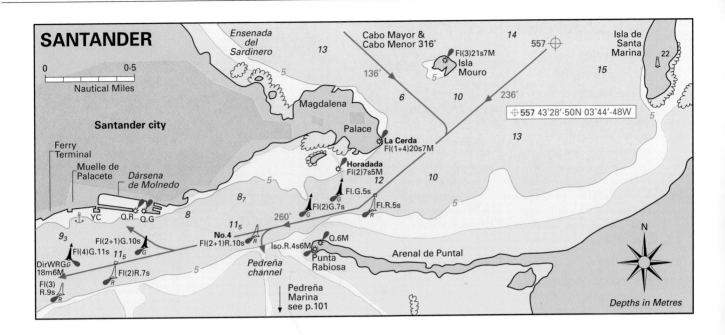

PILOTAGE

Approaches

From NE

By day or night

From ⊕557 to the W of Isla de Santa Marina identify the leading marks bearing 236° on the end of the low-lying Punta Rabiosa (front Q, rear Iso.R.4s). The marks are spindly metal tripods but Arenal de Puntal's white beach leading to Punta Rabiosa makes identification easy by day.

On this line Isla Mouro (Fl(3)21s7M) with a conspicuous white lighthouse will be passed ¼M to starboard with the Magdalena peninsula with its massive palace on the top ahead fine on the starboard bow. Leave La Cerda (Fl(1+4)20s) which looks like a red-roofed chapel well to starboard and identify the first port hand buoy (Fl.R.5s). Turn short of this to 260° onto the next leading line (front Iso.3s, rear Oc.R.4s). The marks are very difficult to see by day but the line of port and starboard buoys on either side of the line lead up harbour.

For Pedreña Marina turn to port short of the next (No.4) port hand buoy(Fl(2+1)R.10s) down the buoyed and lit channel (see plan).

From the W

By day or night

This passage past Cabos Mayor and Menor and to the W of Isla Mouro is clear and free from dangers but has a least depth of 6m. It should not be attempted in gale conditions and/or a heavy swell; the bottom rises quickly from 14m to 7m to a ridge between the island and the Magdalena peninsula and the swell soon builds up and breaks between the two.

In fine weather, align Cabo Mayor and Cabo Menor to pass through and avoid the shallowest 6m area. At night the lights on Isla Mouro (Fl(3)21s) and La Cerda (Fl(1+4)20s) will help and although the latter is obscured when bearing less than 160°, the house lights on the Magdalena peninsula will indicate the S shore.

Passage inside Isla de Santa Marina

In fine weather, with no swell and a rising tide a passage may be possible through the narrow channel to the E of Isla de Santa Marina where BA chart 1145 shows a least depth of 1.1m but with rocks close on either side.

Entrance to Darsena de Molnedo and to Yacht Club anchorage

The entrance to Darsena de Molnedo (least depth 2m) is opposite No.5 starboard hand buoy (Fl(2+1)G.10s) and the entrance is lit by a Q.R and Q.G. This basin provides the only alongside berths in the city centre and is always packed. It will be fruitless to charge in hoping for the best but a temporary berth may be solicited if available either from the yacht club or the fuel berth attendant at the basin's head (12m max).

There are moorings off the yacht club (Real Club Maritimo de Santander) but most are private. Do not anchor to seaward of them or near the club's starting line, but upstream between the club and Muelle de Palacete whence all the cross-harbour ferries run (from 0700 to 2000). This is not peaceful but it is near the shops, yacht club, ferry terminal, train and bus stations.

See below for Ashore in Santander City, Travel, Leisure and Fiestas

Marina del Cantabrico, Parayas

Approaches

By day or night

The main channel up-harbour is wide and deep and there is no need to follow the second leading line of 260° (front Iso.3s, rear Oc.R.4s) but follow the buoys round the curve of the Río Astillero, past the long and prominent oil pier (2 x Q.R) to port until No.15 buoy (Fl(2)G.7s) is reached when the entrance to the marina will be open to starboard. Identification is aided by a conspicuous glass pyramidal building just to the W of the entrance. If you reach No.17 buoy (Fl(2+1)G.10s) you have overshot.

Entrance

The entrance transit of 236° is difficult to see by day and consists of two tall spindly posts just to the left of the Jet pontoon (see photo on page 102). By night the leading line of front Iso.5s and rear Oc.5s should be between a Q.R and a Q.G at the outer entrance. When past the conspicuous octagonal marina building, turn to port into the marina and pick up the first available berth.

Berthing

At pontoons with fingers in perfect shelter, least depth 2.2m. Berths are kept free near the entrance for arrivals and someone will come from the office to allocate a more permanent one depending on the stay. If not, walk up to the office or call on Ch 09.

Ashore at Parayas

The trouble with this marina is that it is miles away from anywhere civilised. It is in the middle of an industrial estate and the wrong side of the airport and motorway. However it is pretty well self-contained, has a selection of eating places and a social club, good repair and haul-out facilities and would be an excellent place to leave a boat, to change crews or even overwinter.

The nearest *supermercado* is Eroski across the airport; it can be reached by bicycle via a cycle track round the airport and over the motorway, by a scheduled bus service from the marina (0720–2230) or by taxi or hire car; the bus also runs to El Corte Inglés.

Facilities

There are all the expected facilities of a first-class marina; a deposit has to be paid for the electric plug to fit the marina terminals; two travel-lifts of 30 tonnes and craneage; repair facilities, mechanical and electric maintenance on site. The fuel berth has both diesel and petrol (it is also a car filling station) and there is water on all the pontoons.

See below for Ashore in Santander City, Travel, Leisure and Fiestas.

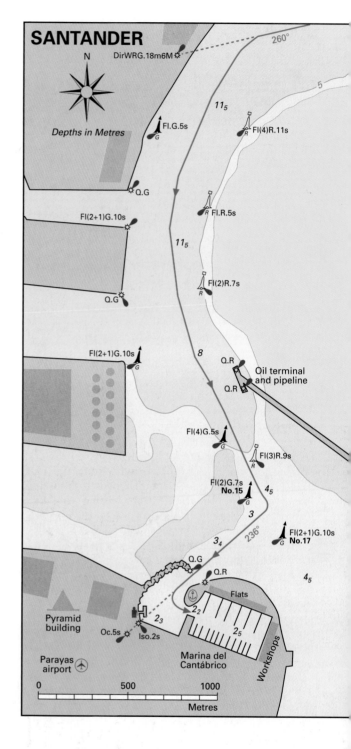

Pedreña Marina

Approach

See above for outer approach to No.4 buoy.

By day or night

A night entry is not recommended unless it has been done by day and there is enough light to see all the unlit starboard hand buoys.

Turn to a track of 163° just to the E of No.4 buoy and identify the first two lateral buoys (Fl.G and Fl.R.5s) at the N end of the channel; on the same bearing sight Punta del Rostro (Fl(2)G.7s) and keep

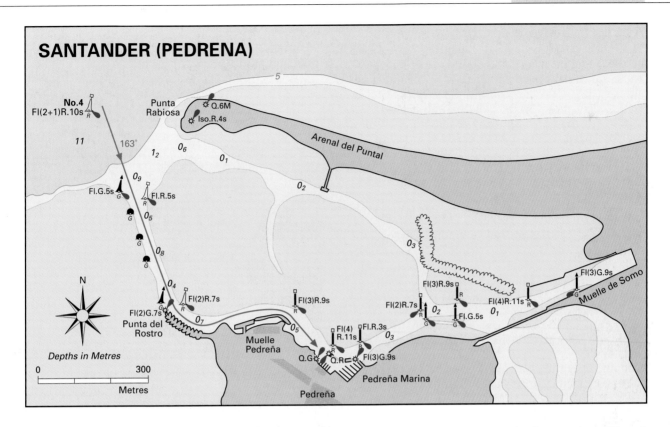

SANTANDER (PEDRENA)

No.4
Fl(2+1)R.10s

Punta
Rabiosa

Q.6M

Iso.R.4s

Arenal del Puntal

11

163°

1₂

0₆

0₁

0₂

5

Fl.G.5s G

Fl.R.5s R

0₉

0₅

0₈

0₃

Fl(3)G.9s

Muelle de Somo

N

0₄

Fl(2)R.7s R

Fl(3)R.9s R

Fl(2)R.7s R

Fl.G.5s G

0₂

0₁

Fl(4)R.11s R

Fl(2)G.7s G

Punta del
Rostro

0₇

Muelle
Pedreña

0₅

Fl(4)
R.11s R

Fl.R.3s R

0₃

Depths in Metres

0   300

Metres

Q.G

Q.R

Fl(3)G.9s

Pedreña Marina

Pedreña

The marina entrance looking SE

Marina looking E. Office and restaurant on right

it on this bearing, leaving the five starboard hand buoys on their right side. The least depth in this channel is 0.4m although claimed to be dredged to 2m. Leave the training wall at Punta del Rostro about 20m to starboard and continue round past the Pedreña wharves until the marina entrance opens up.

Entrance and berthing

Enter slowly and with care as there is not much room inside. The entrance is marked by a Q.R and Q.G. Call before arrival if near or over the limit of 9m on Ch 09 or ☎ 942 50 02 25, English spoken. There is reputedly 2m inside.

Anchoring

Prohibited in the channels.

Ashore in Pedreña

The marina is new and in attractive and peaceful surroundings with a golf course nearby and an up-market village 10 minutes' walk away. There is a café/restaurant in the small marina building if you don't want to walk that far. There are regular ferries between 0700 and 2030 to Santander city and to the beach at Arenal de Puntal.

See below for Ashore in Santander, Travel and Fiestas

Facilities

Water and fuel on the pontoons; no lifting facilities apart from small crane; chandlery and the usual WCs and showers; a good variety of better class shops in the village and the golf course is on the doorstep.

Ashore in Santander City

Santander is the provincial capital of Cantabria, besides being the principal port and major industrial and commercial centre with a thriving shipbuilding industry. It is near the centre of the province and is an excellent place to hire a car and explore the further reaches of Cantabria. For those limited to a shorter stay there are many sights and amusements in this large, modern city.

Communications are excellent and it is one of the best places to change crews, leave the boat or overwinter.

Leisure

The nearest Tourist Office is in the Jardinés de Pereda across the road from Muelle de Palacete and well worth a visit to find out what is on offer.

There are several excellent sandy beaches; Playa de Sardinero is rather like an English resort and across the ria Arenal de Puntal is a vast area of sand with some cafés which can be reached by ferry. There are several churches of note and museums, and further afield are the prehistoric caves of Santián, Altamira and El Pendo; also the well preserved medieval town of Santillana del Mar which has a zoo nearby.

Facilities

Fuel from the pontoon at the head of Darsena de Molnedo; water from a hose at the front of the yacht club but best to ferry by cans and dinghy from there; WCs and showers in the yacht club who welcome reasonably dressed visitors; there is a restaurant in the club and many more in the surrounding streets; shops of all sizes and qualities including some mini *supermercados* within easy walking distance.

Travel

Both railway stations and the bus station are in the square up one block from the ferry terminal; the airport is a 15-minute taxi ride with flights to Madrid and some European destinations; there are twice weekly ferries to Plymouth.

Fiestas

27 July to 4 August for St James the Elder; 21–22 September for La Virgen de la Bien-Aparecida is the major festival for the city, when everything closes.

RCMS clubhouse in centre. The yacht is in the visitors' anchorage

Front leading mark

Rear leading mark

Leading line into Marina del Cantabrico

Octagonal marina building *Flats*

Entrance to Marina del Cantabrico looking E from fuel berth

III. San Pedro del Mar to Avilés
Cabo Mayor to Cabo Peñas

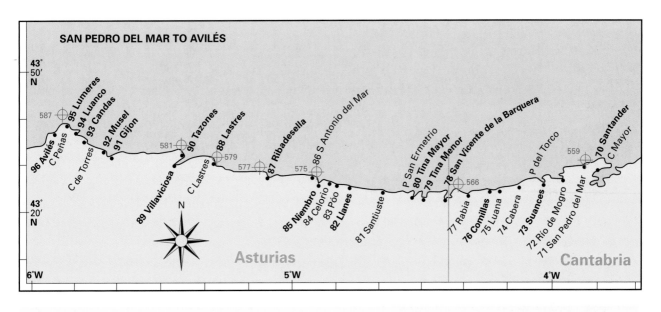

WAYPOINTS

⊕559	S. Pedro del Mar	43°30′.00N	03°50′.40W	⊕579 Cabo Lastres	43°33′.00N	05°17′.70W
⊕566	C. Oriambre	43°25′.20N	04°20′.09W	⊕581 P. Olivo	43°33′.90N	05°24′.70W
⊕575	S. Antonio del Mar	43°28′.40N	04°55′.30W	⊕587 Cabo Peñas	43°41′.07N	05°51′.25W
⊕577	P. de la Sierra	43°29′.50N	05°07′.09W			

Typical coastline looking E over Ribadesella with the lower outliers of the Picos de Europa on the right

Planning Guide
Distances between ports in nautical miles
Ports with marinas in **bold** type

	Port	Santander	S Pedro del Mar	R de Mogro	Suances	E de Cabrera	E de Luaña	Comillas	R de Rabia	S V de la Barquera	R Tina Menor	R Tina Mayor	R de Santiuste	Llanes	E de Póo	E de Celorio	R de Niembro	P de S Antonio	Ribadesella	Lastres	R de Villaviciosa	Tazones	Gijón (ML)	Gijón (Musel)	Candas	Luanco	E de Lumeres	Avilés
A	**Santander**		4	11	13	18	22	24	26	29	32	34	37	45	47	48	49	50	59	69	74	75	86	88	92	94	97	104
D	R de S Pedro del Mar	4		7	9	14	18	20	22	25	28	30	33	41	43	44	45	46	55	65	70	71	82	84	88	90	93	100
D	R de Mogro	11	7		2	7	11	13	15	18	21	23	26	34	36	37	38	39	48	58	63	64	75	77	81	83	86	93
C	**Suances**	13	9	2		5	9	11	13	16	18	21	24	32	34	35	36	37	46	56	61	62	73	75	79	81	84	91
D	E de Cabera	18	14	7	5		4	6	8	11	14	16	19	27	29	30	31	32	41	51	56	57	68	70	74	76	79	86
D	E de Luaña	22	18	11	9	4		2	4	7	10	12	15	23	25	26	27	28	37	47	52	53	64	66	70	72	75	82
C	**Comillas**	24	20	13	11	6	2		2	5	8	10	13	21	23	24	25	26	35	45	50	51	62	64	68	70	73	80
D	R de Rabia	26	22	15	13	8	4	2		3	6	8	11	19	21	22	23	24	33	43	48	49	60	62	66	68	71	78
B*	S V de la Barquera	29	25	18	16	11	7	5	3		3	5	8	16	18	19	20	21	30	40	45	46	57	59	63	65	68	75
C	R Tina Menor	32	28	21	19	14	10	8	6	3		2	5	13	15	16	17	18	27	37	42	43	54	56	60	62	65	72
C	R Tina Mayor	34	30	23	21	16	12	10	8	5	2		3	11	13	14	15	16	25	35	40	41	52	54	58	60	63	70
D	R de Santiuste	37	33	26	24	19	15	13	11	8	5	3		8	10	11	12	13	22	32	37	38	50	52	56	58	61	68
C	Llanes	45	41	34	32	27	23	21	19	16	13	11	8		2	3	4	5	14	24	29	30	42	44	48	50	53	60
D	E de Póo	47	43	36	34	29	25	23	21	18	15	13	10	2		1	3	4	13	23	28	29	41	43	47	49	52	59
D	E de Celorio	48	44	37	35	30	26	24	22	19	16	14	11	3	1		1	3	12	22	27	28	40	42	46	48	51	58
C	R de Niembro	49	45	38	36	31	27	25	23	20	17	15	12	4	3	1		1	11	21	26	27	39	41	45	47	50	57
D	P de S Antonio	50	46	39	37	32	28	26	24	21	18	16	13	5	4	3	1		9	19	24	25	37	39	43	45	48	55
C	**Ribadesella**	59	55	48	46	41	37	35	33	30	27	25	22	14	13	12	11	9		10	15	16	28	31	34	36	39	46
C	**Lastres**	69	65	58	56	51	47	45	43	40	37	35	32	24	23	22	21	19	10		5	6	18	21	24	26	29	36
C	R de Villaviciosa	74	70	63	61	56	52	50	48	45	42	40	37	29	28	27	26	24	15	5		1	13	16	19	21	24	31
B*	**Tazones**	75	71	64	62	57	53	51	49	46	43	41	38	30	29	28	27	26	16	6	1		11	14	17	19	22	29
B*	**Gijón (ML)**	86	82	75	73	68	64	62	60	57	54	52	50	42	41	40	39	37	28	18	13	11		2	5	7	10	17
A	**Gijón (Musel)**	88	84	77	75	70	66	64	62	59	56	54	52	44	43	42	41	39	31	21	16	14	2		4	6	9	16
C	**Candas**	92	88	81	79	74	70	68	66	63	60	58	56	48	47	46	45	43	34	24	19	17	5	4		2	5	12
C	**Luanco**	94	90	83	81	76	72	70	68	65	62	60	58	50	49	48	47	45	36	26	21	19	7	6	2		3	10
D	E de Lumeres	97	93	86	84	79	75	73	71	68	65	63	61	53	52	51	50	48	34	29	24	22	10	9	5	3		7
A	**Avilés**	104	100	93	91	86	82	80	78	75	72	70	68	60	59	58	57	55	41	36	31	29	17	16	12	10	7	

WAYPOINTS

⊕559	S. Pedro del Mar	43°30'.00N	03°50'.40W
⊕560	Río Mogro	43°27'.70N	03°58'.60W
⊕561	Suances	43°27'.10N	04°02'.75W
⊕562	Cabera	43°26'.40N	04°04'.65W
⊕563	Luaña	43°24'.60N	04°13'.20W
⊕564	Comillas	43°23'.80N	04°16'.98W
⊕565	Rabia	43°24'.40N	04°19'.16W
⊕566	C. Oriambre	43°25'.20N	04°20'.09W
⊕567	S. V. de la Barquera	43°23'.80N	04°22'.92W
⊕568	Tina Menor	43°24'.30N	04°28'.20W
⊕569	Tina Mayor	43°24'.50N	04°30'.70W
⊕570	Santiuste	43°24'.70N	04°34'.17W
⊕571	Llanes	43°25'.30N	04°44'.00W
⊕572	Póo	43°26'.55N	04°46'.81W
⊕573	Celorio	43°26'.75N	04°48'.55W
⊕574	Niembro	43°27'.10N	04°49'.50W
⊕575	S. Antonio del Mar	43°28'.40N	04°55'.30W
⊕576	Ribadesella	43°28'.51N	05°04'.00W
⊕577	P. de la Sierra	43°29'.50N	05°07'.09W
⊕578	Lastres	43°30'.85N	05°15'.20W
⊕579	Cabo Lastres	43°33'.00N	05°17'.70W
⊕580	VillaviciosaTazones	43°33'.04N	05°23'.00W
⊕581	P. Olivo	43°33'.90N	05°24'.70W
⊕582	Gijón	43°33'.70N	05°40'.18W
⊕583	Musel	43°34'.00N	05°40'.00W
⊕584	Candas	43°36'.43N	05°44'.60W
⊕585	Luanco	43°37'.35N	05°45'.12W
⊕586	Lumeres	43°39'.43N	05°48'.50W
⊕587	Cabo Peñas	43°41'.07N	05°51'.25W
⊕588	Avilés	43°35'.83N	05°57'.30W

This section of the coast is distinguished by the spectacular range of mountains, the Picos de Europa, some 30km inland between San Vicente de la Barquera and Ribadesella. They are snow-covered for much of the year and visible in clear weather far out to sea (see photograph page 52). They are fronted by a low and parallel coastal range of hills having near vertical cliffs interspersed with many small gaps with sandy beaches. The coast to the E and W of this area consists of low hills intersected by a few river estuaries with points and capes that are relatively inconspicuous. There are no outlying dangers and almost all the coast is steep-to.

Warning
Winds from the S quarter can sweep down from the hills in ferocious gusts much stronger than the mean wind speed.

71 Ria de San Pedro del Mar

Cat D

⊕**559** S Pedro del Mar 43°30´.00N 03°50´.40W

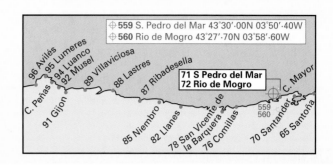

⊕**559** S. Pedro del Mar 43°30´.00N 03°50´.40W
⊕**560** Rio de Mogro 43°27´.70N 03°58´.60W

71 S Pedro del Mar
72 Rio de Mogro

This ria is entered between Los Cañones, a flat-topped, steep-sided promontory with a battery on top, and Punta del Mesa. The entrance has rocks in it and is exposed to the N and NW. It can be entered by shallow draught craft with caution at HW and provides complete shelter once inside.

72 Río de Mogro

Cat D

Pretty estuary which can only be enjoyed by shoal draught vessels

⊕**560** Río de Mogro 43°27´.70N 03°58´.60W

A wide, shallow bay with an entrance negotiable from HW–0200 to HW+0200 provided there is no swell, which breaks with violence right across the bay.

Once inside the entrance, the channel wanders randomly until it deepens in the SE corner where it rounds a golf course on a bluff and where there may be enough water to stay afloat over LW.

Masted navigation ceases ½M further on at a low railway bridge.

It is an attractive estuary but only for shoal draught vessels, preferably after a recce and in fine weather.

There are no shops or other facilities within walking distance.

Río de Mogro looking SE. The outer entrance is indicated, but inside that the channels change continually

III. SAN PEDRO DEL MAR TO AVILES

73 Suances

Cat C

Fearsome entrance in any weather or swell from the N quarter; there is a small harbour on the W side of the río which leads to a port for coasters 5M up; extensive bird life on the marshes

Location
43°27′.00N 04°02′.00W

Shelter
Good inside

Warning
Entrance breaks across in any swell

Depth restrictions
1m on the bar
0.9m in harbour

Night entry
Lit but not advised

Tidal information
HW PdG –0015
LW PdG –0000

Mean height of tide (m)

MHWS	MHWN	MLWN	MLWS
3.9	2.9	1.5	0.4

Tidal stream
Up to 3 knots on the ebb; more in a heavy spate which may reverse the flood

Berthing
Alongside in harbour

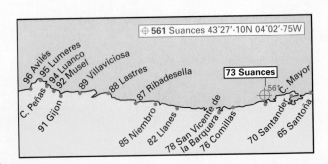

Facilities
A few shops and cafés

Charts
BA 1150 (12.5), 1105 (200)
Spanish 4012 (10)

Weather
Santander Ch 24 0840, 1240, 2010
Navtex A or D

Radio and telephone
None

Suances looking S at 1 hour before LW

PILOTAGE

Approaches

By day

From ⊕561 pick out the two leading marks on 150°; they are both white masonry towers, the rear one low down on the bluff. Isla de los Conejos has steep cliffs and is flat-topped to port and the peninsula of Punta del Torco will be conspicuous on the starboard bow with its blocks of flats and lighthouse. Assess conditions in the entrance before proceeding further.

By night

Not recommended mainly due to the difficulty of picking out the unlit beacon on the end of the training wall in time; also there are no lit channel indications above the first leading line.

Warning

Not an entrance to be attempted except in good conditions, with a reliable engine or a constant fair wind and in the last half of the flood. The 30m wide entrance channel leaves no room for mistakes between the rock training wall and the breakers on the sands.

Entrance

Identify the spindly beacon on the end of the training wall. The outer end of the training wall covers above half tide but the leading line, if accurately held, will lead the right side of it. Keep 20m off the training wall to port until just before the harbour is reached. The deep water is all on the E side of the channel. Turn then into the entrance to seek a berth or proceed further upriver to anchor.

Berthing

There is 0.9m over most of the basin, more in the NW corner. On the W wall is a pontoon for small boats only. Find a berth on the N or W sides; the inside of the E walls have 0m. A fender board will be needed as the walls are steel piled.

Anchoring

An anchorage in mud and 2m can be found just above the harbour on the SW side of the channel above the moorings.

An anchorage for a lunch stop or in fine weather overnight can be found to the S of Punta del Torco as close in as depth allows on sand. There is a strong N-going set along this shore on the ebb. There is a small 3.5m hole just above Punta del Hornillo; two anchors needed.

Further upriver

The training walls are marked by spindly posts or beacons but the former cover at about HW−0200 and the little left showing of the latter is difficult to see. Apart from this, the river follows a straightforward course some 5M up to La Requejada where it splits, but it would be wise to have either BA 1150 or Spanish 4012 charts on board if going this far.

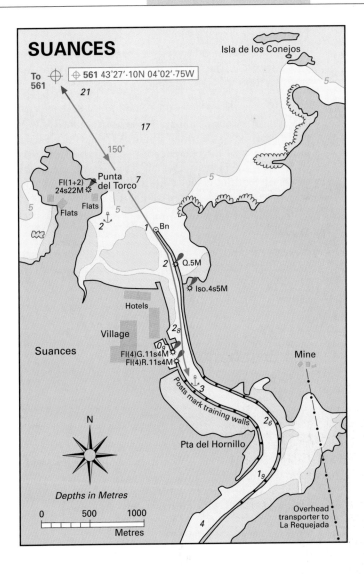

The stretch above Punta del Hornillo is pleasant, wooded and secluded except for a house and a few moorings halfway along. This stretch and the following one are of particular interest to bird watchers as there is an indigenous population of unusual wetland birds. ¾M above Punta Hornillo and below a wooded bluff is a disused harbour (reputed to have 1m in it) which may provide an anchorage out of the channel.

The final stretch starts rurally but the industry and works at La Requejada become increasingly oppressive, as does their smell.

Some 30 coasters a year come here for the export of hornblende and calamine, the product of the Solvay mine. This is taken by an interesting overhead transporter 2¼ miles to the works at La Requejada.

There are various jetties at La Requejada but they are all commercial and it is no place for a yacht.

Ashore in Suances

The main town is up the hill from the village by the harbour but there are probably enough distractions below to satisfy the casual visitor.

Facilities

Water taps on the quays; no fuel nearby; a variety of small shops in the village and a good sprinkling of cafés, restaurants and hotels.

Leisure

The beach fronting Suances tends to get crowded but those on the W side of the Punta del Torco peninsula and to the E of the entrance are less frequented.

A visit by taxi to the well preserved medieval town of Santillana del Mar (8km and not on the sea), where there is also a small zoo and prehistoric caves nearby, is worthwhile.

Travel

Nearest air and ferry port Santander (20km). Buses to and from Suances town.

Solvay mine and quarry at the start of the transporter. Yellow buckets carry ore

74 Ensenada de Cabera
Cat D

⊕**562** 43°26´.40N 04°04´.65W

Shelter may be found here under the lee of Punta Ballota from SW to NW winds in up to 10m sand; tuck well in under Punta Ballota.

This anchorage is sometimes used by coasters waiting suitable conditions to enter Suances.

Suances harbour looking NW. Best berths on W or N walls

Typical Costa Verde coastline. Looking over Punta Ballota and Ensenada de Cabera eastwards

75 Ensenada de Luaña
Cat D

⊕**563** 43°24′.60N 04°13′.20W

A deep and relatively narrow bay with an extensive beach at its head on the W side of Punta Ruiloba. It is backed by a ravine and these two features make it identifiable from seaward.

Sheltered from winds from between SW and NW.

76 Comillas
Cat C

Small drying port with a rocky approach; the village restaurants are popular as a lunch stop

Location
43°23′.00N
04°17′.00W

Shelter
None unless small enough to dry out inside

Warning
Rock encumbered approach

Depth restrictions
2m in approach
Harbour dries

Night entry
Well lit but not advisable

Tidal information
HW PdG −0040
LW PdG −0025

Mean height of tide

MHWS	MHWN	MLWN	MLWS
3.9	2.9	1.5	0.4

Tidal stream
Not significant off the port

Berthing
Dry out in harbour; anchor off

⊕**564** Comillas 43°23′·80N 04°16′·98W

Facilities
Those of a small fishing village

Charts
BA 1105 (200)
Spanish 938 (40), 939 (40)

Weather
Santander Ch24 at 0840, 1240, 2010

Radio and telephone
None

COMILLAS
⊕ 564 43°23′·80N 04°16′·98W
To 564 ⊕
Depths in Metres

PILOTAGE

Approaches

By day

The bay lies 2½M west of the prominent Cabo Oriambre. From ⊕564 identify the first leading line on 194°. The marks are halfway up the hill just to the right of a Victorian-style house. Follow these closely until the second set of similar appearance just to the S of the port and to the right of the conspicuous red brick seminary up the hill are in line on 245° and turn down them. Follow the breakwater end round at about 20m.

By night

Not recommended as although the leading lines are well lit there is little light inside the small crowded harbour.

Berthing

Dry out in the outer part of the harbour; the bottom is uneven mud. For the deeper keeled it may be possible to dry out alongside the E wall inside or outside the entrance but a recce first is preferable.

There is a shallow sill across the entrance.

Anchoring

In a suitable depth near the leading lines; do not stray far from them inside the 5m line as the survey is uncertain and it is very rocky.

Ashore in Comillas

The shallow sill across the entrance not only keeps the mud in but takes the blocking boards to close the harbour entrance in heavy weather. The crane appears to be dedicated to this purpose.

III. SAN PEDRO DEL MAR TO AVILES

245°

Comillas looking W

Entrance

Harbour looking N

Facilities

Water from a point on the W quay; fuel from garage in the village; the shops are about ½ mile away; there is a substantial slipway capable of taking medium-sized fishing boats.

Leisure

The resort is a favourite of the richer from Santander and there is a good selection of restaurants headed by El Capricho de Gaudi; the beach is popular, but long enough not to be crowded; the prehistoric caves at Cueva las Aguas near Novales and the Pontifical University Palace of the Marquis de Comillas (the Seminary) which dominates the village are worth a visit.

Travel

Local buses connect with the coastal services. Nearest railway station 12km. Nearest air and ferry port Santander (40km).

Fiestas

30 March, 29 June, 15 July, 25 July.

Gaudi's extravagant house, now a gourmet restaurant

77 Ria y Ensenada de Rabia

Cat D

⊕565 Rabia 43°24′.40N 04°19′.16W

The prominent Cabo Oriambre gives good shelter from the W and its offlying rocks some protection from any swell. There is good holding mainly on sand to the SSE of the cabo.

There is a 5m bank (Bajo de Molar) ½M to the NNW of the cabo which should be left to the S if approaching from the W. The 5m line with rocks extends 0.4M to the E from the cabo.

The ria at the E end of the bay is narrow and obstructed by a sand bar at the entrance which is just to W of the rocks of Peña de la Barra (see Spanish charts 938, 939). A recce first would be needed to enter but it deepens inside and there is said to be water to lie afloat in shelter above the bar. A low bridge crosses the ria ½M from its entrance.

78 San Vicente de la Barquera

Cat B*

Very busy fishing port with some concessions to yachts; a lively town; a gateway to the Picos

Location
43°24´.00N 04°23´.00W

Shelter
Adequate inside

Warning
The sea may break in the entrance in northerly weather

Depth restrictions
6.0m in outer entrance
2.0m+ alongside fish quay

Night entry
Possible but no lit leading line

Tidal information
HW PdG −0040
LW PdG −0025

Mean height of tide

MHWS	MHWN	MLWN	MLWS
3.9	2.9	1.5	0.4

Tidal stream
Ebb runs at up to 3 kts at springs, 2kts at neaps in río

Berthing
Alongside quay or fishing boat; communal mooring buoy

Facilities
Good eating and shopping; no specific yacht facilities

Charts
BA 1150 (12.5)
Spanish 4021 (10)

Weather
Santander Ch 24 at 0840, 1240, 2010
Navtex A or D

Radio
The capitanía may answer on Ch 12

San Vicente de la Barquera looking SW; river in spate

East head   Fish quay

220°

West head and Isla Peña   Punta de Silla lighthouse

PILOTAGE

Approaches

By day

The white Punta de Silla lighthouse and the long white Playa de Merón indicate the entrance. Do not cut the corner round the W breakwater if coming from the W due to the 1.3m on Bajo de la Plancha.

By night

From ⊕567 a track of 220° should lead between the breakwater (Fl.WG.2s) and the training wall (Fl(2)R.8s) heads. Note that the W head light will change from G to W when about 200m from the light and that Punta de Silla (Oc.3.5s) obscures as the W head is passed.

Entrance

Warning

The depths indicated on the plan were taken in late 2004 during dredging operations. These appear to take place every three years so shoaling from these depths in the channel can be expected to 2007.

In October 2005 a dangerous wreck awash at CD was in position 43°23'.90N 04°23'.87W close to ⊕567 and this should be given a wide berth.

By day or night

From the entrance a track of 220° should be followed towards Punta de la Espina (F.G), a green conical masonry tower. When this is abeam the fish quay or its lights will become visible; continue on 240° to the quay or secure to the large white mooring buoy at the entrance to the creek to port. Note that the E training wall mostly covers at HW.

Berthing

The most likely place to find a berth is on the new quay just below the bridge either alongside or outside a 'resting' fishing boat. Take care in turning below the bridge on the flood, the stream runs at up to 3 knots. An alternative is to raft up on the boats secured to the bridge but beware of extensive footings on the bridge supports which cover at half tide, and go bow-to-bridge.

Mooring

There are a number of private moorings to the S of the bridge and opposite Punta de la Espina, and a large communal white buoy to which yachts raft up. The problem with the latter area is that there are considerable eddies on the ebb and boats swing in all directions.

Anchoring

For those not needing the proximity of the town, a peaceful anchorage can be found in the creek leading to Casa de la Maza. There are a number of moorings here in a reported 2m but still space to anchor clear of them.

Anchoring off the main channel can only be a temporary option as the channel sides are steep.

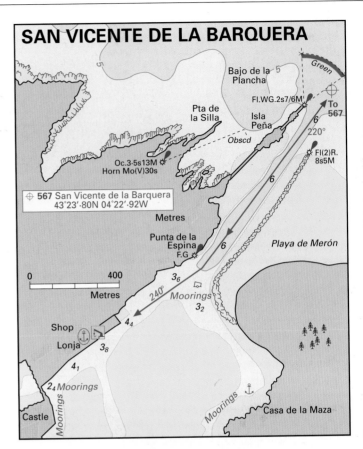

The approach to the fish quay

Ashore in San Vicente de la Barquera

It is a vigorous town with many restaurants and cafés but on the main road and hence noisy. The main part lies S over the bridge. The fishing fleet has expanded steadily over the last few years together with the quays and slip; one can see this expansion continuing along the N bank towards the old and disused boatyard. The port is at the mouth of an extensive, sandy estuary draining a large area of the hinterland through which rivers rush down from the Picos – hence the need for regular dredging.

Facilities

Water from taps on the quays; fuel in cans from a garage up the road; engineers and electricians able to deal with fishing boats; a large slip and 10-tonne crane; ice from the *lonja*; there is a good little *supermercado* behind the *lonja* and many other shops in town.

Leisure

The fine Gothic basilica of Santa Maria de los Angeles and the Castillo del Rey in which there is a visitor centre are well worth a visit, as is a stroll round the castle walls. The Playa de Merón is a huge beach and big enough not to be crowded. A taxi trip round the two Tinas to the W to Cueva del Pindal, a prehistoric cave with paintings may amuse.

San Vicente de la Barquera is a good place to take off for the Picos but sadly, like Ribadesella at the western end of the range, is no place to leave a yacht unattended in safety, with no better options in between. For enthusiastic walkers and climbers the longer trip to the Picos from Gijón or Santander is the only possible alternative unless the less energetic can be left on board as boatkeepers.

Travel

The town is on the main bus routes E and W, and S into the Picos. The railway is 5km south. Nearest air and ferry port Santander (60km).

Fiestas

20 April for La Virgen de la Barquera; 10 August song festival; 8 September for La Santissima Virgen de la Barquera.

Castle Bridge berths Basilica

The berths on the new jetty just below the bridge

Looking down harbour from above the town. Casa de la Maza on the right

The anchorage/mooring area off Casa de la Maza looking N

Picos de Europa

The Picos are a small limestone massif rising to 2600m, 40km across and 30km from the coast, which the Asturians regard as their own but which extend into Cantabria. They are a firm favourite with climbers, trekkers, canoeists, potholers and ramblers, in a beautiful and unspoilt area from Potes in the E to Cangas de Onis in the W near where the Moorish invasion of Spain was turned at Covadonga in 714 AD. The area is crowded in July and August but the springtime is delightful, with wild flowers crowding the valleys and the higher peaks still snowbound.

For further information contact *Turismo* in the main road in San Vicente de la Barquera (☎ 942 71 07 97) or Federacion Cantabria de Montaña in Santander (☎ 942 37 33 78).

79 Ria de Tina Menor

Cat C

Attractive and deserted ria with no facilities

⊕**568** 43°24´.30N 04°28´.20W

PILOTAGE

This ria is only for yachts drawing 2m or less and prepared to dry out, although there is one very small pool of 2m near the entrance and another reported further up. The entrance is only possible in settled weather and no swell.

Approaches

By day only

From ⊕568 identify the entrance, which is a steep gash in the cliffs which rise 200+m on either side. Close to the W is a squat and prominent television tower on the crest. Approach on a track of about 180° to leave Punta de la Vigia about 150m to starboard.

Entrance

At or just before HW, from abeam of Punta de la Vigia head for the W side of the gap until the largest house on the W bank bears SW and the wooden ramp up to the house is seen, then turn towards it and keep very close to the W bank where the deepest water lies. The sand spit from Isla Canton extends almost across.

Anchorages

Sound carefully forward towards Pena del Pinto until there is enough water, and anchor. There is very little room to swing so bow and stern anchors will be needed and the stream runs hard both on ebb and flood.

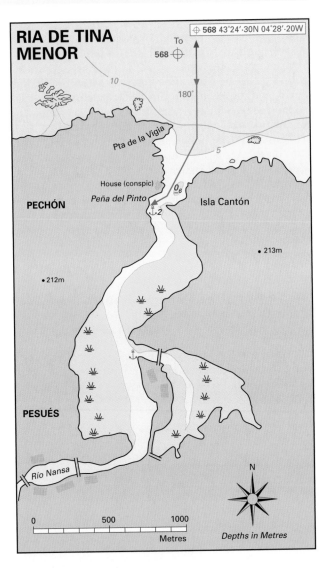

Looking SSE up the ria with the Picos rising above the clouds in the background

Another anchorage is reported at the junction of a small stream coming in on the E bank about ½M up as shown on the plan. Otherwise anchor and dry out on firm sand.

Ashore

Facilities

The small villages of Pechón and Persués have basic shops but they are some distance from the ria. A dinghy trip up to Persués may be the best way if desperate for provisions.

Travel

The main coastal road and railway pass across the head of the ria and are noisy in the upper reaches.

80 Ria de Tina Mayor

Cat C

Beautiful estuary which mostly dries; a few facilities

⊕569 43°24´.50N 04°30´.70W

PILOTAGE

Approaches

Like its neighbour Tina Menor, this ria is only for shallow draught boats or for a lunch stop near HW in fine weather.

By day only

The entrance may be identified from ⊕569 from the prominent squat television mast on the crest just to the E and from the caravan site on the E side of the entrance. Approach well to the W of the entrance so that the final track past Punta de la Tina is southeasterly.

Entrance

The middle of the entrance is obstructed by Baja de San Mateo drying 0.4m, so Punta de la Tina must be passed 50m off on a SE track until inside the cliffs. Keep then to the centre of the ria for 350m until just short of the drying spit on the port side, then hug the W bank where the deep water is.

Anchoring

Sound carefully forward until enough water is found to anchor close to the W bank; there is reported to be a 1m hole here but depth and channel vary greatly depending on the winter storms. Bow and stern anchors may be needed if staying over a tide. The

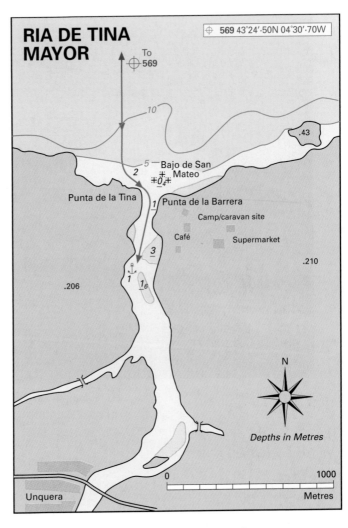

Looking S up the ria at HW–0100. Campsite on left, Punta de la Tina in the centre

streams run at 3+knots and will be much stronger in a spate when there will be no noticeable flood.

Boats dry out on the spit which is all hard sand; in any swell go to the S side of it.

Ashore

Facilities

There is a small *supermercado* and café in the camp site above Punta de la Barrera where Camping Gaz is available, also showers. Land on the beach just above the spit and walk up.

A dinghy trip up the río to the rather dull town of Unquera will find shops, restaurants, garage and supplies.

Travel

The motorway, with its bus services E and W, passes across the top of the ria and there is a railway station at Unquera.

81 Ria de Santiuste

Cat D

Open bay well sheltered from the W with a good beach and small stream

⊕**570** 43°24′.70N 04°34′.17W

Isolote de Castron de Santiuste

Ria de Santiuste lying 2M W of Punta San Emeterio looking SW at HW+0200

82 Llanes

Cat C

Attractive little port and popular resort; 0m in entrance but 1.9m at berths

Location	**Mean height of tide**			
43°25′.30N 04°45′.00W	MHWS	MHWN	MLWN	MLWS
Shelter	4.0	3.0	1.5	0.5
Good inside	**Tidal stream**			
Depth restriction	Minimal in harbour			
0m in entrance	**Berthing**			
Night entry	Alongside in 1.9m			
Lit but no leading	**Facilities**			
lights	Those of a small town.			
Tidal information	A lifeboat is based here			
HW PdG –0030				
LW PdG –0035				

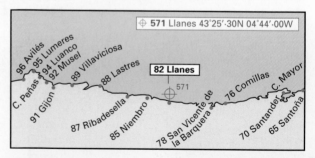

⊕ **571** Llanes 43°25′.30N 04°44′.00W

96 Avilés 95 Lumeres 94 Luanco 92 Musel 89 Villaviciosa 88 Lastres **82 Llanes** 571 76 Comillas C. Mayor C. Peñas 91 Gijón 87 Ribadesella 85 Niembro 78 San Vicente de la Barquera 70 Santander 65 Santoña

Charts
BA 1105 (200)
Spanish 938 (40)

Weather
Santander Ch 24 at 0840,
1240 and 2010

Cabo Peñas Ch 26 at 0840,
1240 and 2010
Navtex A and D

Radio and telephone
None

PILOTAGE

With little flow down the small río the harbour has silted considerably in the last few years and is unlikely to be dredged with such a small resident fishing fleet. Nevertheless, once in, there are deeper berths but don't get caught in here in a northeasterly.

Approaches

By day or night

A straightforward and danger-free approach from ⊕571 on a track of 250° on St Anton lighthouse (Fl(4)15s). There is no leading line but the town lights and Dique de la Osa (Fl.G.5s) will assist.

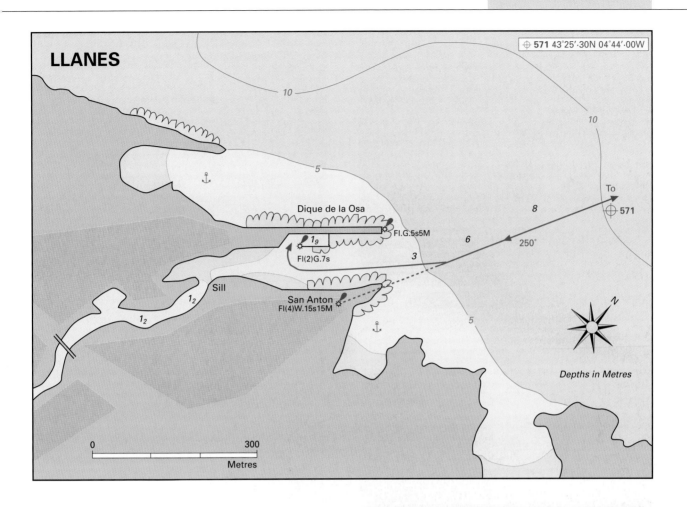

LLANES

571 43°25'·30N 04°44'·00W

Dique de la Osa

Fl.G.5s5M

1₉

Fl(2)G.7s

To
571

8

6

250°

3

Sill

1₂

1₂

San Anton
Fl(4)W.15s15M

5

N

Depths in Metres

0   300
Metres

Entrance

The concrete blocks on the end of Dique de la Osa have been painted in varied and bright colours and are conspicuous from seaward. At HW–0100 to HW depending on draught, turn off 250° when the entrance is open and pass up the channel, keeping well over to the S side where the deeper water of 0m is; turn to starboard into the basin when the entrance is almost abeam (pier end Fl(2)G.7s).

Berthing

There is 1.9m along the N wall, 1.4m along the E and less along the pier although the lifeboat lies afloat at its outer end. The walls are flat but high except for the pier, and a ladder will be needed if there is not a berth next to one.

Anchoring

Anchorages with some shelter from the W may be found in the bays N and S of the entrance.

Inner basin

The lifting sill to the inner harbour dries 2m and notionally retains 1.2m inside where it is crowded with small boats. There appears to be no pattern to the opening of the sill, which can be left open for long periods and the harbour dries out. If needing shelter in here, ask at the capitanía which is in the town.

San Anton light

250°

Painted blocks on La Osa

Llanes looking WSW

Brightly coloured blocks at end of Dique de la Osa

Looking WSW up harbour. Best berth in foreground

Facilities

Water at hydrant on N quay; fuel from garage in town; a slip and 5-tonne crane; good shops close by and a variety of restaurants, including one well known one at end of N quay.

Travel

On the main railway and close to the main E/W motorway for buses which also run S to the Picos. Nearest airport Asturias just to the W of Gijón (65km).

Leisure

The 15th-century church and castle in the old town are worth a visit, also Caverna de Avia and Cueva del Pindal nearby prehistoric cave dwellings. Good beaches on either side of town.

Fiestas

21 July, 12–31 August, 7–8 September.

83 Ensenada de Póo

Cat D

Enchanting, landlocked and drying bay with a fine-weather anchorage outside

⊕572 43°26´.55N 04°46´.81W

Approaches to Póo looking WSW

PILOTAGE

Approach and entrance

By day only

From ⊕572 identify Isoletes Palo de Póo and the island just to the W of the entrance on a track of 195°. Islet A should soon be picked out; this is steep-to all round to 7m depth and is bare rock. From abeam of this, sound in to an anchorage on sand under the island. For those able to dry out, the channel to the inner bay shoals gradually and it is all flat.

Sadly, the privacy and remoteness of Póo has become more widely known and the sands are crowded in the summer, although there has been no further building apart from the small hotel.

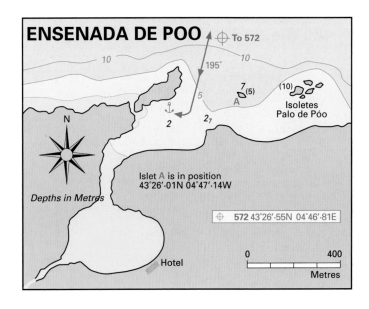

ENSENADA DE POO
To 572
Isoletes Palo de Póo
Islet A is in position
43°26'·01N 04°47'·14W
572 43°26'·55N 04°46'·81E
Depths in Metres
Hotel
0   400
Metres

84 Ensenada de Celorio

Cat D

Open bay suitable for a lunch stop in fine weather

⊕573 43° 26'.75N 04°48'.55W

PILOTAGE

The bay lies 1M to the W of Póo, 1½M to the E of Ria de Niembro and S of ⊕573 from where it should be possible to identify the bay and beach. Sound carefully in and anchor as the depths allow, mostly sand. No protection from the swell.

Ashore

There is a small but well-stocked *supermercado* ½M inland, a hotel and a sprinkling of restaurants and *sidrerias* in the vicinity, any of which are good enough reason to come here. There is a railway station and the bus route is close.

Celorio looking SSW. Quay on N side of headland in foreground

85 Ria de Niembro

Cat C

Little-frequented and beautiful ria with entrance only passable in fair weather near HW

Location
43°27'.00N 04°50'.00W

Shelter
Good inside

Depth restrictions
0.5m on bar; dries inside

Night entry
No lights

Tidal information
HW PdG –0010
LW PdG –0000

Mean height of tide

MHWS	MHWN	MLWN	MLWS
4.0	3.1	1.5	0.6

Tidal stream
2 knots ebb in entrance

Berthing
Drying alongside quay or on sands

Facilities
None, except some small restaurants

Charts
No large-scale
BA 1105 (200)
Spanish 403 (50)

Weather
Cabo Peñas Ch 26 at 0840, 1240 and 2010

Radio and telephone
None

⊕ **574** Niembro 43°27'·10N 04°49'·50W

96 Avilés
95 Lumeres
94 Luanco
92 Musel
89 Villaviciosa
88 Lastres
87 Ribadesella
⊕ 574
C. Peñas
91 Gijón
85 Niembro
82 Llanes
78 San Vicente de la Barquera
76 Comillas
C. Mayor
70 Santander
65 Santoña

Church

210°

Niembro entrance looking S

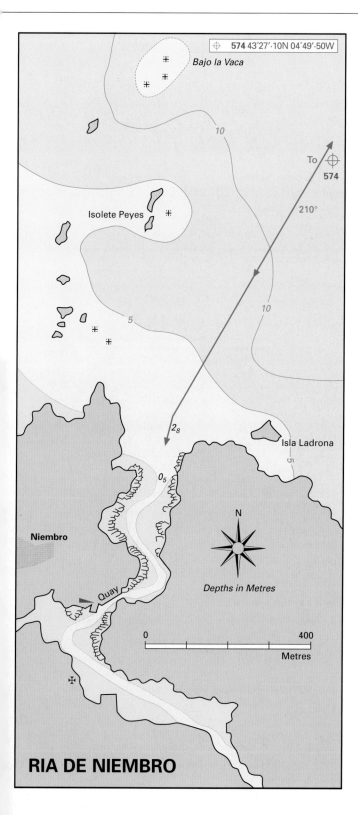

⊕ **574** 43°27'·10N 04°49'·50W

Bajo la Vaca

10

Isolete Peyes

To ⊕
574

210°

10

5

2₈

Isla Ladrona

0₅

5

Niembro

N

Depths in Metres

Quay

0   400

Metres

RIA DE NIEMBRO

The bar near LW looking N. Isolete Peyes on left beyond

The imposing church on the S bank

PILOTAGE

Approach

By day only

From ⊕574 make good a track of 210° and do not get to the W of it where Bajo la Vaca and the rocks of Isolete Peyes lie in wait. Isla Ladrona is steep-to and may help in identifying the entrance, which does not fully open up until it bears S.

Entrance

The bar has 0.5m or less on it. The best time to enter is HW–0100 to HW but it tends to break in any swell at any state of the tide. A wait in deep water to observe the conditions before commitment to the entrance will be prudent.

Berthing

Keep to the outside of the sharp bends after entry. There is a substantial quay around the second bend drying from 1.5m to 0.9m, sandy bottom and deeper at the inner end by the slip. It has ladders and bollards and is suitable to dry out alongside.

Otherwise sound in along the channel to find a hole to anchor in or dry out on the sands. Beware the occasional rock which can be seen on the latter in clear water.

Facilities

There are no shops, but three small restaurants/cafés in the village.

Leisure

The pretty estuary is asking for exploration by dinghy and the church is worth a visit.

III. SAN PEDRO DEL MAR TO AVILES

86 Playa de San Antonio del Mar

Cat D

⊕575 43°28′.40N 04°55′.30W

A small inlet with a sandy beach at its head on the E side of Cabo del Mar, a prominent steep-to Cape 6M from Ribadesella and 4M from Niembro.

There is good holding and shelter in W to NW winds and it is a traditional place of shelter for the local fishermen.

87 Ribadesella

Cat C

Most attractive fishing port in beautiful surroundings with alongside berths in the town. Entry not viable in a heavy swell or strong onshore winds; the main gateway to the Picos

Location
43°28′.00N 04°56′.00W

Shelter
Good inside in all weathers

Warning
A narrow entrance subject to swell

Depth restrictions
2.0m in entrance;
1–4m at berths

Night entry
Possible but few lights

Tidal information
HW PdG –0010
LW PdG –0000

Mean height of tide

MHWS	MHWN	MLWN	MLWS
4.0	3.1	1.5	0.6

Tidal stream
2 knots ebb, more when in spate

⊕576 Ribadesella 43°28′·51N 05°04′·00W

96 Avilés 95 Lumeres 94 Luanco 92 Musel 89 Villaviciosa 88 Lastres 576
C. Peñas 91 Gijón **87 Ribadesella** 85 Niembro 82 Llanes 78 San Vicente de la Barquera 76 Comillas C. Mayor 70 Santander 65 Santoña

Berthing
Alongside town quay in 1–4m

Facilities
Those of a small town

Charts
BA 1150 (12.5)
Spanish 4031 (10)

Weather
Cabo Peñas Ch 26 at 0840, 1240 and 2010
Navtex D

Radio and telephone
None

PILOTAGE

Approaches

By day

From ⊕576 the entrance below Punta del Caballo with the prominent white hermitage on it can be easily identified; approach on a track of 170° to leave the white light tower on the knuckle close to port.

By night

There is only one light (Fl(2)R.6s) but this should be sufficient to lead in with the street lights providing direction on the port side up to the berths.

Entrance

In other than good conditions, entry should not be attempted outside HW–0200 to HW. A heavy swell will break right across the bay out to the 5m line and the channel will be impassable.

Leave Punta del Caballo light 50m to port and then keep 20m off the shore up to a berth.

Berthing

There are no visitors' berths in the small marina which is not normally manned, and egress can only be obtained with a card. Proceed up the quay past the *lonja* until a space is found; the depths alongside gradually shallow from 4m to drying 1m by the

bridge; there is 1m by the crane. A fender board will be needed on the first piled section of jetty, and a ladder to get ashore at LW.

Anchoring

Not allowed in the harbour.

Travel

On the main E/W rail and bus routes; nearest airport Asturias beyond Gijón (60km).

Ashore in Ribadesella

Facilities

Water from the *lonja*; fuel from a filling station at the E end of the bridge; ice from the *lonja*; good selection of shops and restaurants close to the quay; some repair facilities at the marina.

Leisure

Ribadesella is one of the main entry points into the Picos up the Río Sella via Cangas but is not a place where a yacht can be left unattended even for a few days. Gijón is the nearest safe port for the walkers, potholers or mountaineers to take off from.

Playa de Santa Marina is a good surfing beach and not usually too crowded. There are a number of prehistoric caves nearby, details from the Turismo in town.

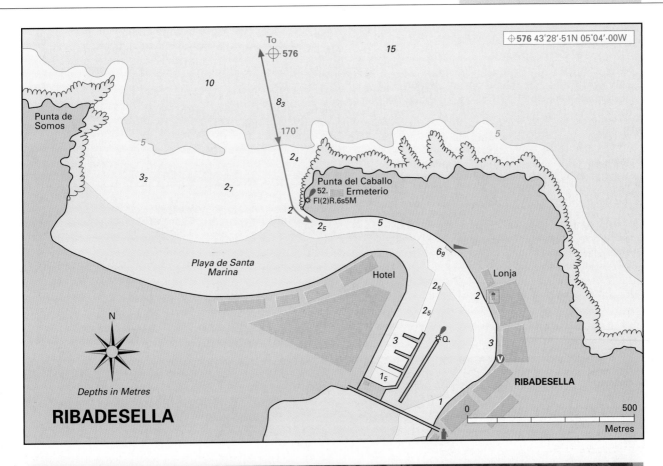

RIBADESELLA

Punta de
Somos

Playa de Santa
Marina

Punta del Caballo
52. Ermeterio
FI(2)R.6s5M

Hotel

Lonja

RIBADESELLA

N

Depths in Metres

RIBADESELLA

0   500
Metres

576 43°28'·51N 05°04'·00W

Ribadesella looking SE

88 Lastres

Cat C

Very pretty unspoilt fishing village clinging to the hillside above a small harbour, with some facilities for yachts

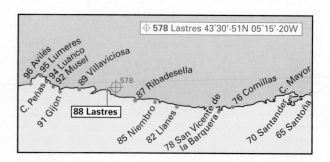

⊕ **578** Lastres 43°30'·51N 05°15'·20W

Location
43°31'.00N 05°16'.00W

Shelter
Adequate but not in easterlies

Warning
Bajo de la Plancha breaks in heavy seas; it should be avoided

Depth restrictions
2m+ at alongside berths

Night entry
Possible

Tidal information
HW PdG –0018
LW PdG –0010

Mean height of tide (m)

MHWS	MHWN	MLWN	MLWS
4.4	3.0	1.7	0.3

Berthing
Alongside in 1–3m; anchored off

Facilities
Those of a large village

Charts
BA 1150 (12.5)
Spanish 4041 (15)

Weather
Cabo Peñas Ch 26 at 0840, 1240 and 2010
Navtex D

Radio and telephone
None

Radio/TV tower

Possible alongside berths

Lastres looking W

PILOTAGE

Approaches

By day

The harbour is readily identified by the prominent red and white lattice TV tower above it. From the W pass to the NE of Bajo de la Plancha and approach the breakwater with the 9-legged concrete structure bearing 220° or more. From the E proceed from ⊕578 on a westerly track to the harbour.

By night

As above but keep the outer breakwater light (Fl(3)G.9s) bearing between 230° and 290° on the approach.

Entrance

The outer breakwater is high so do not cut the corner too close in case of leavers.

Berthing

Alongside berths can often be found on the outer wall as indicated in between 2 and 6m. Do not use the pontoon at the head of the harbour.

Mooring

There are often fishing boats moored in the middle of the harbour and it may be possible to raft up on them.

Anchoring

Just outside the harbour clear of the entrance in 2m, sand as indicated and clear of the rock ledges.

Ashore in Lastres

The capitanía is well disposed towards yachtsmen, the fishermen less so but quite a number of yachts visit and there is reasonable co-operation for berths.

Facilities

Water tap on the W quay; fuel is 5km away towards Colunga; adequate shops and good restaurants in the old and pretty village (5 minutes' walk uphill); there is a slip and 10-tonne crane at the harbour.

Leisure

There are fine views from the vicinity of the TV tower and a good beach at Playa de Colunga ½M to the SE. The sea breaks across the mouth of Río de Colunga below half tide but a dinghy trip up the río the 4M to Colunga around HW is through pleasant countryside.

Travel

The main road is 4M S at Colunga, the railway runs to the S of the coastal hills. Nearest airport Asturias to the W of Gijón (45km).

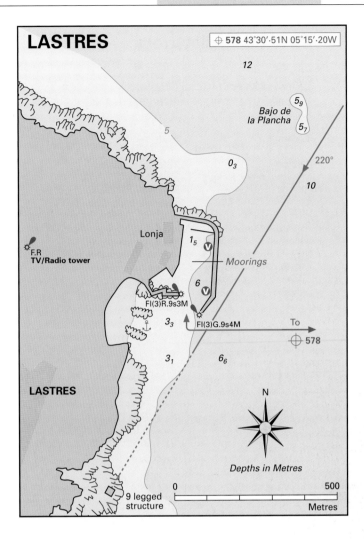

LASTRES

⊕ 578 43°30'·51N 05°15'·20W

Bajo de la Plancha

220°

Lonja

F.R
TV/Radio tower

Moorings

Fl(3)R.9s3M

Fl(3)G.9s4M

To
⊕ 578

LASTRES

N

Depths in Metres

0   500

Metres

9 legged
structure

The outer breakwater looking SSE

The 9-legged day mark

III. SAN PEDRO DEL MAR TO AVILES

89 Ria de Villaviciosa

Cat C

Canalised river entrance only for fine weather, with a large estuary winding inland; a good place for bird watchers

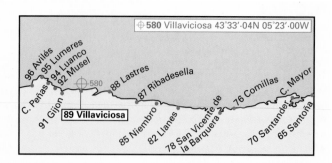

Location
43°33'.00N 05°23'.00W

Shelter
Sheltered anchorage inside

Warning
Entry should only be attempted from HW–0200 to HW and not in a swell

Depth restrictions
2.0m in entrance and channel

Night entry
No lights

Tidal information
HW PdG –0015
LW PdG –0010

Mean height of tide (m)

MHWS	MHWN	MLWN	MLWS
4.4	3.0	1.6	0.3

Tidal stream
Up to 3 knots ebb at springs, more with a spate

Berthing
Anchor only

Facilities
Minimal; small shop

Charts
BA 1105 (200)
Spanish 4041 (15)

Weather
Cabo Peñas Ch 26 at 0840, 1240 and 2010

Radio and telephone
None

Rodiles caravan park

White house (front) in transit with block of flats

Ria de Villaviciosa entrance from the N on leading line ½ hour after LW, illustrating the need to keep close to the W training wall

PILOTAGE

Approaches

By day only

From ⊕580 identify the leading line of a small, low off-white house directly in front of a block of flats between two stands of trees. This leads between the training walls; do not stray off this line to the W where there are the many rocks off Bajas de la Mesnada.

Entrance

There is 2m outside the entrance which deepens inside. Enter between HW–0200 and HW and check that any swell is not breaking across. Favour the W side of the channel as far as the first bend to starboard and then keep in the centre. The soundings on the plan were taken in 1998 and may have shoaled since.

Berthing

None; the small pontoon on the Rodiles side is for dinghies only and the pontoon in the basin for small local boats.

Anchoring

Above the basin at El Puntal as indicated or by the entrance to the basin on sand and mud.

Above El Puntal

The río winds for 4M through an estuary rich in wild life to an old quay at El Gaitero in Villaviciosa town. This is one of Spain's better known *sidra* factories, whence it used to be shipped out downriver. Spanish chart 4041 gives some indication of the lower part of the channel, otherwise it is for dinghy exploration on a rising tide only.

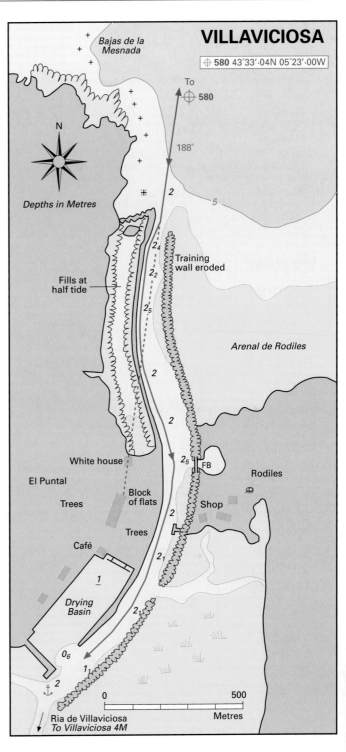

Looking S up the ria towards Villaviciosa from above Rodiles

Ashore in El Puntal and Rodiles

Facilities

Water from tap at slip in basin and from the cafés at El Puntal and Rodiles; no fuel; small shop and showers at Rodiles caravan site, land at the pontoon jetty; there is a slip and small crane at the end of El Puntal basin.

Travel

Villaviciosa is on the main E/W road and rail routes; nearest airport Asturias to the W of Gijón (25km).

90 Tazones

Cat C

Pretty little ex-fishing village much taken over by restaurants; shelter only from the W in a rolly anchorage

Location
43°33′.00N 05°24′.00W

Shelter
Only from the W

Depth restrictions
Up to 3m alongside

Night entry
Adequate lights for anchoring

Tidal information
HW PdG –0015
LW PdG –0010

Mean height of tide (m)

MHWS	MHWN	MLWN	MLWS
4.4	3.0	1.6	0.3

Berthing
Alongside berth possible

Facilities
Modest shops, many restaurants

Charts
BA 1105 (200)
Spanish 404 (50)

Weather
Cabo Peñas Ch 26 0840, 1240 and 2010

Radio and telephone
None

PILOTAGE

Approaches

By day

From the W there are no outlying dangers. Keep outside the 10m line to round Punta Tazones. From the E the red roofs of the village will be conspicuous from ⊕580.

By night

From the W or E Tazones light (Fl.7.5s20M) and the breakwater end light (Fl.G.3s) will assist.

Entrance and berthing

There may be a berth available inside the breakwater but good fendering will be needed if there is any swell. There is 3m at the outer end, shoaling inwards.

Anchoring

The bay shoals gradually and is mostly sand but any swell will find its way in.

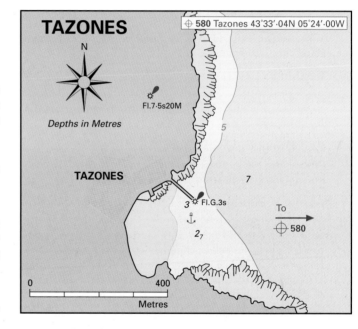

Ashore in Tazones

Fishing is now confined to a few small boats and has been replaced by a thriving restaurant trade fuelled from Gijón. Very crowded at weekends and all a bit twee (including a shell house). Some basic shops, and water from the *lonja*. Not many leisure opportunities except eating and watching others eating.

Tazones looking W

The *lonja* and breakwater looking N

91 Gijón (Muelles Locales)

Cat B*

The main port of Asturias, with a major marina. Doubtful access in really bad weather but an all-weather alternative at Musel across the bay

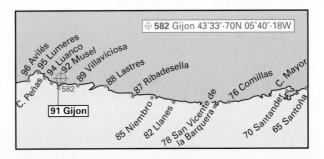

Location
43°33′.00N 05°40′.00W

Shelter
Good in the marina

Warning
Offlying banks break in a swell or bad weather

Depth restrictions
3.5m in approaches, 3m in marina

Night entry
Well lit but no leading lights

Tidal information
HW PdG –0020
LW PdG –0010

Mean height of tide (m)
MHWS	MHWN	MLWN	MLWS
4.4	3.0	1.7	0.3

Tidal stream
Negligible in approaches

Berthing
On fingers on pontoons

Facilities
Those of major city and marina

Charts
BA 1153 (10), 1154 (10)
Spanish 404 (50), 404A (25), 4042 (10)

Weather
Cabo Peñas Ch 26 at 0840, 1240, 2010

Radio
Ch 09 Marina (Spanish only)

Telephone
Marina ☎ 34 985 34 45 43
www.puertogijon.es

Gijón marina looking SE

PILOTAGE

Approaches

Warning

In a really heavy swell or gale from the N sector the sea in the approaches to Gijón will break on the 5m lines and entry will be impassable; in this event use 92 Puerto de Musel.

From the W

By day

Once the prominent Cabo Peñas is rounded, Cabo de Torres with its spherical white tanks and red and white chimneys will be seen with the high breakwaters of Puerto del Musel and the city of Gijón beyond; the way is then clear to ⊕582 leaving Musel to starboard.

From the E

By day

The high-rise buildings of Gijón will be visible from a distance and once Cerro de Santa Catalina with its distinctive sculpture is identified the corner can be cut keeping outside the 5m line to join the 170° track to the marina.

By night

There are many lights but from ⊕582 identify Piedra del Sacramento (Fl(2)G.6s) and the end of Dique de Liquerica (Fl(2)R.6s) to pass between them on a track of 170°.

By day or night

From ⊕582 pass between Serrapio del Mar and Piedra de San Justo, which break in any swell, on a track of 170° to enter the dredged channel of 3.5m leading between Piedra del Sacramento and Dique de Liquerica.

An alternative approach is to pass S of Piedra de San Justo with the ends of Dique de Liquerica (Fl(2)R.6s) and Malecón de Fomento (Fl(3)G.10s) in transit on 145°; the difficulty here is that both lights and structures are the same height.

Entrance

Once Dique de Liquerica has been passed turn to port in to the wide entrance. The reception berth is ahead on the S side of the spur. If this is full, go into the next basin to the fuel berth. Beware of the fingers on the reception pontoon which are small and unstable.

Berthing

Once cleared in, visitors are usually allocated a berth on the pontoons on Dique de Liquerica in 3m.

Anchoring

Anchoring is not allowed in the marina but an anchorage outside in settled weather may be found as indicated, or further W; nearly all sand.

Ashore in Gijón

The city was completely rebuilt after destruction in the civil war when it was subject to a heavy

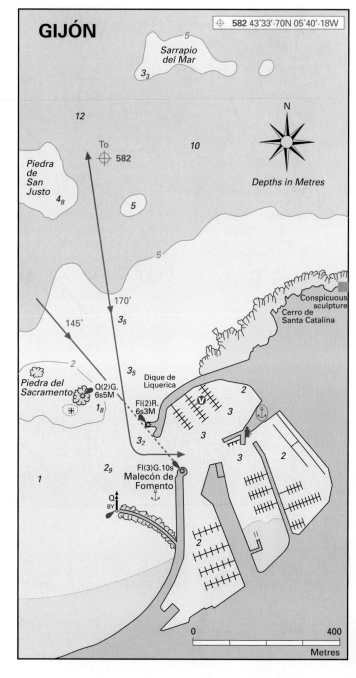

bombardment from the sea, fierce fighting in the streets and round the Nationalist Barracks, which miners armed with sticks of dynamite stormed in August 1936. The only part of the town that escaped was on the peninsula of Cerro de Santa Catalina just to the NE of the marina. Since then the city has gone from strength to strength and is now the major port, industrial and commercial centre on the north coast.

The marina was built on the site of the old harbour when Musel was developed as the new commercial port.

Facilities

Water and electricity on the pontoons; Gasoleo A and petrol at the fuel berth; 20-tonne travel-lift and 5-tonne crane (although reliability of the former is suspect); a large slip, and most repairs can be effected. It may be possible to lay up here. The large yacht club on the E side of Cerro de Santa Catalina, Real Club Astur des Regates, is mainly a social club and does not welcome non-members, particularly foreign ones. The main shopping centre is a short walk to the SE of the marina.

Leisure

The main *Turismo* is in the square immediately to the S of the marina and worth visiting. The city is blessed with a variety of museums from Roman antiquities and art from various eras to railways and even bagpipes.

This is one of the best places to leave the boat in safety if an extended visit to the Picos de Europa is planned, even though they are 2 hours' drive away to the SE.

There is a wide variety of restaurants to suit all tastes and purses within walking distance; the nearest, one of the better and more expensive ones, is in the marina above the reception berth. The Cerro de Santa Catalina area is the centre of the late and lively nightlife.

Travel

The city is on the main S, E and W rail and bus routes. Nearest airport is Asturias 25km to the W with flights to Madrid and thence onwards. Nearest ferry port is Santander with twice weekly ferries to Plymouth.

Fiestas

24 June St John the Baptist and blessing of the sea; 29 June St Peter and a procession of boats; 11–18 August Feast of the Assumption.

92 Puerto de Musel

Cat A

Large commercial port of no interest to yachtsmen, except for emergency shelter when Muelles Locales is impassible

Location
43°34'.00N 05°40'.00W

Shelter
Good

Warning
Banco las Amasucas with 14m over it lies ½M to the NE of the entrance and is marked with cardinal buoys and should be avoided

Depth restrictions
15m in entrance
5m in harbour

Night entry
Well lit but no leading lights

Tidal information
HW PdG –0015
LW PdG –0010

Mean height of tide

MHWS	MHWN	MLWN	MLWS
4.4	3.0	1.7	0.3

Berthing
Alongside or at anchor

Facilities
None specifically for yachts

Charts
BA 1153 (10), 1154 (10)
Spanish 404A (25), 4042 (10)

Weather
Cabo Peñas Ch 26
0840,1240, 2010

Radio
Ch 11, 12, 14, 16 (24hrs)
Call sign *Gijón Practicos*

Telephone
Capitanía ☎ 985 35 49 45

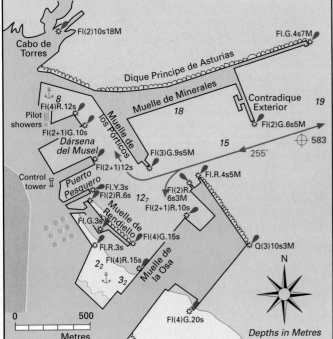

PUERTO DE MUSEL ⊕ 583 43°34'.00N 05°40'.00W

PILOTAGE

Approach

See *Warning* above.

From N

The end of Dique Principe de Asturias (Fl.G.3s) can be rounded at about 100m and course then shaped to pass the Contradique Exterior (Fl(2)G.6s).

From ⊕583 a track of 255° should lead between all the outer breakwaters.

Before entering call *Gijón Practicos* on any of the channels above to request a sheltered berth or give intentions; English is generally spoken. The capitanía is situated in a large glass building rather like an airport control tower.

Berthing

There are many alongside berths available in an emergency but all are high with bollards a long way apart. Anchorages can be found in the NW corner in about 8m or behind Muelle de Rendiello in 2m+, or a berth alongside a fishing boat in Puerto Pesquero.

Ashore

Nothing of interest to yachtsmen except some showers in the NW corner; shops are a long hike.

93 Candas

Cat C

Small fishing port with limited depths; at present being developed

Location
43°35′.00N 05°46′.00W
4M WNW of Musel

Shelter
Indifferent

Warning
Avoid 5m shoals on
approach in any swell

Depth restrictions
Inner half of harbour
dries

Night entry
Possible but not
recommended

Tidal information
HW PdG –0025
LW PdG +0005

Mean height of tide (m)

MHWS	MHWN	MLWN	MLWS
4.0	3.1	1.5	0.6

Berthing
May be alongside berth on new
quay; anchor in outer harbour

Facilities
Those of a small fishing port

Charts
BA 1153 (10)
Spanish 404A

Weather
Cabo Peñas Ch 26 0840,
1240, 2010

Radio and telephone
None

PILOTAGE

Approaches

By day or night

To avoid the 5m patches which break in any swell approach the big new breakwater end (Fl(2)G.7s) from ⊕584 on a track of 230°. If coming from Gijón or the SE an alignment of a white tower (F.R) on Punta del Cuerno with the lantern on the roof of a house on the next headland (both F.R) on 291° will lead to the N of any 5m patches until the breakwater end can be approached on 230° as above.

Entrance

Straightforward, but do not cut too close as the rocks at the breakwater end extend some way.

Berthing

Depths along the new mole are not known but there was at least 2m along the outer 50m of the old mole.

Anchoring

In 2–3m in the outer part of the harbour or outside the entrance in the same depths.

Ashore in Candas

The harbour is being developed (2005) for the benefit of fishermen and whether there will be any spin off for yachtsmen is not yet known.

Facilities

Water from a tap on the mole; there are adequate shops in the village; the yacht club Sociedad

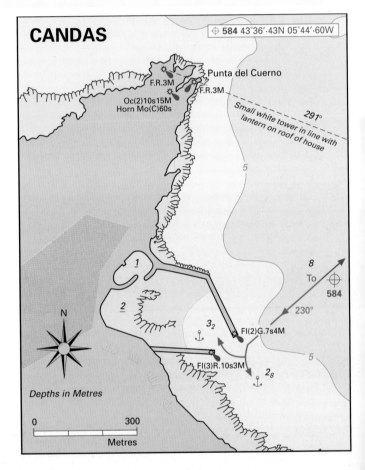

CANDAS

⊕ 584 43°36′·43N 05°44′·60W

Punta del Cuerno

F.R.3M

F.R.3M

Oc(2)10s15M
Horn Mo(C)60s

Small white tower in line with
lantern on roof of house

291°

5

8
To ⊕
584

230°

5

N

1

2

3₂

Fl(2)G.7s4M

Fl(3)R.10s3M

2₈

Depths in Metres

0   300
Metres

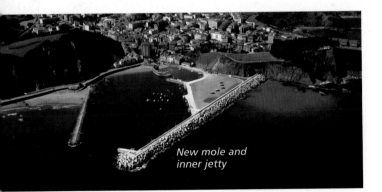

*New mole and
inner jetty*

Candas looking WSW

Polideportivo Nautico Carreño has a clubhouse near the harbour with showers and a bar.

Leisure

A good sprinkling of restaurants and cafés round the harbour; it is a pleasant walk to Punta del Cuerno with its hermitage. There is the small Ria Perán 1M to the SE as a day anchorage or to swim. Bullfights sometimes take place in the small inner harbour at LW.

Travel

Local buses to Avilés whence connections may be made to the coastal rail and bus services; nearest airport Asturias (20km).

Fiestas

14 September El Cristo de Candas.

94 Luanco

Cat C

Small fishing harbour which dries, and minor holiday resort with fine-weather anchorages

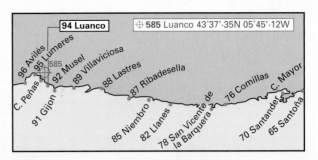

Location
43°38'.00N 05°47'.00W

Shelter
Only from the W, open to the E

Warning
Rocks and shallows break to N and S of the approach line

Depth restrictions
Inner harbour dries

Night entry
Possible to the anchorages

Tidal information
HW PdG –0020
LW PdG –0015

Mean height of tide (m)

MHWS	MHWN	MLWN	MLWS
4.0	3.1	1.5	0.6

Tidal stream
Negligible

Berthing
In calm weather it may be possible to berth on outer side of outer wall

Facilities
Those of a fishing village

Charts
BA 1153 (10) (old 1151)
Spanish 404A (25)

Weather
Cabo Peñas Ch 26 at 0840,1240, 2010
Navtex D

Radio and telephone
None

Rear leading mark   Harbour   Breaking offliers

Juan de Melao

255°

Luanco looking WSW

PILOTAGE

Approaches

From N

Keep at least 600m from the shore or outside the 10m line to avoid Bajo Sierra del Peon which extends to the E ½M to the N of Juan de Melao.

From E or S

From ⊕585 pick up the leading line of the whitened breakwater end (Fl.R.3s) and the white conical tower (Oc.R.8s) 255° amongst the houses. This line is hard to see by day but the conspicuous church tower will give an indication.

Entrance

The harbour dries and there are very unlikely to be any berths on the inside walls.

Anchoring

Either in 2m+ to the S of the approach line before the moorings are reached or at Juan de Melao in the same depth behind the breakwater; the bottom is sand and flat but with rock patches. The latter is probably more protected from any sea or swell but it is a 10-minute walk to the bright lights.

Berthing

In calm weather it may be possible to lie alongside the E face of the harbour breakwater which is used by coasters, and where there are some steps and a crane.

Ashore in Luanco

Luanco always seems more pretentious than it actually is, but it is a happy little resort with a small fishing fleet which is still active. Good for an overnight or lunch stop in good weather.

Facilities

A water tap by the inner harbour; diesel pump by the YC on the basin; a slip and a 2.5-tonne crane; a

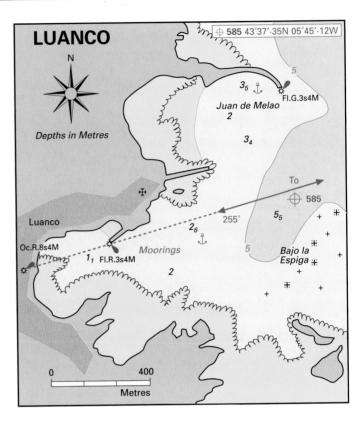

number of good restaurants round the harbour and an adequate variety of shops; *supermercado* 5 minutes by taxi.

Leisure

Good beaches to the N and S. The Maritime Museum of Asturias by the harbour is worth a visit.

Travel

Local buses to Avilés connect with the coastal rail and bus services; nearest airport Asturias (15km).

95 Ensenada de Lumeres

Cat D

Bay with good holding and sheltered from the W, 1 mile S of Cabo Peñas

⊕586 Lumeres 43°39′.43N 05°48′.50W

Old BA chart 1151 is the largest-scale chart of the area.

The centre of the bay lies about 1M S of Cabo Peñas and is bounded by the high Isla del Castro to the N and Punta de la Narvata to the S. From ⊕586 a track of about 240° will lead in to the centre and an anchorage in a suitable depth selected, on a reported clean sandy bottom.

The bay is sheltered from winds from the NW through W and S to SE.

In the SW corner there is an old masonry ore exporting quay which is reputed to give shelter from the N and NW.

Luanco inner harbour looking NE. Church on right

Rounding Cabo Peñas

⊕**587** 43°41'.07N 05°51'.25W

Cabo Peñas is one of the most salient points on the coast and, as well as rocks and shallows off, it has a rough and uneven bottom extending N. A good offing should always be allowed and ⊕587 makes a prudent allowance.

The tidal stream off the cape sets SE when the tide is rising and SW when it is falling and increases the seas.

Opposing winds often occur in the vicinity, with strong NE or E winds to the E and SW or W winds to the W.

The lighthouse is a pale grey octagonal tower on a building (Fl(3)15s115m35M) near the point with the air radio beacon (PS 297.5, 50 miles, H24) in it.

96 Avilés

Cat A*

Considerable industrial and commercial port which has recently introduced some facilities for yachts up river

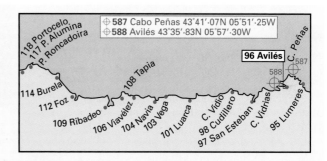

Location
43°36'.00N 05°57'.00W

Shelter
Good round the first bend

Warning
Bajo el Peton 3M to the E breaks in heavy weather; in the red sector of Punta del Castillo light

Depth restrictions
8m in entrance; 7m in channel

Night entry
Very well lit but no leading lights

Tidal information
HW PdG –0050
LW PdG –0030

Mean height of tide (m)

MHWS	MHWN	MLWN	MLWS
4.2	2.8	1.6	0.3

Tidal stream
Up to 2½ knots on the flood, more on the ebb

Berthing
On pontoons 2½M up river

Facilities
Those of a major city

Charts
BA 1108 (200), 1142 (7.5)
Spanish 405A (25), 4052 (7.5)

Weather
Cabo Peñas Ch 26 at 0840, 1240, 2010
Navtex D

Radio
Ch 12, 16 call sign *Avilés Practicos*

Telephone
Turismo ☎ 985 54 43 25

PILOTAGE

Approaches

Warning

A danger in the approaches is Bajo el Peton with 6.9m on it which breaks in heavy weather. It is covered by the red sector of Punta del Castillo light. ½M to the SSE of it lies Los Anuales with 0.7m which is just outside the red sector but is also just off a direct track from the W.

From ⊕588 the harbour entrance bearing 095° should be visible and obvious by day or night. There are no leading marks or lights but Punta de la Forcada (Fl.R.5s), the white sector of Punta del Castillo (Oc.WR.5s) and a succession of Fl.R lights up the N side of the entrance channel, together with a Fl(2)G.7s) on the end of the S training wall, followed by a succession of Fl.G lights up the S side of the channel, should make the way clear.

Entrance

Watch should be kept on Ch 12 and 16 before and during entry. There are also visual signals displayed at the station at Punta del Castillo and the Pilot House which is at the E end of the S bank of the entrance channel; they are:

3 vertical red lights or balls – Port closed
1 red light or ball – Caution bad weather.

Having regard to these, proceed up the centre of the entrance channel on 095° keeping to starboard if any shipping is met.

The power line halfway up Fundeadoro del Monumento has 48m clearance.

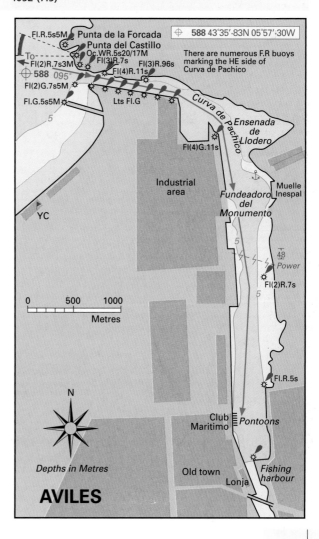

AVILES

Berthing

There are no alongside berths suitable for yachts until the new pontoons are reached 2½M up the river on the W bank. They are situated 400m short of where the river narrows into the fishing harbour below the low bridge which ends the navigation. They have fingers on them but anything longer than 12m may find difficulty, although there is reported to be plenty of water at the fingers.

Fishing boats go past here at speed.

Moorings

None available for visiting yachts.

Anchoring

The openings on the N bank in the outer channel and Ensenada de Llodero all dry and have steep sides. The best anchorage is at the N end of Fundeadoro del Monumento on the W bank as indicated on the plan in 4m clear of moorings. There is a landing stage here and the bus route to Avilés town is ½M inland.

With the exception that an ebb stream into a westerly gale would not be a propitious time to enter, Avilés is an all-weather port.

It is not a particularly attractive harbour, with a 3-mile haul up through drab and sometimes derelict surroundings.

Nevertheless, yachting is now recognised with the provision of pontoons up near the old town and some allocation for visitors up to about 12m in a good depth. The Club Maritimo de Balandran behind the pontoons is a sports fishing club but glad to see visiting yachts.

The historic centre of the old town close by is a pleasant contrast to the grubby industrialisation of the rest.

Ashore in Avilés

Facilities

Water on the pontoons and electricity expected; Gasoleo A from a pump at the fishing harbour; good variety of shops in the old town and an excellent market especially on Mondays; chandlers generally catering for the fishermen by the *lonja*; repair facilities of all kinds but mainly orientated to fishing and commercial. There is a first-class yacht club (Real Club Náutico de Salinas) which welcomes visitors if a UK membership card is produced and a tie is worn – but it is good 2M walk to get there.

Leisure

The old town and the 12th-century church of Sabugo are worth a visit and there is a great variety of restaurants and cafés.

Fiestas

The main festival is on Ash Wednesday when the whole town is given over to the event. Also on 8 April, 18–20 August and 20–31 August.

Punta del Castillo

Avilés looking ESE

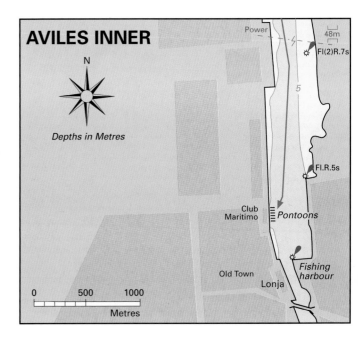

Avilés pontoons on W bank looking SE towards fishing harbour

IV. San Esteban to Puerto Alumina Española

Cabo Peñas to Punta Roncadoira

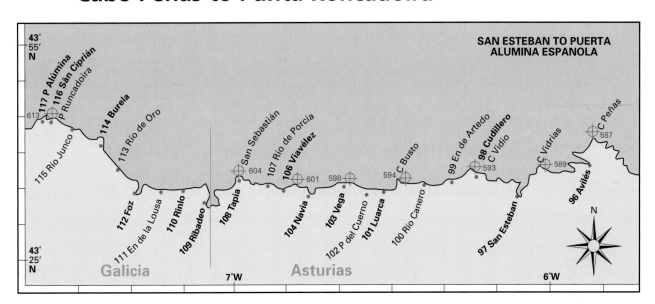

On the eastern half of the coast the high mountains are some distance inland and while the coast is only slightly indented, the river mouths are steep-to with low rocky cliffs and a few outlying islands. The major port is Avilés but this is a doubtful entrance in westerly storms. There are several small ports for use in moderate and fair weather.

The western half, W of Tapia, has high mountains near the coast, which becomes more and more indented with deep estuaries, the first of the Rias Altas. The only port of refuge in storm conditions is Puerto Alúmina Española, a huge commercial harbour at the W end of this section; but Burela, a major fishing port, is well protected and Ria de Ribadeo can be entered in nearly all conditions and there are now good facilities for yachts there.

There are also a few minor ports which can only be used under suitable conditions of fair weather and little swell.

Warnings

There are no distant offlying dangers on this coast but the main problem can be the enormous swell which occasionally comes from far out in the Atlantic and breaks with fury over any banks, rocks and beaches, making many entrances impassable and some harbours untenable.

In N or NE winds the clouds may come low enough to obscure or limit the ranges of the higher lighthouses.

The prevalence of fog increases the further W especially in the summer months.

Under storm and gale conditions all promontories

WAYPOINTS

⊕587	Cabo Penas	43°41′.07N	05°51′.25W
⊕589	C. Vidrias	43°35′.08N	06°01′.75W
⊕593	C. Vidio	43°36′.33N	06°14′.69W
⊕594	C. Busto	43°35′.15N	06°29′.10W
⊕598	Romanellas	43°34′.93N	06°37′.79W
⊕601	P. Engaramada	43°34′.94N	06°46′.09W
⊕604	San Sebastián	43°35′.00N	06°57′.08W
⊕613	Los Farallones	43°42′.55N	07°23′.59W

should be given a wide berth due to the confused seas off them which extend some miles offshore.

Lifeboats and lifesaving equipment are maintained at Avilés, Luarca and Ribadeo.

Tidal streams

Tidal streams close to the coast are E-going on the flood, W-going on the ebb.

Currents

Currents are modified by the effect of recent or prevailing winds which may nullify or reverse the tidal flow. With NE winds, strong W-going currents will be experienced; with NW winds the reverse. These winds, when prolonged, will also effect the depth of water; NW winds increase the depth, NE winds decrease it, the effects being most noticeable in ports and estuaries.

Coastal Radio Stations

There are VHF coastal radio stations at Cabo Peñas and Navia. Details of services and the weather forecasts can be found in *Technical and navigational information* above and in each port.

Planning Guide

Distances between ports in nautical miles
Ports with marinas in **bold** type

		Avilés	S Esteban	Cudillero	E de Artedo	R de Camnero	Luarca	P del Cuerno	Vega	Navia	C Ortiguera	Viavélez	R de Porcía	Tapia	Ribadeo	Rinlo	E de Lousa	Foz	R de Oro	Burela	R Junco	S Ciprian	P Alumina
A	Avilés		6	9	11	27	30	33	35	39	40	45	46	50	54	57	58	63	65	68	71	73	74
C	S Esteban	6		3	5	21	24	27	29	33	34	39	40	44	48	51	52	57	59	62	65	67	68
C	Cudillero	9	3		2	18	21	24	26	30	31	36	37	41	45	48	49	54	56	59	62	64	65
D	E de Artedo	11	5	2		16	19	22	24	28	29	34	35	39	43	46	47	52	54	57	60	62	63
D	R de Canero	27	21	18	16		3	6	8	12	13	18	19	23	27	30	31	36	38	41	44	46	47
C	Luarca	30	24	21	19	3		3	5	9	10	13	14	18	22	25	26	31	33	36	39	41	42
D	P del Cuerno	33	27	24	22	6	3		2	6	7	10	11	15	19	22	23	28	30	33	36	38	39
C	Vega	35	29	26	24	8	5	2		4	5	8	9	13	17	20	21	26	28	31	34	36	37
C	Navia	39	33	30	28	12	9	6	4		1	7	8	12	16	19	20	25	27	30	33	35	36
D	C Ortigueira	40	34	31	29	13	10	7	5	1		5	6	10	14	17	18	23	25	28	31	33	34
C	Viavélez	45	39	36	34	18	13	10	8	7	5		1	5	9	12	13	18	20	23	26	28	29
D	R de Porcía	46	40	37	35	19	14	11	9	8	6	1		4	8	11	12	17	19	22	25	27	28
C	Tapia	50	44	41	39	23	18	15	13	12	10	5	4		4	7	8	13	15	18	21	23	24
B	Ribadeo	54	48	45	43	27	22	19	17	16	14	9	8	4		3	4	9	11	14	17	19	20
C	Rinlo	57	51	48	46	30	25	22	20	19	17	12	11	7	3		1	8	10	13	16	18	19
D	E de Lousa	58	52	49	47	31	26	23	21	20	18	13	12	8	4	1		5	7	10	13	15	16
C	Foz	63	57	54	52	36	31	28	26	25	23	18	17	13	9	8	5		2	5	8	10	11
D	R de Oro	65	59	56	54	38	33	30	28	27	25	20	19	15	11	10	7	2		3	6	8	9
A*	Burela	68	62	59	57	41	36	33	31	30	28	23	22	18	14	13	10	5	3		3	5	6
D	R Junco	71	65	62	60	44	39	36	34	33	31	26	25	21	17	16	13	8	6	3		2	3
C	S Ciprian	73	67	64	62	46	41	38	36	35	33	28	27	23	19	18	15	10	8	5	2		1
A	P Alumina	74	68	65	63	47	42	39	37	36	34	29	28	24	20	19	16	11	9	6	3	1	

To the east it is 7 miles to E de Lumeres from Avilés

To the West it is 3 miles to R de Portocelo from P Alumina

WAYPOINTS

⊕587	Cabo Peñas	43°41′.07N	05°51′.25W
⊕588	Avilés	43°35′.83N	05°57′.30W
⊕589	C. Vidrias	43°35′.08N	06°01′.75W
⊕590	San Esteban de Pravia	43°34′.60N	06°04′.50W
⊕591	Cudillero	43°34′.54N	06°06′.20W
⊕592	Ens de Artedo	43°35′.20N	06°11′.40W
⊕593	C. Vidio	43°36′.33N	06°14′.69W
⊕594	C. Busto	43°35′.15N	06°29′.10W
⊕595	Río Canero	43°33′.54N	06°29′.18W
⊕596	Luarca	43°33′.45N	06°32′.32W
⊕597	P. del Cuerno	43°34′.08N	06°35′.68W
⊕598	Romanellas	43°34′.93N	06°37′.79W
⊕599	Vega	43°34′.43N	06°39′.13W
⊕600	Navia	43°34′.14N	06°43′.42W
⊕601	P. Engaramada	43°34′.94N	06°46′.09W
⊕602	Viavélez	43°34′.42N	06°51′.05W
⊕603	R. de Porcia	43°34′.25N	06°52′.90W
⊕604	San Sebastián	43°35′.00N	06°57′.08W
⊕605	Tapia	43°34′.35N	06°57′.39W
⊕606	Ribadeo	43°33′.76N	07°02′.27W
⊕607	Rinlo	43°34′.23N	07°06′.28W
⊕608	En de la Lousa	43°34′.23N	07°07′.59W
⊕609	Foz	43°34′.73N	07°14′.20W
⊕610	Río de Oro	43°35′.44N	07°16′.28W
⊕611	Burela	43°39′.24N	07°19′.08W
⊕612	Río Junco	43°42′.20N	07°24′.10W
⊕613	Los Farallones	43°42′.55N	07°23′.59W

New wall at San Juan

97 San Esteban de Pravia

Cat C

A former coal exporting port now given over to shipbreaking; a limited entrance with few attractions inside

Location
43°33´.00N 06°05´.00W

Shelter
Good inside

Warning
Entrance dangerous in strong N winds; variable depths in channel

Depth restrictions
2m in entrance
0.5m in basin entrance

Night entry
Well lit plus leading lights

Tidal information
HW PdG –0020
LW PdG –0010

Mean height of tide (m)

MHWS	MHWN	MLWN	MLWS
4.0	3.1	1.7	0.6

Tidal information
Ebb up to 5 knots at entrance at springs or in spate

Berthing
Alongside berth possible in basin

Facilities
Some shops and restaurant; fuel

Charts
BA 1133 (15)
Spanish 934 (40)

Weather
Cabo Peñas Ch 26 0840, 1240, 2010

Radio and telephone
None

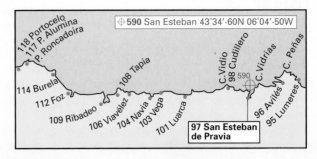

590 San Esteban 43°34´·60N 06°04´·50W

118 Portocelo
117 P. Alumina
P. Roncadoira
114 Burela
112 Foz
109 Ribadeo
106 Viavélez
104 Navia
103 Vega
101 Luarca
108 Tapia
C. Vidio
98 Cudillero
C. Vidrias
C. Peñas
96 Avilés
95 Lumeres
97 San Esteban de Pravia

Juan
Basin entrance
Contradique
206°

San Esteban de Pravia looking SSW at HW+0100

PILOTAGE

Warning

The depths shown on both BA and Spanish charts and this plan must not be relied on as they change constantly depending on how busy the resident dredger has been. Any swell breaks readily on the steep gradient at the entrance. HW–0100 to HW is best time to enter.

Approach

By day or night

A first approach by night is not recommended as the leading lights are limited. From ⊕590 identify the end of Dique del Oeste (Fl(2)12s15M) and the first leading line (both white cylindrical towers with red stripes, front Q, rear Iso.4s) 206°. Pass between the ends of Dique del Oeste and the end of the E training wall (truncated pyramid tower Fl(4)G.11s) on this track.

Entrance

Once past the head of Dique del Oeste, close the W wall to 50m and keep this distance off it past the first elbow, the first two leading lights and a Fl.G.5s. Between this and the next F(2)G.7s the second lot of leading lights (both F.R on grey poles) on 182° may become visible but they are inconspicuous and the lights very dim. Whether identified or not, continue to favour the W bank until the entrance to the basin opens up beyond the Fl(4)G.11s and the old overhead loading towers; do not cut the corner but enter in the middle of the opening on a track of about 270°.

Berthing

When not working, the dredger berths in the first corner beyond the overhead loaders in one of the deeper parts of the quay and can be doubled up on. The pontoon beyond the red brick railway station is not suitable for larger yachts as the fingers are very short. The next pontoon is private. Otherwise select any free space on the long W wall, which is reasonably flat, in a suitable depth which varies

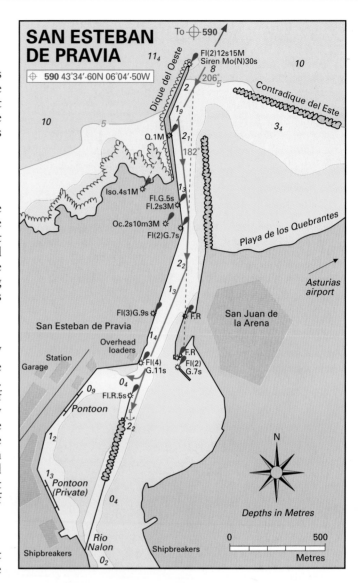

from 0.9m to 1.3m. Stay close to the W wall as the channel between it and the large drying area is narrow.

Anchoring

There is good holding in the main channel above the basin entrance in mud and sand; sound around until a suitable depth is found.

There is also a deeper anchorage 1M further up the river in better depths and prettier surroundings There is reputed to be 1m+ in the channel beyond the ship-breakers on the E side. Continue until a castle is seen on the top of a bluff to port and anchor just beyond it well over on the NE side in 2–3m. The river turns back to the W after this and is crossed by a low bridge reachable by dinghy; there is a small *supermercado* by the crossroads here.

Ashore in San Esteban and San Juan

This was once a busy coal harbour and much work to quays and breakwaters has been done since this trade ceased some 15 years ago; this and the presence of a resident dredger indicate that perhaps there is a future for the port and area.

The dredger at its berth, with the old overhead loading towers on its port bow. San Juan is through the basin entrance beyond

San Esteban de Pravia looking WSW. Behind the red brick station can be seen the red garage sign

Facilities

Water points on the quay and pontoon; fuel by cans from the garage behind the railway station; some shops and the occasional restaurant in both San Esteban and San Juan; there are several cranes (which look in working order) and slips at the ship-breakers.

Leisure

Few exciting opportunities, although the cave paintings at La Peña and Candamos nearby are worth seeing and a dinghy trip up the river goes into nicer country.

Travel

The railway branch line joins up with the main E/W line and the motorway is close to the S. Asturias airport which is at the top of the hill above San Juan, with flights to Madrid.

98 Cudillero

Cat C

Busy fishing port which provides some pontoons for local yachts in the new harbour but little provision for visitors

Location
43°34′.00N 06°09′.00W

Shelter
Good inside

Warning
Not an entrance in strong northerlies

Depth restrictions
5m in entrance and inside

Night entry
There are leading lights

Tidal information
HW PdG –0010
LW PdG –0010

Mean height of tide

MHWS	MHWN	MLWN	MLWS
4.1	3.2	1.6	0.5

Tidal stream
Negligible

Berthing
Pontoon space may be available

Facilities
Those of a small fishing port

Charts
BA 1108 (200)
Spanish 405A (10)

Weather
Cabo Peñas Ch 26 at 0840,1240, 2010

Radio and telephone
Turismo ☎ 985 59 01 18

Lonja and industry

Old harbour

Village

Punta Rebollera

200°

Yacht pontoons

Cudillero looking WSW

PILOTAGE

Approach

The only dangers near the approach are Islotes las Colinas which must be given a good berth if coming from the W.

By day or night

From ⊕591 off Punta Rebollera with its white tower and red roof (Oc(4)16s), the entrance can be identified. The leading line by day to the W of the lighthouse is not so conspicuous but at night the front light is Fl(3)G.9s and the rear Fl(3)R.9s.

Entrance

Leave the leading line as indicated on the plan and round Isla Osa at about 20m off, keeping a good look out for vessels leaving. Turn to starboard at the end of the narrow channel to avoid the rocks on the S side and head round the moorings to the NW of Isla Osa before heading for the pontoon.

Berthing

There are no visitors' berths and the fingers are short so the chances of finding a suitable berth are small. The gate from the pontoon is usually locked so the dinghy must be used to get ashore anyway (this is the quickest way to the village).

Moorings and anchoring

There are a number of private and fishing boat moorings which can be picked up or doubled up on but ask at the *lonja* before settling down. There are some open spaces to anchor in, but do not obstruct the channel between entrance and fish quay. A trip line would be prudent.

Ashore in Cudillero

The old harbour to the S of the entrance is not used now and the arched quays make an uncomfortable berth. The fishing complex is quite detached from the old village which has charm and provides a modicum of entertainment.

Facilities

Water on the pontoons; Gasoleo B is still available (2005) to all comers at the fish quay; there are a number of shops and a good variety of restaurants; market day Friday; repairs, slipping and craneage in the fish complex.

Leisure

13th- and 16th-century churches and a nice climb to the top of the hill or to the lighthouse.

Travel

The main rail and bus routes pass close to the S of the village; nearest airport Asturias 15km to the E with flights to Madrid.

Fiestas

The big fiesta is on St Peter's day (29 June) when the village is given over to L'Amuravela, a public speech in the local *pixueto* language, after which there are extensive celebrations.

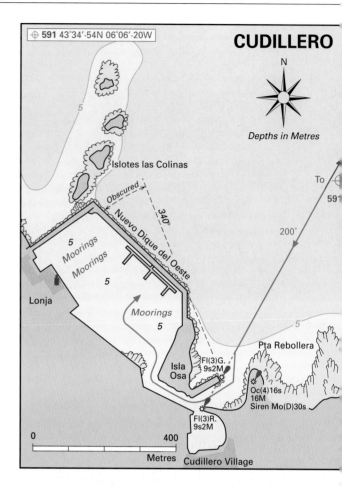

Looking NNW into harbour; pontoons behind rocks on right

Looking from pontoons S towards entrance; roofs of village visible above Isla Osa

Ensenada de Artedo looking SW

99 Ensenada de Artedo

Cat D

⊕592 43°35′.20N 06°11′.40W

This wide bay with a long beach lies 3M to the W of Cudillero under Punta Austera which provides good shelter from the S to NW. It has a clean and sandy bottom with good holding in 2–10m.

The motorway crosses the head of the bay above the beach.

Ensenada y Río de Canero looking SE

100 Ensenada y Río de Canero

Cat D

⊕595 43°33′.54N 06°29′.18W

A handy anchorage lying 2M E of Luarca, under Cabo Busto, to take refuge from the NE winds in the summer, 5–10m in sand.

The río entrance is obstructed by a sand spit and a bar that dries.

101 Luarca

Cat C

Very attractive town in a steep valley, with a busy fishing fleet and arrangements for visiting yachts

Location
43°33′.00N 06°32′.00W

Shelter
Reasonable at yacht berths

Warning
Stay close to leading line on entry

Depth restrictions
5m in entrance; 2.6m inside

Night entry
Well lit

Tidal information
HW PdG –0005
LW PdG +0005

Mean height of tide (m)

MHWS	MHWN	MLWN	MLWS
4.2	3.3	1.6	0.7

Berthing
On buoys, stern to wall

Facilities
Those of small fishing port

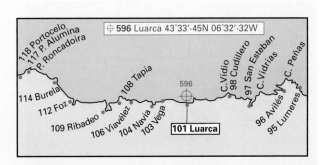

⊕ 596 Luarca 43°33′·45N 06°32′·32W

Charts
BA 1133 (15)
Spanish 933 (40),4061 (10)

Weather
Navia Ch 60 at 0840, 1240, 2010

Telephone
Turismo ☎ 985 64 00 83

A lifeboat is maintained here

PILOTAGE

Approach

By day or night

At ⊕596 align the two leading marks/lights (white columns with red bands front Fl.5s rear Oc.4s) which will almost be in line with the E breakwater light (white concrete tower Fl(3)R.9s) on 170° and keep very close to this line until course has to be altered round the E breakwater end.

Entrance

Deep (4m+) and straightforward; turn to port once inside to visitors' berths or inner entrance.

Berthing

There are 6 visitors' buoys along the inner side of the E breakwater; they are 6m apart and 35m from the wall; secure bow-to and take a stern line to the wall but do not haul in too close as the rubble at the base extends 3m. A disturbed berth in northerlies. There are no berths for yachts in the inner harbour which is usually full of fishing boats.

Anchoring

Outside as indicated on the plan in 2–3m. Anchoring is prohibited inside.

Ashore in Luarca

A very attractive town dating from the 13th century and nestling up the valley of the Río Negro. A whaling and trading port in the past, it is now a busy minor fishing harbour.

Facilities

Water from a tap by the *lonja*; Gasoleo A from pump as indicated but there is only 0.2m alongside and the wall has haul-off moorings from it; the attendant must be found at the Gasoleo B pump at

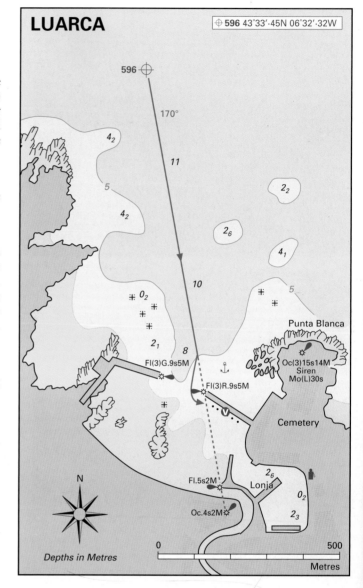

the *lonja*. Good variety of shops and an excellent market; usual fishing port slipping, craneage and repair facilities; good selection of restaurants.

Leisure

Lovely cliff walks and good beaches; a climb through the old village to the lighthouse past or through the cemetery is worthwhile.

Travel

The railway station is 1½M S and the main E/W road about the same distance; nearest airport Asturias 80km to the E.

Fiesta

Main fiesta 15–22 August; also 28 July.

Punta Blanca lt Cemetery   Lifeboat

170°

Luarca looking ESE

102 Punta del Cuerno

Cat D

⊕**597** 43°34′.08N 06°35′.68W

The anchorages under the E side of Punta del Cuerno lie 3M W of Luarca and are well sheltered from the W off Playa de Arnela or Playa de Sebugo.

Approach from ⊕597 on at least 180° to avoid Baja la Vaquiña which has 0.4m over it and breaks in the least swell. Otherwise it is clean sand and good holding.

The small village of Sebugo lies on the main road ¾M S of the bay.

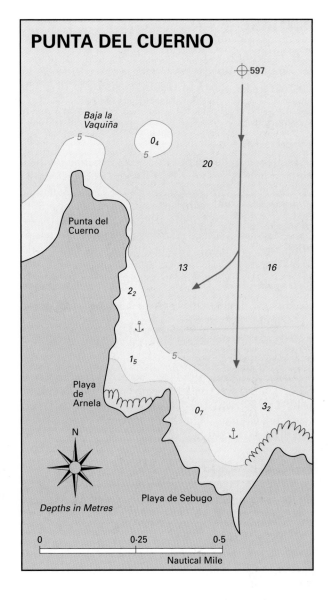

PUNTA DEL CUERNO

Vega looking S at half tide

103 Vega

Cat C

Tiny old whaling port recently enlarged but with narrow entrance and very subject to swell; only simple shops and cafés ashore

Location
43°34′.00N 06°36′.00N

Shelter
Exposed to swell in outer harbour

Warning
Stay close to leading line

Depth restrictions
2m in entrance;
1.4–2.2m alongside

Night entry
Possible but not recommended

Tidal information
HW PdG –0005
LW PdG +0005

Mean height of tide (m)

MHWS	MHWN	MLWN	MLWS
4.1	3.1	1.5	0.5

Berthing
Alongside inner side of breakwater

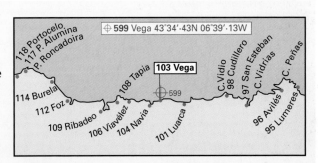

Facilities
Few

Charts
No large-scale
BA 1108 (200)
Spanish 933 (40)

Weather
Navia Ch 60 0840, 1240, 2010
Navtex D

Radio and telephone
None

PILOTAGE

Warning

It would be unwise to attempt this entrance in northerly conditions of strong winds or swell when there will be a considerable surge inside.

Approach

By day or night

A first time night entry is not recommended as the leading lights are only 1M visibility and the line is critical in the later stages. Between HW–0200 and HW from ⊕599 identify the leading marks on 150°: the front is a tall white triangle which often has flags flying from it and the rear a white mast on a white building; they should just be open of the end of the breakwater.

Entrance

Round the breakwater closely keeping close to it once rounded.

Berthing

There is 2.2m at the outer end of the breakwater shoaling to 1.6m near the steps; there are two ladders and some bollards with a new and smooth wall. The SW wall has 1.4m but is often encumbered with small boats. The inner harbour dries and is usually full of fishing boats.

Ashore in Vega

It is hard to believe that this tiny place was once a thriving whaling port although the small fishing fleet is still very active.

Facilities

Water from the *lonja* or cafés; only Gasoleo B by pump; limited shops and restaurants; usual fishing boat support at *lonja*.

Leisure

Nice walks, simple meals.

Travel

The main road and railway are 5km south.

Fiesta

22 May Santa Rita.

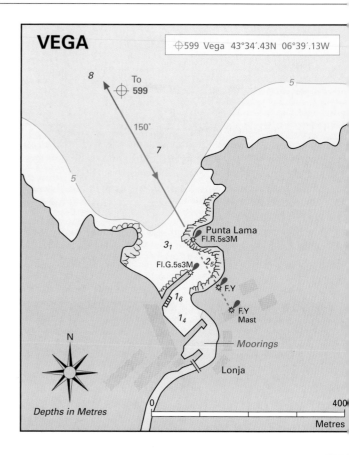

VEGA

⊕599 Vega 43°34'.43N 06°39'.13W

To 599

150°

Punta Lama Fl.R.5s3M

Fl.G.5s3M

F.Y

F.Y Mast

Moorings

Lonja

N

Depths in Metres

0 400 Metres

Outer harbour looking NE; berths on the left

Entrance to inner harbour with the imposing *lonja* beyond

A harpoon gun is the only relic of the whaling past of Vega

104 Navia

Cat C

Small provincial town with an active shipbuilding industry, entry at around HW only with no swell; some facilities and few recreations

Location
43°34′N 06°44′W

Shelter
Good inside

Warning
Bar has 0m on it and varies

Depth restrictions
As above, 2m in channel, 3m at pontoon

Night entry
No lights

Tidal information
HW PdG −0000
LW PdG +0005

Mean height of tide (m)

MHWS	MHWN	MLWN	MLWS
4.1	2.9	1.4	0.2

Tidal stream
Up to 3 knots on the ebb

Berthing
On pontoon or anchor off town

Facilities
None specifically for yachts

Charts
BA 1108 (200)
Spanish 4061 (10)

Weather
Navia Ch 60 at 0840, 1240, 2010
Navtex D

Radio and telephone
None

⊕ **600** Navia 43°34′·14N 06°43′·42W

118 Portocelo
117 P. Alumina
P. Roncadoira
114 Burela
112 Foz
109 Ribadeo
106 Viavélez
103 Vega
108 Tapia
104 Navia
600
101 Luarca
C. Vidio
98 Cudillero
97 San Esteban
C. Vidrias
C. Peñas
96 Avilés
95 Lumeres

Ship waiting off the bar

Shipbuilding yard

Pontoon for yachts

Basin for local boats

Navia looking NNW at half tide

PILOTAGE

Approach

By day only

Cabo de San Augustin with its black and white banded lighthouse is conspicuous on the approach from ⊕600 on a track of 190°. If there is any swell, stand off and observe the bar to see if it is breaking; allow a depth of 0m but there may be more. If in doubt, anchor as indicated to the SE of Cabo de San Augustin in 2–3m sand and good holding.

Entrance

The E training wall covers near HW as does the outer end of the W one. Provided there is no swell and enough depth of water, head for the middle, favouring the W bank initially. Depths increase once inside.

Berthing

There is 3m at the seaward end of the pontoon outside the basin, 1.4m at the bridge end and visitors are expected to berth here. The basin is for locals only drawing less than 1.3m.

Anchoring

Anchor in 2–3m mud off the basin entrance if the pontoon is full.

Ashore in Navia

With its limiting bar it is a surprising place to find a thriving shipbuilding yard which produces large fishing boats, tugs and service craft. Apart from this and some good restaurants the town has little to offer.

Facilities

None on the pontoon; water from a tap in the basin; fuel by can from a garage over the bridge; slips, cranes and all repairs facilities at the shipyard. An adequate variety of shops and restaurants in the town.

Leisure

The town is only commercial but there are some good beaches nearby. The best diversion is probably a dinghy trip up the river which runs for many miles through pleasant country.

Fiestas

11 and 17 August water festivities.

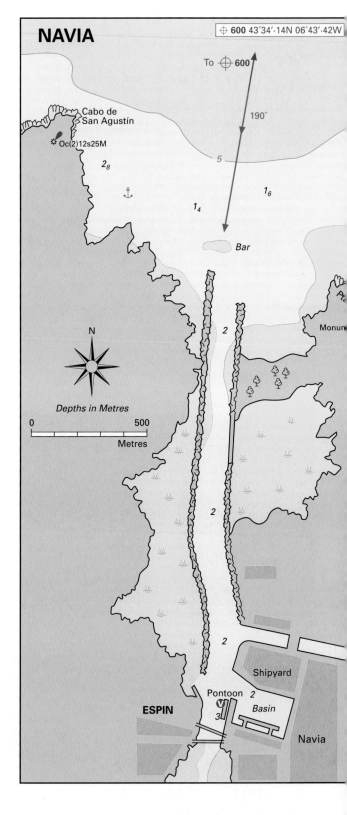

105 Cabo de San Augustin

Cat D

⊕600 43°34′.14N 06°43′.42W

The cape provides some shelter from the E and the W. The anchorage to the E of the Cape is shown on the plan above. The anchorage to the W in Cala de Ortiguera gives some shelter from the E if tucked well in to the small río, 1–3m sand.

106 Viavélez

Cat C

Small rock-bound harbour with an entrance only for the brave or rash except in the calmest conditions

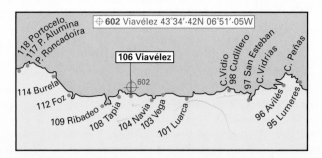

Location
43°34´.00N 06°50´.00W

Shelter
Minimal in any swell

Warning
Narrow and dangerous entrance

Depth restrictions
1–3m in entrance, 0.5m inside, 0m at quay

Night entry
Lit but not recommended

Tidal information
HW PdG –0005
LW PdG +0005

Mean height of tide (m)

MHWS	MHWN	MLWN	MLWS
4.1	2.9	1.4	0.2

Berthing
Drying alongside; possibly anchor

Facilities
One crane, one restaurant

Charts
BA 1108 (200)
Spanish 933 (inset (5))

Weather
Tapia Ch 60 at 0840,1240, 2010
Navtex D

Radio and telephone
None

Viavélez looking S

PILOTAGE

Approach

By day

From ⊕602 it may be possible to identify the entrance from the houses at the back of the harbour or pick out the light structure on the N breakwater which is a truncated conical masonry tower with a red top. Make good a track of about 140° keeping the two breakwater light structures open.

Entrance

The decision to continue or retire needs to be made before the N breakwater end is reached. If all is well, round the S breakwater end at about 20m off and pass through the gap with the inner breakwater.

Berthing

Muelle de Gudin has an off-lying above-water rock off its end marked by a beacon. The S side of the quay has 0.4m at the end reducing to 0m alongside with a flat bottom; fishing boats dry out alongside it and it may be occupied. The E/W wall is rough and sloping.

Anchoring

It may be possible to anchor behind the inner breakwater but a stern line will be needed and a sandy area between the rocky patches should be selected.

Ashore

Water tap on quay; small restaurant by the slip; nearest shops in Caridad village 2km up the hill.

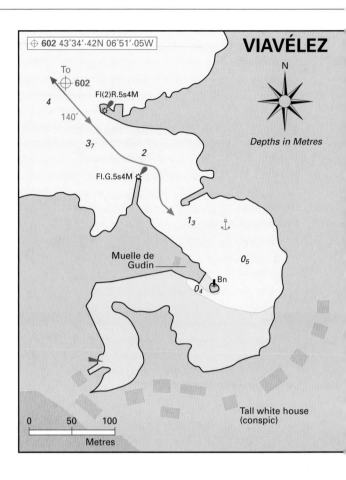

VIAVÉLEZ

⊕ 602 43°34'·42N 06°51'·05W

To ⊕ 602

Fl(2)R.5s4M

140°

Fl.G.5s4M

Muelle de Gudin

Bn

Tall white house (conspic)

N

Depths in Metres

0   50   100

Metres

The entrance looking N in moderate conditions

Muelle de Gudin with fishing boat alongside

107 Ensenada y Río de Porcia

Cat D

Rock-encumbered bay giving some shelter from the E

⊕**603** 43°34´.25N 06°52´.90W

Ensenada y Río de Porcia looking SSW

Approach and entrance

Spanish chart 933(40) is the only one showing some details of this río.

Bajo las Devesas with 3m lies 600m N of Isoletes del Boy in the centre of the photo and should be avoided

From ⊕603 make good a track of 140° until Isoletes del Boy can be identified and leave them to port on a track of about 120° to find an anchorage in a suitable depth clear of rocks.

Not an easy anchorage and for fine weather only. The río was used for many years for the export of ore.

108 Tapia

Cat C

Uncomfortable harbour in any swell from the N or W with few berths for yachts; attractive town with lively bars and restaurants

Location
43°34´.00N 06°57´.00W

Shelter
Not good in W or NW conditions

Warning
Strong surge in harbour in W or NW winds

Depth restrictions
4m in entrance, 2–4m in outer harbour

Night entry
Lit but no leading lights

Tidal information
HW PdG –0005
LW PdG +0005

Mean height of tide (m)

MHWS	MHWN	MLWN	MLWS
4.1	2.9	1.4	0.2

Berthing
Alongside the E end of fuel quay

⊕ **605** Tapia 43°34´.35N 06°57´.39W

118 Portocelo
117 P. Alumina
P. Roncadoira
114 Burela
112 Foz
109 Ribadeo
106 Viavélez
104 Navia
103 Vega
101 Luarca
C. Vidio
98 Cudillero
97 San Esteban
C. Vidrias
C. Peñas
96 Avilés
95 Lumeres

108 Tapia 605

Facilities
None for yachts; usual shops, etc.

Charts
No large-scale
BA 1108 (200)
Spanish 933 (40)

Weather
Navia Ch 60 at 0840, 1240 and 2010
Navtex D

Radio and telephone
Turismo ☎ 985 47 29 68

San Sebastián light · Fuel berth · Slip

Tapia looking E

PILOTAGE

Approach

In fine or easterly weather only.

From the E

By day or night

Cabo San Sebastián (Fl(2+1)19s) must be given a berth of at least ½M, or pass through ⊕604 to clear the shoals before turning S and leaving Islote Orrio de Tapia ¼M to port to join the entry track.

From the W

The lighthouse and buildings on Cabo San Sebastián, and the church above the town, are both conspicuous. From ⊕605 make good a 090° track towards the entrance keeping the breakwater ends (Fl(2)R.7s and Fl.G.5s) just open.

Entrance

Straightforward in 4m; give the breakwater ends at least 20m.

Berthing

The only possible alongside berths are from the fuel pump inwards but this is uncomfortable in any swell and often occupied by small fishing boats.

Anchoring

The N part of the harbour is the only possible anchoring space but it is rocky and foul. Worth a risk with a tripping line for a short stay if there is no alongside berth available.

Moorings

All private and all for small boats.

Ashore in Tapia

A pretty town of little historical interest, it is well patronised by surfers who keep it lively in the summer. The fishing fleet is small and apparently in decline which is not, perhaps, surprising with the insecurity of the harbour.

Facilities

Water tap on the quay; Gasoleo B only from the jetty pump; garage in village; crane and a substantial patent slip capable of taking large fishing boats; good selection of shops and restaurants.

Leisure

Good walks and beaches.

Travel

Close to the main E/W road, 5km to the railway. Nearest airport Asturias 130km to the E.

TAPIA

⊕ **604** San Sebastián 43°35'·00N 06°57'·08W
⊕ **605** Tapia 43°35'·00N 06°57'·08W

N

Depths in Metres

Islote Orrio de Tapia

Cabo San Sebastián

Fl(2+1)19s18M

Fl(2)R.7s4M

To ⊕ **605**   090°

Fl.G.5s3M

Moorings

0   400

Metres

Islote Orrio de Tapia   Cabo San Sebastián

Possible anchoring area   Fuel berth

Tapia looking NW over the harbour

109 Ribadeo

Cat B

Large and scenic estuary with a new marina below a bustling provincial town; a wide all-weather entrance

Location
43°33′N 07°02′W
The ria is the boundary between Asturias and Galicia

Shelter
Good in the marina

Warnings
The leading lines are hard to see. Banks above the bridge constantly change

Depth restrictions
Deep approach; 3-5m in marina; bridge clearance 30m

Night approach
Well lit plus leading lights

Tidal information
HW PdG –0005
LW PdG +0005

Mean height of tide (m)

MHWS	MHWN	MLWN	MLWS
4.1	2.9	1.4	0.2

Tidal stream
Up to 3 knots on the ebb past marina entrance

Berthing
Up to 18m on pontoons in 3–5m

Facilities
Most marina facilities; good shops

Charts
BA 1108 (200), 1122 (25)
Spanish 4071 (10)

Weather
Navia Ch 60 0840, 1240, 2010
Navtex D

Radio
None

Telephone
Club ☎ 982 13 11 44
Turismo ☎ 982 12 86 89

⊕ **606** Ribadeo 43°33′·76N 07°02′·27W

118 Portocelo
117 P. Alumina
P. Roncadoira
114 Burela
112 Foz
606
109 Ribadeo
108 Tapia
106 Viavélez
104 Navia
103 Vega
101 Luarca
C. Vidio
98 Cudillero
97 San Esteban
C. Vidrias
96 Avilés
95 Lumeres
C. Peñas

Castropol   Vegadeo   Porcillan marina

205°

Las Carrayas

140°

Pancha light

Ribadeo estuary. Entrance looking S

PILOTAGE

Approaches to Ribadeo

By day or night

⊕606 is on the outer leading line of 170° Punta Castrelius/Bridge Centre/Castropol spire At night proceed on 170° between Isla Pancha light (Fl(3+1)20s) and Punta de la Cruz light (Fl(4)R.11s) until the next leading line 140° of two red and white beacons (front Iso.R, rear Oc.R.4s) aligns. Continue on this line of 140° until Las Carrayas are abaft the beam and identify the final leading line 205° under the right hand arch of the bridge; this (front white column with red diamond VQ.R on Porcillan breakwater, rear white square on end of octagonal house Oc.R.2s) is not easy to identify by day or night. If in doubt by day the conspicuous red domed church on Ribadeo town skyline is almost on the same line on 205°. At night the Fl(2)G.7s and Fl(4)R.11s lights marking the centre arch of the bridge will assist.

Entrance to Porcillan

The bridge (clearance 30m) can be passed either under W or centre arches but keep to the W side if using the latter. Turn parallel to the Porcillan breakwater and enter between a Fl.G.5s and Fl.R.5s. There is at least 3m up to 300m from this breakwater.

Berthing at Porcillan

A *marinero* will usually meet arrivals and indicate a berth. There are 200 berths with some 20 kept for visitors up to about 20m. If in doubt or in a larger yacht, berth on one of the pontoon ends just inside the entrance. There is a reception berth under the offices by the slip.

Anchoring

The main channel runs close to the W bank and up to and beyond the fishing port in Darsena de Mirasol and an anchorage may be found in peace and quiet beyond.

Berthing at Figueras

There is an unmarked channel carrying 3m close along the NE shore to the town and shipbuilding yard at Figueras where there is a small boat harbour, some moorings with water and room to anchor in the channel.

Berthing at Castropol

The channel to Castropol from Figueras is reported to have shifted and shoaled and BA chart 1122 and Spanish 4071 cannot be relied on until the results of the survey (due in 2005) are published. The pontoon pier off the club used to have 1.4m alongside it and there was anchoring space in the channel off it in about 2m. The bottom is all sand and mud so an exploration on a rising tide would be possible.

Upstream to Vegadeo

There are no charts above Ribadeo but the estuary winds through attractive countryside some 5M to the country town of Vegadeo which is worth a visit at least by dinghy on the flood.

Banco Berlinga

Castropol spire

Front leading mark 205°

Porcillan marina looking SSE towards Castropol

RIBADEO

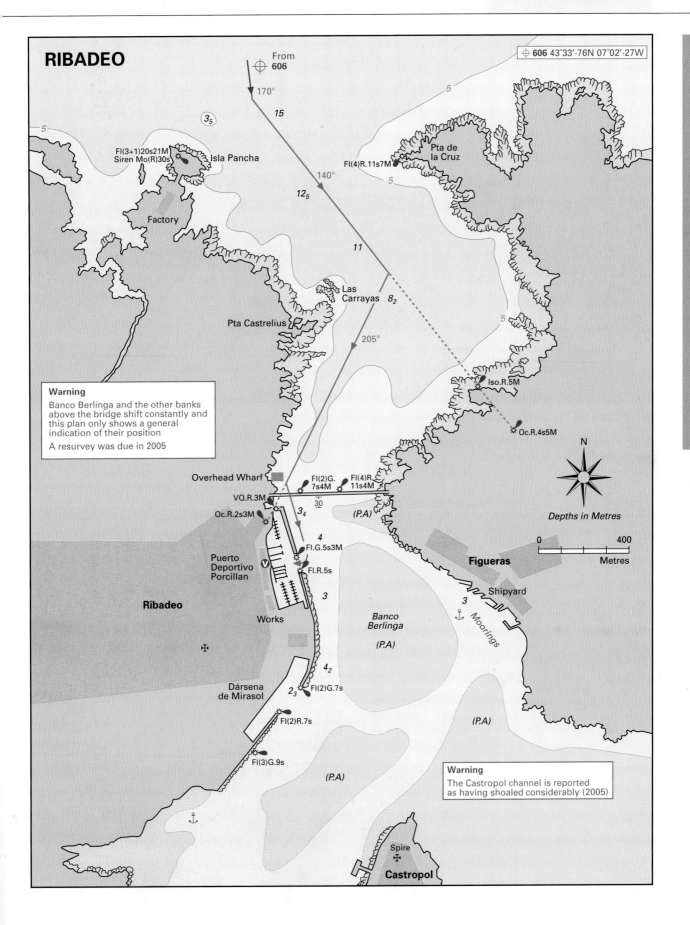

606 43°33'·76N 07°02'·27W

From **606**

170°

15

3₅

140°

Fl(3+1)20s21M
Siren Mo(R)30s   Isla Pancha

12₅

Factory

Pta de
la Cruz

Fl(4)R.11s7M

5

11

Las
Carrayas

Pta Castrelius

8₂

205°

5

Iso.R.5M

Warning

Banco Berlinga and the other banks
above the bridge shift constantly and
this plan only shows a general
indication of their position

A resurvey was due in 2005

Oc.R.4s5M

N

Overhead Wharf

Fl(2)G.
7s4M

Fl(4)R.
11s4M

VQ.R.3M

30

Oc.R.2s3M

3₄

(P.A)

Depths in Metres

0   400

Metres

4

Fl.G.5s3M

Puerto
Deportivo
Porcillan

Ⓥ

Fl.R.5s

Figueras

Shipyard

Ribadeo

3

3

Works

*Banco
Berlinga*

(P.A)

Moorings

Dársena
de Mirasol

4₂

2₃   Fl(2)G.7s

Fl(2)R.7s

(P.A)

Fl(3)G.9s

(P.A)

Warning

The Castropol channel is reported
as having shoaled considerably (2005)

Spire

Castropol

Front leading mark   Rear leading mark 140°

Estuary looking N near LW showing extent of Banco Berlinga. Figueras right centre

Ashore in Ribadeo

The town is worth the walk although there are also several hostelries en route, and a Parador above Mirasol. It was once a considerable trading port going back to Roman times. More recently fishing, and being an important country town, have kept it going and now there is also a good marina.

Facilities

Water and electricity on the pontoons; fuel pumps at the N entrance; travel-lift expected in the SE corner; 8–1 tonne cranes; slip; ask at the office for repair work; plenty of good shops in the town and a *supermercado* N from the square; many restaurants with a good one behind Mirasol.

Leisure

The red-domed 18th-century church is worth a visit and the club náutico are friendly; they have a local class with an interesting rig of a standing lugsail very like a lateen.

Travel

On the main E/W road, 2M to the railway station; nearest airport La Coruña 160km.

Fiestas

16 July; first Sunday in August is a (Galician) bagpipe festival; 7 September Santa Maria del Campo.

Ashore in Figueras

Ship- and boatbuilding are the principal occupations; there are some shops and simple restaurants.

Ashore in Castropol

Castropol was where the better-off merchants and ship-owners lived and is worth a visit with its picturesque houses and streets; there are regular ferries across the ria from Ribadeo, which is probably the easiest way to reach it as the ferrymen know the latest shift of the sands and channels. There is an enthusiastic rowing club by the pontoon whose members have provided many of the Spanish national rowing teams.

Facilities

2 *supermercados* and a good variety of shops and some restaurants; water tap near the pontoon.

Club   *Old overhead loading wharf*

Porcillan marina looking N

110 Rinlo

Cat C

Gap in the rocks with quay and small village; only the adventurous need contemplate it in fine weather only

Location
43°34′.00N 07°06′.00W

Shelter
None

Warning
Enter entirely at own risk

Depth restrictions
3m in entrance; 0.7m alongside

Night entry
Light on breakwater corner

Tidal information
HW PdG −0005
LW PdG +0005

Mean height of tide (m)

MHWS	MHWN	MLWN	MLWS
4.1	2.9	1.4	0.2

Berthing
Quay often obstructed by crane

Facilities
2 shops; tap on jetty

Charts
No large-scale
BA 1108 (200)
Spanish 932 (40)

Weather
Navia Ch 60 at 0840, 1240, 2010
Navtex D

Radio and telephone
None

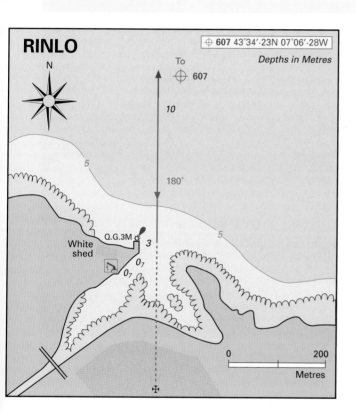

PILOTAGE

Approach

By day in fine weather and no swell

From the vicinity of ⊕607 identify the church and approach the entrance aligned on it on 180°. A white shed just to the W of the entrance also identifies the harbour.

Entrance and berthing

Once past the jetty corner with the light, turn to starboard but from here on there is very little room to turn. The crane often seems to be left turned out over the edge of the jetty, precluding any masted craft of any size getting alongside. The outer E corner of the jetty is probably the last point at which to go astern out of it in safety.

The jetty is relatively smooth and good fenders will suffice. It is surprising that there is relatively little movement alongside here when conditions outside would suggest otherwise. Perhaps the SE arm acts as a baffle.

Ashore

A couple of shops and a water tap on jetty. The village is 2km from the main road and railway.

Rinlo jetty looking N from the bridge

Rinlo looking SW

111 Ensenada de la Lousa

Cat D

One of the few little bays along this stretch offering some shelter from the E

⊕**608** 43°34′.23N 07°07′.59W 1 mile W of Rinlo

Approach on a track of about 150° from ⊕608 and tuck in under Punta Corbeira as close as depth allows, on sand.

There is not much shelter but it might provide respite if battling against easterlies and Ribadeo, another 4M to east, does not appeal.

Ensenada de la Lousa to the right of Punta Corbeira looking E

112 Foz

Cat C

Pleasant little town at the mouth of a large shallow estuary with miles of sands; entry only near HW in reasonable swell and weather states

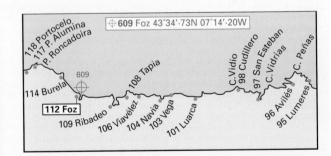

Location
43°35′.00N 07°07′.00W

Shelter
Good inside

Warning
Entry limited to near HW

Depth restrictions
1m in entrance; 1–2m in harbour

Night entry
No leading lights

Tidal information
HW PdG −0000
LW PdG +0005

Mean height of tide (m)

MHWS	MHWN	MLWN	MLWS
3.9	2.9	1.4	0.4

Tidal stream
Ebb at up to 5 knots at springs

Berthing
Alongside in outer basin

Facilities
Those of a small fishing port

Charts
No large-scale
BA 1108 (200)
Spanish 932 (40)

Weather
Navia Ch 60 at 0840,1240, 2010

Radio and telephone
None

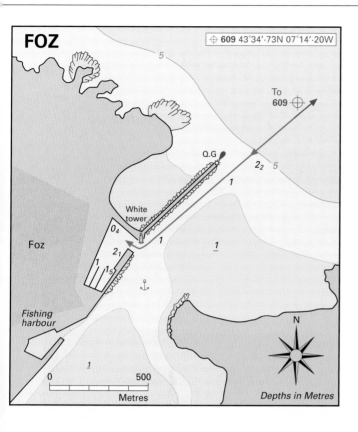

IV. SAN ESTEBAN TO PUERTO ALUMINA ESPANOLA

Anchoring

Outside the basin as far out of the channel as depth allows as the streams run fast.

The estuary

The estuary is large, beautiful and unspoilt and would provide a good exploration area for a multihull or bilge keeler.

Ashore in Foz

With the building of the outer basin, efforts have been made here to attract yachtsmen but few seem to respond and even the fishing fleet seems a little lacklustre.

Facilities

Water tap on the quay; fuel from garage in town; a variety of shops and a scattering of restaurants.

Leisure

Excellent beaches, explorable estuary.

Fiestas

16–17 July, 8–12 August.

PILOTAGE

Approach

By day

From ⊕609 make good a track of 230° with the two towers on the training wall just out of line. The beaches on either side and the town on the hill beyond are conspicuous.

Entrance

The entrance is dredged from time to time but a least depth of 1m should be assumed and arrival timed accordingly preferably before HW. The water is clear so any deeper channel can be seen in the right light.

Keep about 50m parallel to the training wall and turn into the first basin across which there will be a strong set except at slack water.

Berthing

The berth immediately to port inside is the deepest (2.1m) and is sometimes occupied by the dredger. Go alongside here or double up, or elsewhere in the basin as the depth allows. The two pontoons are for small local boats only.

A drying berth may be available in the fishing harbour but the quays are often all occupied.

Foz looking WSW

---

113 Río de Oro

⊕**610** 43°35'.44N 07°16'.28W

This is a narrow canalised stream 25m wide running across an open beach with no shelter off it except from directly offshore, although *Bay of Biscay Pilot NP 22* and BA chart 1108 suggest otherwise.

114 Burela

Cat A*

The major fishing port on this part of the coast in a new and expanding town; it makes no concessions for yachts, who are just tolerated; usual run-ashore amenities and a handy hospital

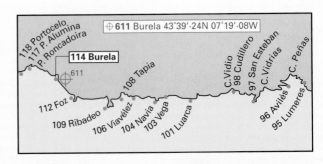

Location
43°40′.00N 07°21′.00W

Shelter
Good inside

Warning
Dangers in approach from the N

Depth restrictions
3m in entrance, 2.5m in harbour

Night entry
Lit but no leading lights

Tidal information
HW PdG −0005
LW PdG +0005

Mean height of tide

MHWS	MHWN	MLWN	MLWS
3.9	2.9	1.4	0.4

Berthing
In NE corner on pontoon ends

Facilities
Those of large fishing port

Charts
BA 1108 (200)
Spanish 932 (40)

Weather
Navia Ch 60 at 0840,1240, 2010

Radio and telephone
Try *Burela Cofradia* on Ch 12

Burela looking W; development continuing to the SW of the *lonja*

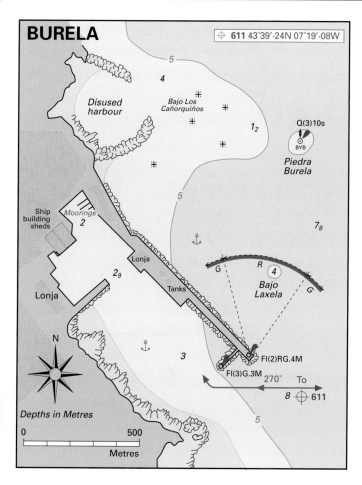

BURELA

611 43°39'·24N 07°19'·08W

Depths in Metres

0   500

Metres

Ashore in Burela

A town of no particular charm or history but with the usual necessities.

Facilities

Water points on quays; fuel from garage in town; usual fishing boat maintenance and repair facilities; good shops and a variety of restaurants.

Leisure

Not much except beaches.

Travel

Railway runs through town, main road round edges; nearest airport La Coruña 120km.

Fiesta

10 June St John the Baptist.

Hospital

Large hospital with A & E.

115 Río Junco

Cat D

Inlet 3 miles to the NW of Burela giving some shelter from E and W

612 43°42'.20N 07°24'.10W

Approaches and entrance

Spanish chart 932 (40) is the largest-scale.

The inlet lies between Punta Rueta to the W and Punta Castro to the E with a reef extending N from the latter to give some protection from the NE.

From 612 approach on a track of about 170° and identify the inlet from the bridge crossing the head of the beach as in the photograph.

Sound in carefully before anchoring in a suitable depth on sand with rocky patches.

PILOTAGE

Approaches

From any direction the shipbuilding sheds are prominent with the town rising up behind them.

From N or W

By day or night

Pass to the E of Piedra Burela (E cardinal Q(3)10s) and avoid Bajo Laxela (4m) which breaks in any swell, approaching the breakwater end (Fl(2)R.G) in the green sector on 210° or more.

From E

By day or night

From 611 make good a track of 270° to the harbour entrance.

Entrance

Straightforward in at least 3m.

Berthing

No particular arrangement for yachts; proceed to the NE corner where there are some pontoons for small boats and a berth may be found on a pontoon end or alongside.

Anchoring

Outside or inside the outer harbour towards the SW shore.

Río Junco looking SSW

116 San Ciprián

Cat C

Two run-down villages with a recently improved jetty behind a detached breakwater

Location 43°43′.00N 07°26′.00W	**Depth restrictions** 5m in entrance; 2m at jetty	**Mean height of tide** MHWS MHWN MLWN MLWS 3.9 2.9 1.4 0.4	**Charts** BA 1122 (15) Spanish 931, 932 (40)
Shelter Marginal	**Night entry** Directional light through entrance	**Berthing** Alongside jetty in 2m; little room to anchor	**Weather** Cabo Ortegal Ch 02 0840, 1240, 2010
Warning Axuela Reef extends well N of breakwater	**Tidal information** HW PdG −0005 LW PdG +0005	**Facilities** A few shops in Figueras	**Radio and telephone** None

PILOTAGE

Approaches

By day or night

From ⊕614 make good a track of 196° in the white sector of the directional light (DirQ.WR) just to the left of Axuela breakwater end (Fl.G.3s). Note that this sector does not entirely cover the gap between Axuela and San Ciprián.

Entrance

Before Axuela breakwater end comes abeam and when it and the inner breakwater end (F.R) are open, alter between the two and enter the red sector of the directional light; round the inner breakwater end.

Berthing

Berth alongside either the new inner breakwater or the jetty at right angles but note that fishing boats also use these berths.

Anchoring

All the area to the S of Axuela is now occupied by small craft moorings and finding an anchorage here is unlikely; use a trip line if space is found as there are a lot of old moorings on the bottom.

There is a fine-weather anchorage in between Los Fallarones in 1–2m. Also in westerlies a sheltered anchorage may be found in the bay to the E of San Ciprian.

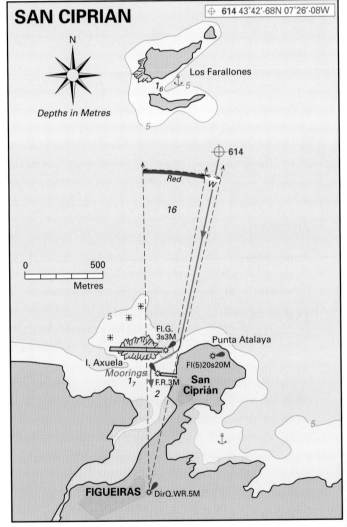

San Ciprián looking SSW at LW

Ashore in San Ciprián

The renewal of the jetty seen on the photo has breathed some new life into the immediate area but there is little to entertain in the two villages of Figueras and San Ciprián. Livelihoods here very much depend on the aluminium works just to the west.

Facilities

Water on the quay; nearest fuel in Figueras where the only shops are; some cafés and small restaurants in both villages.

Leisure

Good beaches on the E side of the peninsula.

Axuela breakwater end   Los Farallones

San Ciprián harbour looking N

117 Puerto Alúmina Española

Cat A

Huge commercial harbour for the aluminium works of no interest to yachtsmen except in an emergency

Location
  1M W of San Ciprián
Shelter
  Protected from W and N
Night entry
  Entrance well lit
Tidal information
  As for San Ciprián

Berthing
  Alongside or anchor off Portino in NW corner
Facilities
  None
Charts
  BA 1122 (15)
  Spanish 931, 932 (40)

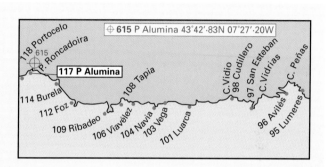

PILOTAGE

The approaches to ⊕615 are clear from the N and E apart from Los Farallones ¾M to the E of the entrance. ⊕615 is due E of the wide and well lit entrance with massive breakwaters (north Fl(2)WG.8s, south Fl(3)R.8s). Proceed through on a westerly track and follow the N breakwater along to the small fishing facility at Portino in the NW corner. An alongside berth in about 2m may be available here; otherwise double up or anchor off.

Apart from a semi-derelict boatyard and a crane there are no facilities here; it is 3M to the main road.

Portino quay looking WNW

Puerto Alúmina looking SE

V. Portocelo to La Coruña

Punta Roncadoira to Torre de Hercules

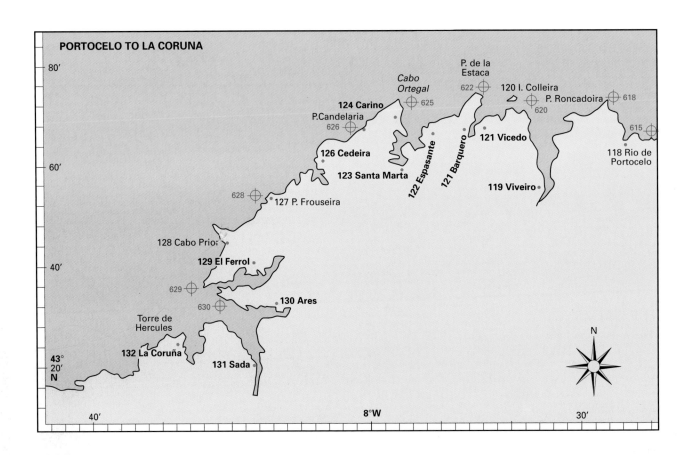

This section of the coastline contains many of the Rias Altas, fjord-like estuaries of considerable size which run inland between high ranges of hills. There are a number of large promontories between these rias and the coast has high, steep cliffs. There are no offlying dangers at any distance from the coast and deep water comes up close to the cliffs.

There are submarine exercise areas and missile firing ranges off El Ferrol and Cabo Ortegal.

Warning

The possibility of a heavy swell arising from distant storms in the Atlantic, and the probability of high lighthouses being obscured by cloud in NE winds, applies particularly to this part of the coast.

Very confused seas will be experienced near the coast in storm conditions due to wave reflection from near-vertical cliffs and uneven bottom. Headlands should be given a berth of at least 5M in these conditions.

A lifeboat is maintained at La Coruña.

Stream and currents

The tidal stream is up to 2 knots on this coast, NE-going on the flood and SW-going on the ebb. In the offing the stream weakens and in general the current is SW and becomes the Portugal, and later the Canary Current.

Planning Guide

Distances between ports in nautical miles
Ports with marinas in **bold** type

		Alumina	Portocelo	Vivero	I Colleira	Barquero	Espasante	S Marta	Cariño	Ortigueira	Cedeira	Frouseira	Cabo Prior	El Ferrol	Ares	Sada/Fontán	La Coruña
A	P Alumina		3	8	10	11	19	21	22	26	41	47	54	62	66	68	70
D	Portocelo	3		5	7	8	16	18	19	23	38	44	51	59	66	66	67
B	**Vivero**	8	5		2	3	11	13	14	18	25	33	39	46	54	61	62
D	I Colleira	10	7	2		1	9	11	12	16	23	31	37	44	52	59	60
B*	**Barquero**	11	8	3	1		8	10	11	15	22	30	36	43	51	58	59
D	Espasante	19	16	11	9	8		2	3	7	14	22	28	35	43	50	51
D	S Marta	21	18	13	11	10	2		1	5	12	20	26	33	41	48	49
B*	**Cariño**	22	19	14	12	11	3	1		4	11	19	25	32	40	47	48
C	**Santa Marta**	26	23	18	16	15	7	5	4		15	21	28	36	43	42	44
B	**Cedeira**	41	38	33	31	30	22	20	19	15		6	13	21	28	27	29
D	Frouseira	47	44	39	37	36	28	26	25	21	6		7	15	22	21	23
D	Cabo Prior	54	51	46	44	43	35	33	32	28	13	7		8	15	14	16
A	**El Ferrol**	62	59	54	52	51	43	41	40	36	21	15	8		7	4	9
D	Ares	66	66	61	59	58	50	48	47	43	28	22	15	7		4	7
A*	**Sada/Fontán**	68	66	60	58	57	49	47	46	42	27	21	14	4	4		7
A*	**La Coruña**	70	67	62	60	59	51	49	48	44	37	29	23	16	8	7	

WAYPOINTS

⊕559	S. Pedro del Mar	43°30'.00N	03°50'.40W
⊕615	P. Alúmina	43°42'.83N	07°27'.20W
⊕616	I. Amarón	43°44'.43N	07°28'.59W
⊕617	Portocelo	43°44'.43N	07°30'.60W
⊕618	I. Runcadoira	43°44'.60N	07°31'.34W
⊕619	Viveiro	43°43'.00N	07°35'.58W
⊕620	I. Coelleira	43°46'.25N	07°38'.00W
⊕621	Barquero	43°46'.34N	07°39'.00W
⊕622	Est de Bares	43°48'.04N	07°40'.15W
⊕623	Espasante	43°43'.38N	07°50'.05W
	E. Santa Marta		
⊕624	Cariño	43°44'.24N	07°50'.68W
⊕625	C. Ortegal	43°47'.68N	07°51'.69W
⊕626	P. Candelaria	43°42'.74N	08°04'.09W
⊕627	Cedeira	43°40'.01N	08°04'.87W
⊕628	C. Frouseira	43°38'.54N	08°10'.79W
⊕629	C. Prior	43°33'.01N	08°20'.08W
⊕630	El Ferrol	43°26''.42N	08°21'.59W
⊕631	Ares	43°24'.60N	08°13'.88W
⊕632	Sada/Fontán	43°21'.63N	08°14'.39W
⊕633	La Coruña	43°22'.00N	08°22'.00W

Viveiro, looking ENE

118 Portocelo

Cat D

Deep, narrow bay sheltered from all but the N with a quay but no other facilities nearby

Location
43°43′.00N 07°31′.00W

Shelter
Little from the N

Depth restrictions
4m in anchorage, 1.5m alongside quay

Night entry
No lights

Tidal information
HW PdG −0005
LW PdG +0005

Mean height of tide (m)

MHWS	HWN	LWN	LWS
4.0	3.1	1.5	0.6

Berthing
Alongside subject to depth and fishing boats

Facilities
Crane and slip

Charts
No large-scale
BA 1108 (200)
Spanish 931 (40)

Weather
La Coruña Ch 26 0840, 1240, 2010
Navtex D

Radio and telephone
None

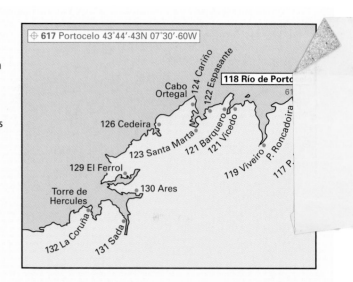

⊕ **617** Portocelo 43°44′.43N 07°30′.60W

118 Río de Porto

Cabo Ortegal — 124 Cariño — 122 Espasante
126 Cedeira
123 Santa Marta — 121 Barquero — 121 Vicedo
129 El Ferrol — 119 Viveiro — P. Roncadoira — 117 P.
Torre de Hercules
130 Ares
132 La Coruña — 131 Sada

PILOTAGE

Approach

There are no particular identifying features to pick out the entrance from ⊕617 but a track of about 180° should lead to it as the final narrow channel to the quay becomes visible. If coming from the W do not cut the headland on the W side of the río where there is a 0.6m patch 100m to the N of it.

Entrance

Favour the W shore to avoid the detached above-water rocks shown on the E shore in the photograph. The inlet extends for about 800m.

Berthing

Treat the rocky and weed-covered area to the N of the narrow entrance channel with caution as the depth here is not known. There is 1.5m on the inner side of the outer end of the pier, shoaling to 0m by the crane, and fishing boats use all the length of it.

Dry out on the sands up the río or in the bay to W beyond the quay.

Anchoring

In 2–4m, as indicated on the photograph, sand.

Ashore

Apart from the slips and crane there are no facilities whatever; this quay is used occasionally by small fishing boats to unload. There are some scattered houses inland but no village nearby.

Quay

180°

Portocelo looking SW

Slip   Crane   Slip

Alongside berth

Looking towards entrance

119 Viveiro

Cat B

The fishing harbour at Cillero is separate from the new marina at Viveiro which is near the town centre

Location
43°43´.00N 07°36´.00W

Shelter
Excellent in marina

Warning
The three shoal patches of Bajo El Co to the NE of Punta Socastro and the two separate patches of 4m and 7m of Cabo de Estiero to the NE of Punta de Faro (not shown on plan) break in any swell or heavy weather

Depth restrictions
None in approaches; 3m+ in harbours

Night entry
Well lit but no leading lights

Tidal information
HW PdG –0005
LW PdG +0005

Mean height of tide (m)

MHWS	MHWN	MLWN	MLWS
4.0	3.1	1.5	0.6

Tidal stream
Up to 3 knots on the ebb in channel

Berthing
On pontoons in marina; at anchor off Cillero

Facilities
Those of a small town and marina; shops close by. Hospital in Viveiro

Charts
BA 1122 (20)
Spanish 931 (40)

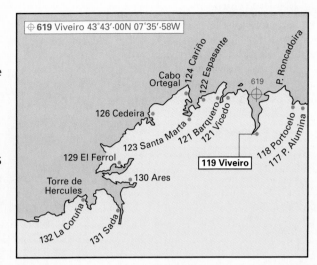

⊕ **619** Viveiro 43°43´·00N 07°35´·58W

Weather
La Coruña Ch 26 at 0840,1240, 2010
Navtex D

Radio
Ch 09 (working hours)

Telephone
☎ 982 56 08 79/982 57 06 10
www.pdviveiro.com

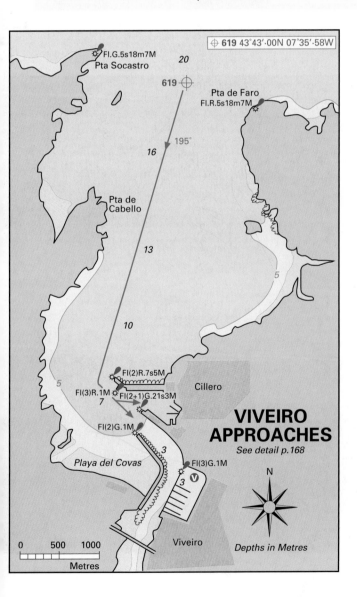

⊕ **619** 43°43´·00N 07°35´·58W

Fl.G.5s18m7M
Pta Socastro

619

195°

Pta de Faro
Fl.R.5s18m7M

Pta de Cabello

Fl(2)R.7s5M
Fl(3)R.1M
Fl(2+1)G.21s3M
Cillero
Fl(2)G.1M

VIVEIRO APPROACHES
See detail p.168

Playa del Covas
Fl(3)G.1M

Viveiro

N

Depths in Metres

0   500   1000
Metres

See detail p.168

PILOTAGE

Approaches

By day or night

Note the Warning above and approach ⊕619 on a track of 195° and continue on this towards the Cillero Breakwater end (Fl(2)R.7s). The ria is wide, deep and clear. Round the breakwater end at 100m and head either for the river entrance or Cillero.

Entrance

The channel running 140° to the marina is dredged to 3m. The marina entrance is not lit.

Berthing

There are 6 pontoons inside with fingers and berths for visitors up to about 15m; most of the basin carries 3m. There are sometimes berths on the NE wall just inside the entrance with 3.2m but this is often taken by laid-up fishing boats; the NE corner of the basin is encumbered with rubble and rocks.

There is a drying berth just below the bridge beside the old *lonja* but it is very noisy.

Anchoring

An anchorage in 3–4m, mud, can be found off the two pontoons (which are for small boats only) off Cillero. Otherwise there are many quiet anchorages in the ria to the N, or off Playa del Covas but several of the bays have fish farms in them.

Ashore in Viveiro and Cillero

The fishing fleet is now all in Cillero and Viveiro has turned to leisure with the expansion of the marina and encouragement of tourism in the town.

Facilties in Viveiro

The amenities of the marina are still developing but diesel and petrol are available, water and electricity on the pontoons; showers, heads and other niceties will no doubt follow when the office upgrades from the present portakabin. 2 *supermercados* within 5 minutes walk and the town centre only a bit further with many shops and restaurants.

Facilities in Cillero

Slips, cranes and chandlery for fishermen; the *capitanía* is here if needed. A less attractive small town than Viveiro.

Leisure

The 9th-century church and old town gates are worth a visit in Viveiro and a dinghy trip up the Río Landrove is through pleasant countryside; good beaches all round the ria; Playa del Covas is popular and crowded.

Travel

On the main rail and bus coastal routes; nearest airport. La Coruña (100km).

Fiestas

15–16 July, 15–16 August Viveiro; 25 July Cillero.

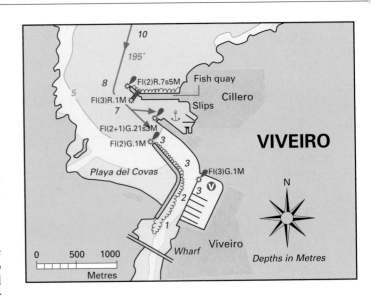

Cillero and Viveiro looking SSE

120 Isla Colleira

Cat D

⊕**620** 43°46′.25′N 07°38′.00W

There is a small cove and landing place on the W side of the island to the SE of the offlying rocks shown on the photo. The island is some 80m high and has a lighthouse (Fl(4)24s7M) and dwelling on the summit.

The channel between the island and mainland is 800m wide, has a 4m patch extending from the S side and is otherwise clean with a least depth of 18m but breaks across in strong N or NW gales.

Río Barquero entrance

Isla Colleira looking SW

121 Ria del Barquero

Cat B*

Deep and wide ria with the anchorage of Bares and the small ports of Barquero and Vicedo; good shelter in one or the other

Location
43°46′.00N 07°40′.00W

Shelter
Good in Vicedo and Barquero; from the W only in Bares

Depth restrictions
1m in río to Barquero, 1.5–2.5m in harbour; 3.1m in Vicedo

Night entry
Directional but no leading lights

Tidal information
HW PdG −0005
LW PdG +0005

Mean height of tide

MHWS	MHWN	MLWN	MLWS
4.0	3.1	1.5	0.6

Tidal stream
3+ knots in río to Barquero

Berthing
Alongside in Vicedo and Barquero

Facilities
See below for each harbour

Charts
BA 1108 (200), 1122 (25)
Spanish 931 (40)

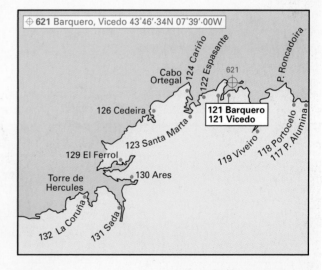

⊕ **621** Barquero, Vicedo 43°46′·34N 07°39′·00W

Cabo Ortegal
124 Cariño
122 Espasante
621
P. Roncadoira
126 Cedeira
121 Barquero
121 Vicedo
123 Santa Marta
119 Viveiro
118 Portocelo
117 P. Alumina
129 El Ferrol
130 Ares
Torre de Hercules
132 La Coruña
131 Sada

Weather
La Coruña Ch 26 at 0840,1240, 2010
Navtex D

Radio and telephone
None

PILOTAGE

Approaches

By day or night

The approaches to ⊕621 are clear from the E to NW; see above if passing S of Isla Colleira. From here it is 2½M to Punta de la Barra in deep and clear water in the white sector of Punta de la Barra light (Fl.WRG.3s). Punta del Castro light (Fl(2)7s) is only visible from 180° or less. Draught permitting, alongside berths may be found in Barquero and Vicedo, otherwise there are several anchorages in the ria. Vicedo breakwater ends are lit (Fl(4)R or Fl(4)G.11s).

Anchorages

Bares See below.

Playa Compelo S of the cove but N of the fish farm in the S part of this bay, in up to 6m, sand.

Playa Castro Vilela S or SW of the islets and clear of shellfish beds.

Río Barquero To S of Barquero harbour in the main channel and N of the 3 bridges.

Off Vicedo To the S of the harbour and clear of the moorings.

Playa de Xilloy A fine-weather anchorage open to the N and any swell.

Bares

Anchoring

A number of moorings now occupy a lot of the bay and it may not be possible to get in out of any swell.

Ashore

Facilities

Water at campsite at end of jetty; bar and two restaurants; small *supermercado* at top of village; mobile baker calls mid-mornings.

Leisure

Nice beach.

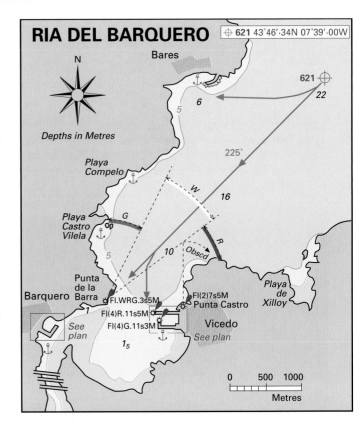

RIA DEL BARQUERO ⊕ 621 43°46′·34N 07°39′·00W

Bares looking W

Ria del Barquero looking SW

Southern part of Ria del Barquero

Vicedo

PILOTAGE

Entrance

There is 4m in the entrance, which has no projections from the ends. Turn sharply to starboard once inside before the pontoons, which are for small boats.

Berthing

Along the W or S walls in depths as indicated. There are some ladders but one may be needed at MLWS if there is no berth alongside one.

Ashore in Vicedo

Facilities

Water on the quay, crane and slip; some shops and simple restaurants. The main E/W road runs through the village. The boatyard and slip ½M to the S appear little used.

Barquero

PILOTAGE

Entrance to river and harbour

By day only

There are no lights once past Punta de la Barra. Approach the latter with its white truncated tower

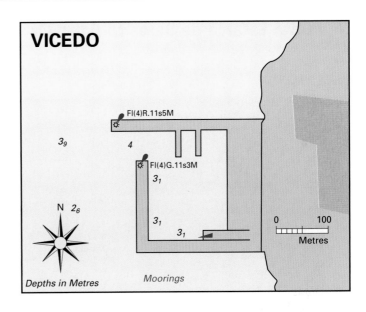

just clear of the previous point on about 225° between HW–0100 and HW. There is 1+m in the channel which is deepest on the W side. When a large red house appears make for it and leave it 25m to starboard, thence for the harbour entrance which has a tall white mast at the S breakwater end.

Berthing

The N outer jetty has the most water as indicated and there is from 2.5–1.5m on the W side of the E wall. Fishing boats use both. The harbour shoals progressively towards the W wall which dries. There are many small-boat moorings in the shallower parts.

Anchoring

There is space and water to anchor in the channel below the bridges and above the harbour if there are no berths. There are some small boat moorings just to the S of the harbour but enough space between them and the bridges. The ebb runs at 3+ knots but more caution is needed on the flood to watch for dragging onto the low railway bridge.

Ashore in Barquero

Facilities

Water on the quay; only Gasoleo B at the harbour; garage up the hill; 3 restaurants on the quay, shops up the hill plus small *supermercado*; mobile baker calls mid-morning.

Leisure

A dinghy trip up the Río Sor leads through unspoilt countryside.

Travel

The village is on the main rail and road running E/W. Nearest airport La Coruña (85km).

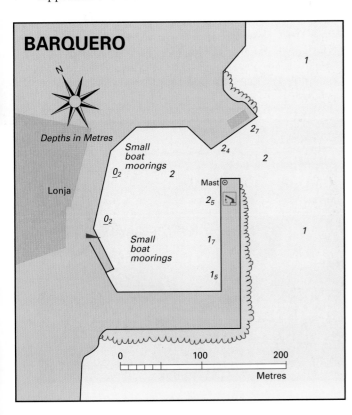

Punta Estarca de Bares to Cabo Ortegal

Entrance to Ens. de Santa Maria   Cariño   Cabo Ortegal

Looking W over Punta Estaca de Bares

122 Espasante

Cat D

Anchorage sheltered from the E off a small harbour and village at entrance to Ensenada de Santa Marta

⊕**623** 43°43′.38N 07°50′.05W

See 123 Ensenada de Santa Marta for data

PILOTAGE

Approaches and anchorage

Make 105° from ⊕623 to the anchorage in 2–4m off the breakwaters if coming from the W, or pass to the E of Piedras Liseiras W cardinal (Q(9)15s) and rocks if coming from the E or N. The breakwater ends have Fl.R and G.5s lights.

Ashore in Espasante

Apart from a slip and crane there are no facilities, and the inner part of the harbour is rock-encumbered while the deeper parts are filled with small boat moorings; the breakwaters are not suitable to dry out against. Simple shop in the village.

Piedras Liseiras buoy

105°
From ⊕623

Espasante looking E

123 Ensenada de Santa Marta

Cat C

Large bay to the E of Cabo Ortegal containing Cariño, a small commercial and fishing port; Espasante an open anchorage and small harbour, and Santa Marta de Ortiguera with a marina at the top of an extensive estuary

The data below applies to Cariño, Espasante and Santa Maria de Ortiguera

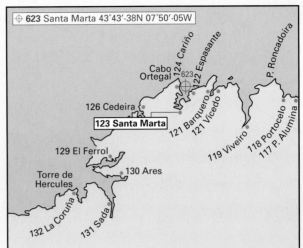

⊕ 623 Santa Marta 43°43'·38N 07°50'·05W

Location
43°43'·00N 07°50'·00W

Shelter
Cariño exposed to the E; Espasante exposed to the W; perfect in Ortiguera

Warnings
In N gales or storms, Cariño provides the only shelter and entry further S into the bay should not be contemplated
Entry into Ria de Santa Marta past Isla de San Vicente should not be attempted with any swell or in strong northerlies

Depth restrictions
3–5m in Cariño; 0.9m on bar to río, deeper inside

Night entry
Possible to Cariño but not well lit; possible to anchor off Espasante; not possible to enter Río de Santa Marta or go to Santa Marta

Tidal information
HW La Coruña +0050
LW La Coruña +0050

Mean height of tide (m)

MHWS	MHWN	MLWN	MLWS
4.1	3.2	1.5	0.6

Tidal stream
Negligible in bay; up to 5 knots in río

Berthing
Alongside in Cariño; in marina in Santa Marta; at anchor off Espasante

Facilities
Provisions, fuel and water at Cariño and Santa Marta; little at Espasante

Charts
BA 1108, 1111 (200), 1122 (25)
Spanish 930 (40)

Weather
La Coruña Ch 26 0840, 1240 and 2010
Navtex D

Radio and telephone
Try *Cariño practicos* on Ch 12

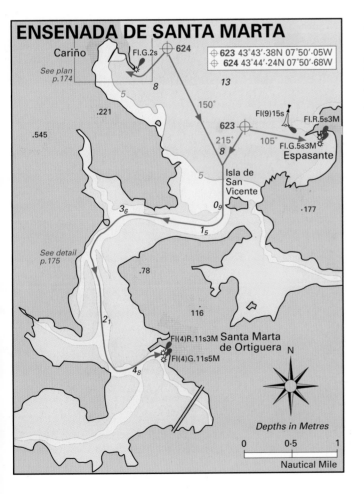

ENSENADA DE SANTA MARTA

⊕ 623 43°43'·38N 07°50'·05W
⊕ 624 43°44'·24N 07°50'·68W

Depths in Metres

0   0·5   1

Nautical Mile

PILOTAGE

Approach

By day or night make good a track of 225° from ⊕624 to round the breakwater end (Fl.G.2s) which is steep-to.

Entrance

Round up towards the pontoon or sound in to an anchorage.

Berthing

The pontoon has 1m+ alongside the middle of the outer side reducing to 0.2 metres at the ends. The N side is full of small boats on outhauls. The problem is to find a way through all the boats at moorings on the approach (see photograph); this will be even more difficult at night as there are no lights on the pontoon.

Anchoring

In the W part of the outer harbour clear of the moorings in from 2–8m, mostly sand.

Moorings

There are none for visitors and are unlikely to be substantial enough for yachts.

124 Cariño

Cat B*

Small commercial and fishing port well sheltered from the N and W with a pontoon for yachts

For data see 123 Ensenada de Sant Marta

Cariño looking N near LW

Ashore in Cariño

Cariño is the most eastern of the harbours that might be a port of call after crossing the Bay before going on further S, and it has just about enough facilities and amenities to refresh and refill. Not a great run ashore.

The commercial wharf is used for the export of timber and aggregates.

Facilities

There is a water tap at the end of the jetty to the pontoon but it may be locked; if so, there is a hose at the *lonja* which may be used; Gasoleo B only at the harbour, diesel and petrol by cans from garage in the village; numerous shops and restaurants in the village; fishermen's chandlery near the *lonja*; a slip for the largest fishing boat plus cranes; repairs can be undertaken.

Travel

It is 10km S to Mera at the head of the estuary which is on the main E/W rail and road routes; nearest airport La Coruña (75km).

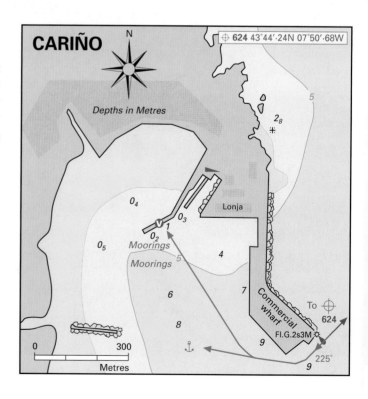

125 Santa Marta de Ortiguera

Cat C

A delightful town four miles up a large unspoilt estuary.
It has a shallow bar but the river is well marked in the upper reaches to a marina with 2m

For data see 123 Ensenada de Santa Marta

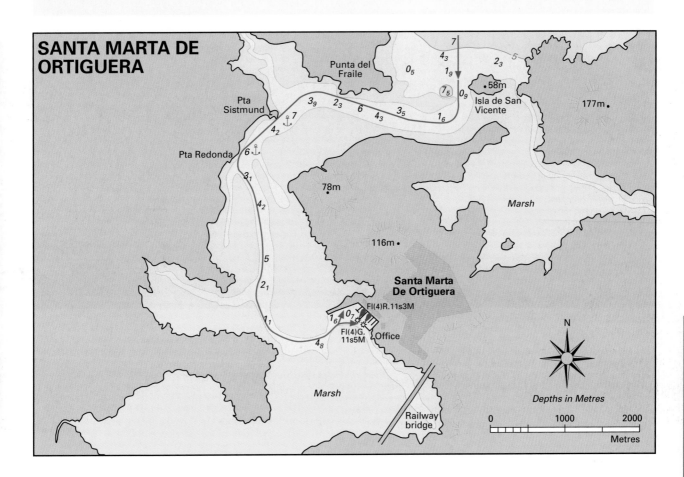

SANTA MARTA DE ORTIGUERA

PILOTAGE

Approach

By day only

Depending on draught enter between HW−0200 and HW but not if there is significant swell or strong northerlies. From ⊕623 make good a track of about 215° until the W side of Isla de San Vicente bears 180°.

Outer entrance

Cross the bar leaving the island 50m to port. Continue towards the dunes and turn parallel to them 100m off and keep this distance on a track of about 290° towards Punta del Fraile. The depths vary on this first reach but at least 2m should be found once round the first bend. There is no buoyage at this stage.

Passage upriver

When Punta del Fraile is well abaft the beam start turning into the next reach towards Punta Sisimund where there is a small basin on the point and the river deepens considerably off it. Keep Punta Redonda fine on the starboard bow and pick up the buoyed channel southwards. The buoys are small red and green unlit conicals and are supplemented by the occasional beacon and withies. The buoys are at close intervals round the final bend to the quay and marina but don't cut too close as many are laid on the drying line.

Berthing

The quay will be recognised by the blue crane at its end. It has 1.5m at the outer end, 1.3m towards the root on the S side and has bollards but no steps. There is a rich growth of mussels on the wall below MTL.

Continue round the corner if going to the marina in which 2+m will be found, rather less towards the E end. There are three pontoons, maximum 12m but only 4 berths over 10m and visitors are catered for.

V. PORTOCELO TO LA CORUNA

Santa Marta de Ortiguera looking E

Anchoring

Off Punta Sisimund in up to 7m, sandy mud.

Off Punta Redonda in 6m.

Note that the streams are at their strongest in these two anchorages and can reach up to 5 knots on the ebb.

Moorings

There are a number of moorings in the river but these are private and mainly for small craft.

Ashore in Santa Marta

Facilities

Water on the pontoons, and electricity expected; diesel and petrol from garage in town; there are many shops and restaurants about ½M away in the town plus a *supermercado*; club náutico by the harbour office near the SE corner of the marina where visitors are welcome.

Leisure

The restored 19th-century church in Casa del Concello is worth seeing otherwise there are some good restaurants.

Travel

The town is on the main E/W road and rail routes, although the services are not frequent; nearest airport La Coruña (70km).

Fiestas

A famous fiesta is held here from 29 July to 2 Aug in honour of Santa Marta. There used to be an earlier International Celtic festival but this appears to have been discontinued.

Looking W along S marina wall towards quay

126 Cedeira

Cat B

Open bay with anchorage sheltered from W; the fishermen, although friendly, use all the facilities; watering, fuelling and provisioning entail some effort

Location
43°40'.00N 08°05'.00W

Shelter
Not too good in NW gale

Warning
Offlying rocks off W entrance

Depth restrictions
Min 6m in approaches

Night entry
Well lit

Tidal information
HW La Coruña +0050
LW La Coruña +0050

Mean height of tide (m)

MHWS	MHWN	MLWN	MLWS
4.1	3.2	1.5	0.6

Berthing
Anchorage only

Facilities
All a dinghy ride away

Charts
BA 1108 (200), 1122 (25)
Spanish 930 (40) (20)

Weather
La Coruña Ch 26 at 0840, 1240 and 2010
Navtex D

Radio and telephone
Try *Cedeira Practicos* on Ch 12

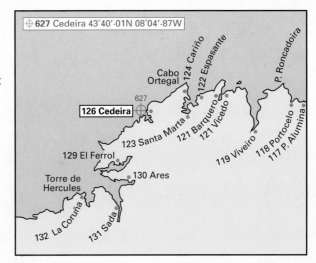

⊕ **627** Cedeira 43°40'·01N 08°04'·87W

Cabo Ortegal
124 Cariño
122 Espasante
P. Roncadoira
627
126 Cedeira
121 Barquero
121 Vicedo
118 Portocelo
117 P. Alumina
123 Santa Marta
119 Viveiro
129 El Ferrol
130 Ares
Torre de Hercules
132 La Coruña
131 Sada

Fish quay   Coaster berth   *Yachts in anchorage*   Old quay   *River entrance to village*

Cedeira looking ENE Punta Promontorio

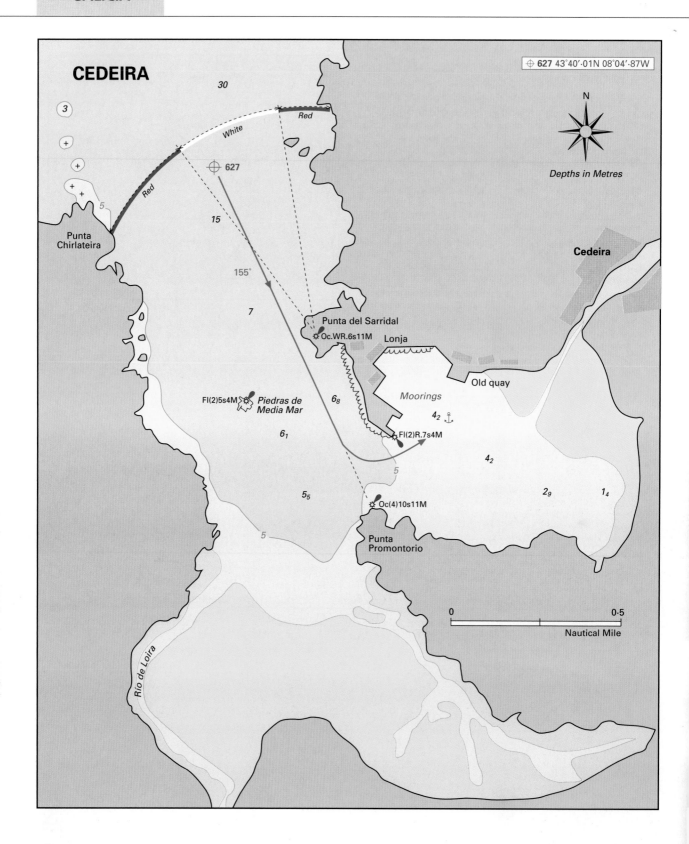

CEDEIRA

Depths in Metres

30

3

+

+

+

Red

White

Red

627

15

155°

Punta Chirlateira

7

Cedeira

Punta del Sarridal

Oc.WR.6s11M

Lonja

FI(2)5s4M

Piedras de Media Mar

Moorings

Old quay

6₈

4₂

6₁

FI(2)R.7s4M

5

4₂

5₅

Oc(4)10s11M

2₉

1₄

5

Punta Promontorio

Río de Loira

0   0·5

Nautical Mile

PILOTAGE

Approaches

By day or night

Give Punta Chirlateira a good ½M berth if coming from the W to avoid the offliers and approach ⊕627 from the N or NW.

Entrance

From ⊕627 proceed down the bearing of 155° on Punta Promontorio (white hexagonal tower, Oc(4)10s) just open of Punta Sarridal (red round tower, Oc.WR.6s) in the white sector of the latter. The track passes shortly after into the W red sector of Punta Sarridal which should be left at least 50m to port. Thence round the breakwater end (Fl(2)R.7s) and proceed to the anchorage.

Anchoring

In 2–4m to SE of the moorings, sand with weed patches.

Moorings

None for visitors.

Berthing

The old quay can be used for embarking fuel and water, and landing; there is from 1.7–2.2m alongside the E half of the S side of it.

Ashore in Cedeira

Cedeira has always welcomed visiting yachtsmen but not done much for them. However, things may be changing; there is now a travel-lift and promises of pontoons to the E of the old quay.

Facilities

Water from old quay; garage (☎ 981 480 34 30) will deliver fuel here if more than 70 litres; 100-tonne travel-lift; shops are a good ½M walk but easier by dinghy near HW; several restaurants in village; ice from the new *lonja*.

Leisure

Good beaches round the ria and the Río Loira is worth a dinghy trip provided it is not breaking at the mouth. Visits to La Concepcion castle, the church of Nuestra Señora Maria del Mar and chapel of San Antonio are worthwhile.

Travel

Occasional local buses to El Ferrol and La Coruña; nearest airport at the latter (60km).

Fiesta

14–30 Aug for Nuestra Señora Maria del Mar, when the port will be full.

127 Punta del Frouseira

Cat D

⊕**628** 43°38´.54´N 08°10´.79W

An open anchorage and one of the few well sheltered from the W behind the Punta in 2–10m, sand.

Punta del Frouseira looking ENE

bo Prior

128 Cabo Prior

Cat D

⊕**629** 43°33´.01´N 08°20´.08W

The only shelter from the E between El Ferrol and Cedeira. A small bay 2M S of Cabo Prior in 2–8m on sand has good protection.

Cabo Prior, looking E

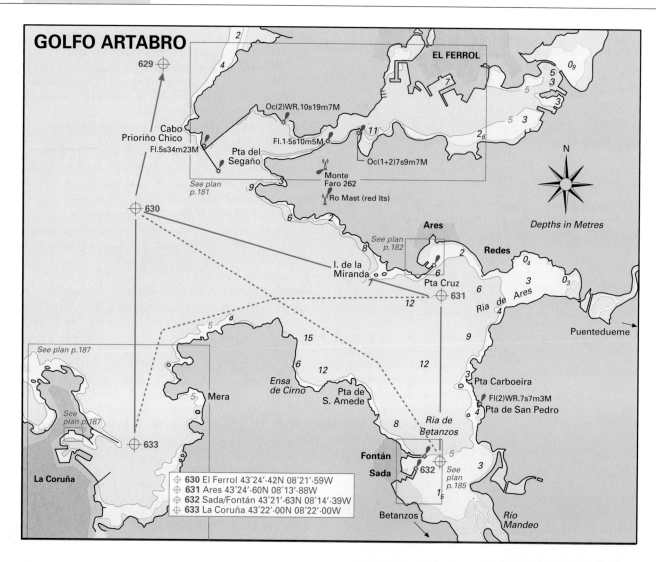

GOLFO ARTABRO

EL FERROL

629

Cabo
Prioriño Chico
Fl.5s34m23M

Oc(2)WR.10s19m7M

Pta del
Segaño

Fl.1·5s10m5M

Oc(1+2)7s9m7M

Monte
Faro 262

Ro Mast (red lts)

*See plan
p.181*

Ares

*See plan
p.182*

I. de la
Miranda

Pta Cruz

Redes

631

Ria de Ares

Puentedueme

Depths in Metres

N

630

See plan p.187

Mera

Ensa
de Cirno

Pta de
S. Amede

Ria de
Betanzos

Pta Carboeira

Fl(2)WR.7s7m3M
Pta de San Pedro

*See
plan p.187*

633

La Coruña

Fontán

Sada

632

*See
plan
p.185*

⊕	**630** El Ferrol 43°24'·42N 08°21'·59W
⊕	**631** Ares 43°24'·60N 08°13'·88W
⊕	**632** Sada/Fontán 43°21'·63N 08°14'·39W
⊕	**633** La Coruña 43°22'·00N 08°22'·00W

Betanzos

*Río
Mandeo*

Sada marina looking SE up river towards Betanzos

Ares and marina looking NE

El Ferrol looking E up harbour with new harbour in foreground

La Coruña looking NW; marina in centre, Torre de Hercules beyond

129 El Ferrol

Cat A

Huge commercial and naval port now having an outer harbour built outside the entrance mainly for container traffic; a few facilities 4M from the entrance for visiting yachts

Location
43°29'.00N 08°18'.00W

Shelter
Perfect inside

Warning
Keep clear of works and shipping in approaches

Depth restrictions
None

Night entry
Very well lit

Tidal information
HW La Coruña +0005
LW La Coruña +0010

Mean height of tide (m)

MHWS	MHWN	MLWN	MLWS
4.2	2.8	1.6	0.3

Tidal stream
Up to 3 knots in the narrows

Berthing
La Graña marina and
Darsena de Curuxeiros

Facilities
Those of a large city

Charts
BA 1117,1118 (10)
Spanish 412A (25)

Weather
La Coruña Ch 26 at 0840,
1240, 2010
Navtex D

Telephone and radio
None

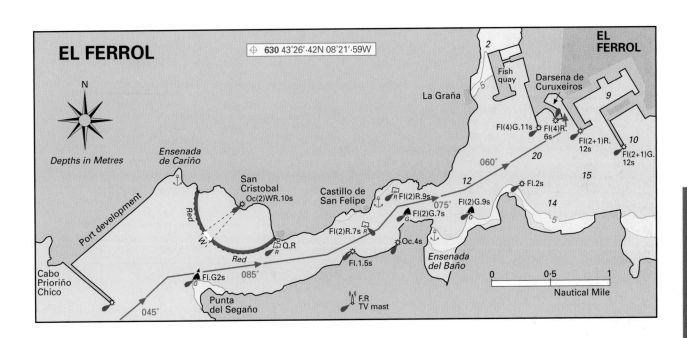

EL FERROL

630 43°26'.42N 08°21'.59W

La Graña

Ensenada de Cariño

Depths in Metres

San Cristobal
Oc(2)WR.10s

Castillo de San Felipe

Port development

Red

W

Red

Q.R

Fl.G2s

045°

085°

Punta del Segaño

F.R
TV mast

Fl(2)R.7s

Fl.1.5s

Oc.4s

Fl(2)R.9s

Fl(2)G.7s

Fl(2)G.9s

Ensenada del Baño

Fl.2s

060°

075°

Fish quay

Darsena de Curuxeiros

Fl(4)G.11s   Fl(4)R. 6s

Fl(2+1)R. 12s

Fl(2+1)G. 12s

2

9

10

20

15

14

12

5

5

Cabo Prioriño Chico

0   0·5   1
Nautical Mile

EL FERROL

V. PORTOCELO TO LA CORUNA

PILOTAGE

Approach and entrance

By day or night

A track of 065° from ⊕630 will clear the outer end of the new breakwater seen on the right to line up 045° in the white sector of San Cristobal light (white truncated tower Oc(2)WR.10s). Before reaching Punta del Segaño align the next marks on 085° (both white truncated towers front Fl.1.5s, rear Oc.4s) taking care to leave the SH buoy and shallows off Pta del Segaño to starboard. Then follow the buoyed channel inwards and identify the entrance to Darsena de Curuxeiros beyond the ro-ro berth (Fl(4)R.11s).

Berthing

The only yacht berths now are in Darsena de Curuxeiros (which is also busy with local ferries) and it will be a question of taking what is available.

The small marina at La Graña has been renovated and can accept the occasional visitor up to 12m in 4-6m but with only a few facilities. Darsena de Curuxeiros is crowded and busy but an alongside berth may be found here.

Anchoring

Temporary anchorages can be found in the following places: Ensenada de Cariño, provided the harbour works have not encroached; to the E of Castillo de San Felipe, and in Ensenada de Baño.

Construction of new harbour to the NE of Cabo Prioriño Chico

130 Ares Marina

Cat A*

Small new marina in a pleasant resort with most facilities and visitors' berths

Location
43°25'.00N 08°14'.00W

Shelter
Good except from NE

Depth restrictions
2–2.5m in marina; deep approach

Night entry
Possible

Tidal information
As for La Coruña (Standard Port)

Mean height of tide (m)

MHWS	MHWN	MLWN	MLWS
4.2	2.8	1.6	0.3

Berthing
On fingers on pontoons

Facilities
Usual marina and small town

Charts
BA 1111 (200)
Spanish 412A (25)

Weather
La Coruña Ch 26 0840, 1240, 2010
Navtex D

Radio
Ch 09 (English spoken)

Telephone
☎ 981 46 87 87
Email
secretaria@nauticoares.com
www.nauticoares.com

PILOTAGE

Approach and entrance

By day or night

From the W in any swell keep S of Bajo de Miranda with 3.7m over it to the SW of Isla de Miranda lying 1M W of Ares breakwater. Otherwise a track of 000° from ⊕631 (see page 180) will clear the breakwater end (Fl(3)R.9s). Round this and call on Ch 09 for a berth (0900–2200; English spoken).

Berthing

On fingers on pontoons, 12m maximum. The pier is for fishing boats. There is 2–2.5m over most of the pontoon area.

Moorings

Are all private.

Anchoring

Moorings take up most of the space to the NE of the marina but anchorage can be found in 2–3m to the E or NE of the breakwater with shelter from the W.

Ashore in Ares

Facilities

Water and electricity on the pontoons; showers and heads in the marina building; craneage available and a 35-tonne travel-lift expected; fuel at the moment only by cans from garage who will deliver in quantity; fuel pumps in marina expected in 2006; repairs by arrangement; shops and provisioning a 10-minute walk into Ares; restaurant and café in marina building and many more in the town.

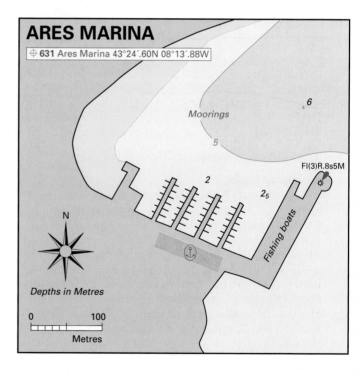

ARES MARINA
⊕ **631** Ares Marina 43°24'.60N 08°13'.88W

Moorings

6

5

Fl(3)R.8s5M

2

2₅

Fishing boats

N

Depths in Metres

0   100

Metres

Leisure

Ares is a modern town and has the usual distractions of a seaside resort with good but crowded beaches.

Travel

Half-hourly bus service to El Ferrol (20 minutes) whence there are bus and rail connections to the rest of Spain. Nearest airports La Coruña (40 minutes) and Santiago de Compostela (1 hour).

Ares Marina looking ESE

Marina looking from end of breakwater

Ria de Ares

The ria extends eastward for 3 miles from Ares to Betanzos and the Río Eume. The N shore is now much obstructed by fish farms and Ensenada de Redes almost entirely taken up by one. It may be possible to anchor to the N of a farm between Isolete Mouron and Punta Modias with some shelter from the W but Spanish charts 4125 or 412A would be needed.

The ria shallows gradually up to the low railway bridge before Puentedueme town where there is 1m but no discernible channel.

Puentedueme is a historical town and worth a dinghy trip at most stages of the tide; the Castelo de Andrade perched over the town is worth a visit.

Ria de Betanzos

Río Mondeo may be entered to the S of Miño peninsula which lies 1M SSE of Sada. There is a small drying harbour on the S side of Miño. From here the río winds 4M to Betanzos, passing under a bridge with a clearance of approximately 20m. Spanish chart 412A is the only guide to the run of the channel and although excursion boats run up to the drying quay at Betanzos on the tide, it would be an adventurous stranger that tried it in a deep-draught masted craft.

Betanzos is an ancient medieval city with many historical attractions including the 12th-century church of Santa Maria de Azogue, an excellent museum and many restaurants around the main square and waterfront.

131 Sada Marina (Fontán)

Cat A

Large expanding marina with all facilities and security; a good place to lay up

Location
43°21′.00N 08°14′.00W

Shelter
Good in the marina

Depth restrictions
4m in entrance, 2.6–2m at berths

Night entry
Well lit, no leading lights

Tidal information
As for La Coruña (Standard Port)

Mean height of tide (m)

MHWS	MHWN	MLWN	MLWS
4.2	2.8	1.6	0.3

Berthing
At pontoons with fingers

Facilities
Those of a large modern marina

Charts
BA 1118 (10)
Spanish 412A (25)

Weather
La Coruña Ch 26 at 0840, 1240, 2010
Navtex D

Radio
Marina Sada Ch 09

Telephone
☎ 981 61 90 15
Fax 981 61 92 87
Marinasada@igatel.net

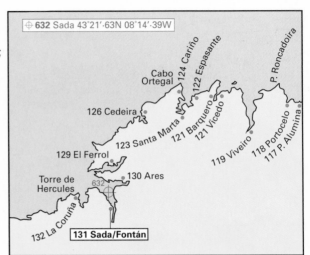

⊕ 632 Sada 43°21′·63N 08°14′·39W

Cabo Ortegal
124 Cariño
122 Espasante
P. Roncadoira
126 Cedeira
123 Santa Marta
121 Barquero
121 Vicedo
119 Viveiro
118 Portocelo
117 P. Alumina
129 El Ferrol
130 Ares
Torre de Hercules
632
132 La Coruña
131 Sada/Fontán

Local berths   Fishing harbour and lonja

Office, fuel and travel-lift   Visitors' berths

Sada Marina and Fontán looking NNW

PILOTAGE

Approaches

By day or night

From ⊕630 off the entrance to El Ferrol there are no offlying dangers provided ½M is kept offshore and a track of 120° on Punta de San Pedro (Fl(2)WR.7s5m3M) maintained until the Sada breakwater (Fl(4)G.11s) is sighted and the way is clear to ⊕632 off the entrance.

Entrance

Wide and straightforward.

Berthing

A prior call on Ch 09 may get a berth allocated. Otherwise select a vacant one on the outer pontoons and check with the office.

Moorings

None for visitors.

Anchoring

Outside clear of the entrance in 1–3m.

Ashore in Sada and Fontán

The fishing harbour in Fontán and the marina at Sada have developed in parallel. Much progress has been made to the marina side in recent years and continues. The scope of the harbour was much enhanced by the removal of La Pulgeira rock and beacon in the middle of the harbour near the end of the pier for the local boats on the W side. There are good laying up facilities and security and this is probably the best place to overwinter along the coast.

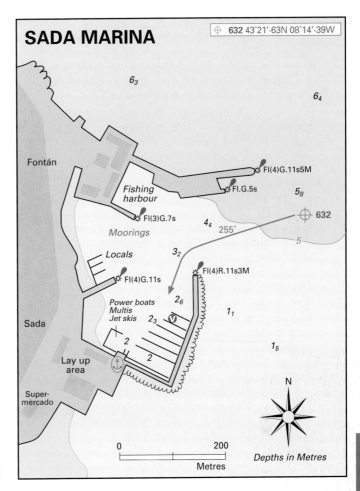

The fuel berth and travel-lift dock looking towards entrance

Facilities

Water and electricity on the pontoons to which access is by card; diesel and petrol at fuel berth; 32-tonne travel-lift; craneage up to 10-tonne; heads and showers; repair facilities under cover if needed; chandlery. Adequate shops within easy walking distance, and a market. Large *supermarcado* S of marina.

Leisure

Sada is a popular seaside resort and there is the usual range of restaurants, shops, cafés and entertainments. Otherwise a dinghy trip up the Río Mondeo to the ancient town of Betanzos on the tide, or by one of the excursion boats that run up the river might amuse. See above for some details of Betanzos. There is a good beach at Playa de Sada.

Fiestas

16 July Feast of Our Lady of Mount Carmel; 15–18 Aug St Roch.

Travel

Sada is off the main rail and motorway routes (but not by much) and buses run to Betanzos to connect. If laying up here, La Coruña airport with occasional flights to UK in the summer, or otherwise via Madrid, is only 15km, with Santiago de Compostela international airport 45 minutes along the motorway.

V. PORTOCELO TO LA CORUNA

132 La Coruña

Cat A*

Large commercial and fishing port with first-class marinas that welcomes visitors. A historical city with good communications and all facilities

Location
43°24′.00N 08°23′.00W

Shelter
Excellent inside

Warning
Outer leading lines must be followed in heavy weather or swell

Depth restrictions
None for yachts

Night entry
Very well lit

Tidal information
A Coruña is a Standard Port

Mean height of tide (m)

MHWS	MHWN	MLWN	MLWS
4.2	2.8	1.6	0.3

Tidal stream
Little in the harbour

Berthing
At fingers on pontoons in marina

Facilities
Those of major city and marina
Hospitals in the city

Charts
BA 1110 (10)
Spanish 412A (25)

Weather
La Coruña Ch 26 at 0840, 1240, 2010
Navtex D. Poor reception reported in harbour area

Radio
Port Control Ch 12
Marina Ch 09

Telephone
Marina ☎ 981 91 41 42
Email administracion@darsenacoruna.com
www.darsenacoruna.com

A lifeboat is maintained here

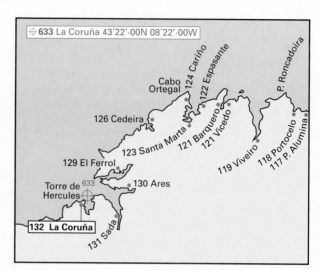

⊕ 633 La Coruña 43°22′.00N 08°22′.00W

Cabo Ortegal — 124 Cariño — 122 Espasante — P. Roncadoira
126 Cedeira
123 Santa Marta — 121 Barquero — 121 Vicedo — 119 Viveiro — 118 Portocelo — 117 P. Alumina
129 El Ferrol
Torre de Hercules — 633 — 130 Ares
132 La Coruña — 131 Sada

If tidal predictions for La Coruña are not available:

	Time differences			Height differences			
HW		LW		MHWS	MHWN	MLWN	MLWS
POINT DE GRAVE							
0000	0600	0500	1200				
and	and	and	and	5.4	4.4	2.1	1.0
1200	1800	1700	2400				
La Coruña							
−0130	−0100	−0045	−0030	−1.6	−1.6	−0.6	−0.5

PILOTAGE

Approaches
By day or night

Warning

The only safe approach in heavy swell or storm conditions is on the Punta Mera leading line S of Banco Yacentes. The latter should be avoided in any seaway.

From N

From ⊕630 pick up the Punta Flateira leading line 182° (front Iso.WRG.2s, rear Oc.R.4s; both RW chequered square towers) and proceed down it to ⊕633; the huge breakwater with the white twin control tower near the root and end light Fl.G.3s will be conspicuous.

From W

To the N of the conspicuous square stone tower of Torre de Hercules (Fl(4)20s) pick up the Punta Mera leading line 108° in the white sector (front Oc.WR.4s, rear Fl.W.4s, both white octagonal towers) and proceed down it until the starboard hand buoy (Fl(3)G.5s) is abaft the beam when course may be altered to SSE to pick up the Punta Flateira line on 182° as above to proceed to ⊕633 and the entrance.

Entrance

Round the breakwater end at about 100m and make good a track of about 280° to leave Castillo de San Anton (Fl(2)G.7s) 100m to starboard. The entrance to the marina (Oc.G.4s and Q.R) will be seen 300m

Torre de Hercules   San Anton   Control

Marina entrance

280°

La Coruña looking NNW

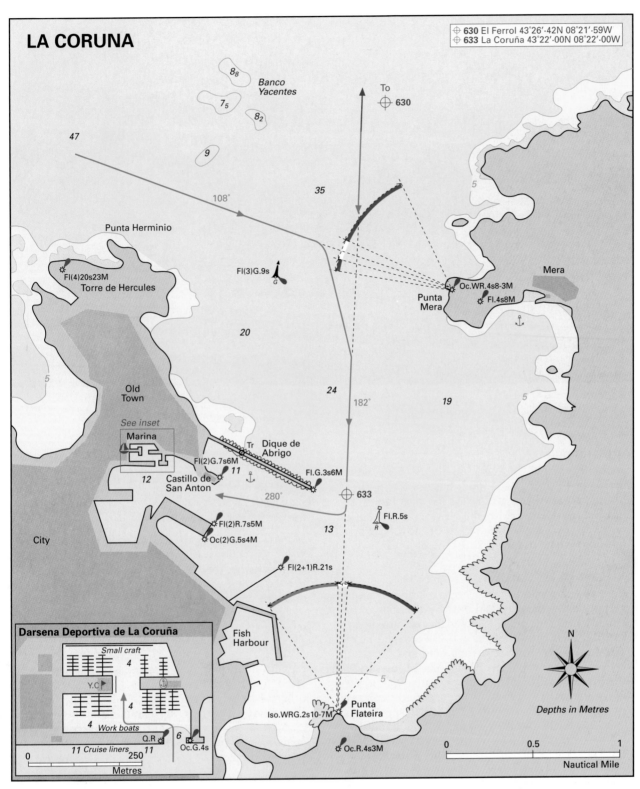

LA CORUNA

⊕ **630** El Ferrol 43°26'·42N 08°21'·59W
⊕ **633** La Coruña 43°22'·00N 08°22'·00W

88

Banco Yacentes

7₅

8₂

9

47

108°

35

To ⊕ 630

Punta Herminio

Fl(4)20s23M
Torre de Hercules

Fl(3)G.9s

20

Old Town

See inset
Marina

24

182°

19

Mera

Oc.WR.4s8-3M
Punta Mera
Fl.4s8M

Fl(2)G.7s6M
11
Castillo de San Anton
12

Tr   Dique de Abrigo

Fl.G.3s6M

280°

⊕ 633

Fl.R.5s

Fl(2)R.7s5M
Oc(2)G.5s4M

13

City

Fl(2+1)R.21s

Fish Harbour

N

5

Darsena Deportiva de La Coruña

Small craft

4

Y.C

4

4 *Work boats*

Q.R   6
Oc.G.4s

11 *Cruise liners* 11
250
0
Metres

Iso.WRG.2s10-7M   Punta Flateira

Oc.R.4s3M

Depths in Metres

0   0.5   1
Nautical Mile

beyond the Castillo; there is often a cruise liner berthed along its outer wall. Turn in to starboard and sharp back to port before turning back to starboard to reach the marina building.

Berthing

Secure alongside the marina building and enquire at the office. Up to 30m, the bigger boats berth to the S of the marina building. Berths are kept for visitors but a prior call on Ch 09 is recommended. There is 4m over most of the basin. The fingers on the pontoons are substantial.

The old berths and marina at the W end of Dique de Abrigo are being renovated and replaced and should be open again for visitors in 2006.

Moorings

There are now no moorings for visiting yachts in the harbour and those to the N of Castillo de San Anton are private.

La Coruña marina looking N

Anchoring

It is still possible to anchor to the S of Dique de Abrigo in 15–10m, thick mud, but use a trip line if to the W as there are a lot of old moorings. Ensenada de Mera 1½M to the NE is a more peaceful anchorage in N and E winds clear of the fishing boat moorings which occupy a lot of the bay.

Ashore in La Coruña

The city has a number of historic connections with the UK. It was the principal port for the start of the Armada in 1588; an ill-founded British attempt to eject the French from Spain in 1809 resulted in the remnants of the army retreating here and the death of the commanding General, Sir John Moore. In the subsequent campaign in the Peninsula War it was one of the main supply ports and has since had busy trading links with the UK. The old town on the peninsula to the N of the marina is now dominated by the high-rise sprawl of the new city to the S. Maritime trade is still active, the port is much favoured by cruise liners and a large new fishing facility has been built in the S part of the harbour at Oza.

Facilities

Water and electricity on the pontoons; fuel at the old fuelling berth to the N of Castillo de San Anton where there is only 1.2m; major repairs to hull, engine, electrics and electronics are possible; 32-tonne travel-lift and craneage; heads and showers in the marina building where there is also a clubhouse (respectable dress expected) and restaurant;

Customs office on site; the city centre with many shops and *supermercados* is within easy walking distance.

Leisure

A visit to the Turismo next to the marina is an essential first stop to see what is on offer. Most visual attractions are nearby in the old town and a climb to the top of Torre de Hercules produces rewarding views. Castillo de San Anton is now a museum and there are several others. The selection of tapas bars, cafés and restaurants will satisfy the most demanding.

Travel

La Coruña airport is just to the S of the city. There are a few direct flights to the UK in the summer, otherwise twice daily to Madrid for onward connections. Santiago de Compostela international airport is 45 minutes away by motorway. The nearest ferry port is Santander, halfway along the coast to the E.

The pilgrim route to Santiago

The final section of the oldest established tourist route in Europe runs S to Santiago de Compostela, where homage is paid to St James. Since medieval times the Camino de Santiago has been thronged with thousands of walkers and riders who still follow the old paths and roads leading S. A visit to the basilica, especially on 25 July (St James's Day) or other holy days, when the huge incense burner (*botafumeiro*) is swung by eight priests, is not to be missed.

Torre de Hercules looking W. A survivor from Roman times, it is reputedly the oldest working lighthouse in the world but little of the original structure now remains

Pilgrims en route to Santiago

Appendix

1. LIST OF LIGHTS

La Gironde

1289 **BXA buoy** Iso.4s7M Red ball on red buoy, white stripes Ra refl Racon

1290 **La Coubre** Fl(2)10s64m28M White tower, red top
Auxiliary F.RG.42m 030°-R-043°-G-060°-R-110° same structure

1293.9 **La Palmyre Ldg lts 081°** *Front* 1.1M from rear
Front DirIso.4s21m20M White pylon on dolphin 080.5°-(intens)-082.5°
Auxiliary Q(2)5s10m2M On same structure

1294 *Common rear* DirQ.57m27M White radar tower 080.7°-(intens)-082.2°
Auxiliary DirF.R.57m17M 325.5°-intens-328.5° On same structure

1294.1 **Terre-Negre** Oc(3)WRG.12s39m18-14M White tower, red top on W side 304°-R-319°-W-327°-G-000°-W-004°-G-097°-W-104°-R-116°

1300 **Cordouan** Oc(2+1)WRG.12s60m22-18M White tower, grey top. 014°-W-126°-G-179°-W-250°-W(unintens)-267°-R-(unintens)-294.5°-R-014° Obscd in estuary when bearing more than 285°

1310 **St Nicolas Ldg lts 063°** *Front* DirQG.22m16M White square tower 061.5°-(intens)-064.5°

1310.1 **Pte de Grave** Oc.WRG.4s26m19-15M White square tower, black corners and top. 033°-W(unintens)-054°-W- 233.5°-R-303°-W-312°-G- 330°-W-341°-W(unintens)-025°.

1312 **Le Chay Ldg lts 041°** DirQR.33m18M White tower, red top 039.5°-(intens)-042.5°

1312.1 **St Pierre** DirQR.61m18M Red water tower 039°-(intens)-043° Synchronised rear with front

Royan

1304 **Jetée Sud head** Fl(2)R.10s11m12M White tower, red brickwork base

1307 **Digue Sud head** Fl(3)G.12s2m6M White metal post, green top

1308 **Digue Ouest head** Fl(3)R.12s8m6M White metal mast, red top

Verdon

1326 **N Dolphin** DirIso.WRG.4s4m12-8M 2 platforms on white dolphin, black top, white bands. 165°-G-170°-W-173°-R-178°

Meschers

Ldg lts 352° 2F

There are many lit buoys and beacons marking the channel to Bordeaux which can be found on SHOM charts 7426 and 7427. The Dordogne above Bourg is not lit. Only lights displayed on or in the vicinity of harbours are shown below.

Pauillac

1358.4 **Breakwater elbow** Fl.G.4s7m5M Green mast
1358.5 **Contre jetée** Q.R.4m2M Red square on red post
1358.6 **Breakwater S head** Q.G.7m4M Green mast

Blaye

1362 **N quay head** Q(3)R.5s6m3M Red mast

Bourg

Dock entrance Fl(4)R.12s

Hourtin

1372 45°08′.5N 01°09′.7W Fl.5s55m23M Red square brick tower, grey top

Arcachon

1378 **Cap Ferret** Fl.R.5s53m27M White truncated tower red top
Auxiliary Oc(3)12s46m14M Same structure.

1379 **Port de la Vigne** Iso.R.4s7m5M White metal post, red top

1379.5 **P d'Arcachon W breakwater** Q.G.6m6M Green metal mast

1379.6 **E Breakwater** Q.R.6m6M Red metal mast

1379.7/8 **Andernos** Fl.G.4s Fl.R.4s

1380 **La Salie wharf** Q(9)15s.19m10M W cardinal mark

1381 **ATT ARC buoy** LFl.10s Ball on red buoy, white stripes, ra refl

1381.2 **La Salie buoy** Fl(2)6s 2 black balls on black buoy, red band

Contis

1382 44°05′.17N 01°19′.2W Fl(4)25s.50m23M White round tower, black diagonal stripes

Capbreton

1384 **Digue Nord** Fl(2)R.6s13m12M Horn 30s White tower, red top

1386 **Estacade Sud** Fl(2)G.6s9m12M White metal post, green top
NE marina head F.R
SW marina head Fl(4)G.4s

L'Adour River, Bayonne and Anglet

1386.5 **BA buoy** LFl.10s5M Red ball on red buoy, white stripes, ra refl

1387 **Digue J Lesbordes** Q.R.11m8M White square tower, red top

1387.2 **Boucau Ldg lts 090°** DirQ.9m19M White pylon, red top 086.5°-(intens)-093.5°

1387.21 *Rear* DirQ.15m19M White pylon, red top 086.5°-(intense)-093.5°

1387.3 **Jetée Nord** Iso.R.4s.12m8M White pylon, red top

1387.4 **Jetée Sud** Iso.G.4s9m10M White square tower, green top

1387.5 **Digue Sud** Q(9)15s15m6M West cardinal

1388 **Entrance Ldg lts 111.5°** DirF.G.6m14M White hut, green band 109°-(intens)-114°.

1388.1 *Rear* DirF.G.10m14M White square tower, green bands, on building 109°-(intens)-114°.

1391 **Marina entrance W side** Fl.G.2s5m2M White pylon, green top.

There are a number of lit buoys and beacons, and two more sets of leading lights up to the first bridge at Bayonne

Pointe Saint-Martin

1410 **Pointe Saint-Martin** Fl(2)10s73m29M White truncated tower, black top

Biarritz

1412.4 **Ldg lts 174°** *Front* Fl.R.2s7m3M White metal mast
1412.41 *Rear* Fl.R.2s19m3M White metal mast

Baie de St Jean-de-Luz

1414   **Ste-Barbe Ldg lts 101°** DirOc(4)R.12s30m18M White triangle on white hut 095°-(intens)-107°

1416   *Rear* DirOc(4)R.12s47m18M Black triangle on white square tower 095°-(intens)-107° Synchronised with front

1417   **Groyne N head** Fl.R.4s7m2M White structure.

1418   **Entrance Ldg lts 150°.42´** *Front* Jetée Est DirQ.G.18m16M White pyramidal tower, red stripe 149°-(intense)-152°

1420   *Rear* Dir.Q.G.27m16M White pyramidal tower, green stripe 149°-(intens)-152°

1422   **Digue des Criquas** Iso.G.4s11m6M Green square tower

1424   **Passe d'Illarguita, Le Socoa Ldg lts138.5°** *Front* Q.WR.36m12/8M White square tower, black stripe shore-W-264°-R-282°-W-shore

1424.1   **Bordagain** *Rear* DirQ.67m20M Black rectangle, white band on white pylon 134.5°-(intens)-141.5°

Baie de Fontarrabie

French side

1425   **Training wall head** LFl.R.10s8m5M White column, red top

1425.5   **Training wall root** Fl.R.2.5s6m4M Red metal column 346.5°-vis-181.5°

1426   **Marina wall elbow** Fl(2)R.6s6m2M White column. Red top 294°-vis-114°

1426.3   **Marina entrance** F.R.2m Strip light

1426.5   **Chenal de Bidasoa** VQ(3)G.5s3m3M Green metal column

1426.6   **Chenal de Bidasoa** LFl.G.10s3m4M Green metal column

1426.7   **Marina jetée sud head** Fl.Y.4s5m4M Yellow metal column

Spanish side

1452   **Cabo Higuer** Fl(2)10s 63m23M Square stone tower, red cupola 072°-vis-340°

Fuenterrabía

1453   **Training wall head** Fl(3)G.9s.9m5M Green tower

1453.5   **Marina N entrance** Fl(4)G.11s.9m3M Green triangle on green beacon

1453.51   **Marina S entrance** Fl(4)R.11s.9m1M Red square on red beacon

1454   **Gurutzeaundi N breakwater elbow** Fl(3)G.9s7m1M Metal post

1454.2   **N breakwater head** Fl(2)R.7s6m3M Masonry tower

1454.3   **N breakwater corner** Q(3)5s13m3M E cardinal

1454.5   **Breakwater head** Fl(2)G.7s7m5M Metal post

1454.6   S **Breakwater head** Fl(3)R.9s7m1M Metal post

Pasajes

1456   **Cabo de la Plata** Oc.4s151m13M White castellated building 285°-vis-250°

1456.2   **Bancha de este** Fl.R.5s18m11M Red metal tower

1456.4   **Bancha del Oueste** Fl.G.5s18m7M Green metal tower

1457   **Punta Arando Grande** Fl(2)R.7s10m11M White masonry tower, red bands

1457.5   **Atalaya Semaforo** 3 Fl.R.2s96m5M plus harbour signals (see plan) Black metal structure Racon

1458   **Senocozulua** DirOc(2)WRG.12s50m6-3M White towers and buildings Racon

1459   **Lts in line 154°49´** *Front* Q.67m18M White masonry tower

1459.1   *Rear* 40m from front Oc.3s86m18M White masonry tower

1460   **Dique de Senocozulua** Fl(2)G.7s12m11M White tower, green bands

1462   **Punta de las Cruces** Fl(3)G.9s9m9M Green and white post

1466   **Castillo de Santa Isabel** Fl(4)R.11s11m8M Red and white metal tower

1468   **Punta del Mirador** Fl.R.5s11m8M Stone arch

1470   **Ermita de Santa Ana** Oc.R.4s32m7M Bracket on masonry hut

1472   **Punta Aroca** Fl(3)R.9s19m10M Red and white metal tower

1474   **Punta Calparra** Fl(4)G.11s9m8M Green and white metal tower on hut

1475   **Torre de San Pedro** Fl.G.5s8m9M White post

There are a number of lights marking the corners and ends of wharves in the commercial and industrial harbours.

San Sebastián (Donostia)

1482   **Isla de Santa Clara** Fl.5s51m9M White round tower on N face of house

1483   **Igueldo or S. Sebastián** Fl(2+1)15s132m26M White round tower on N face of house.

1484   **La Concha Ldg lts 158°** *Front* Q.R.10m7M Grey post 143°-vis-173°
Rear Oc.R.4s16m7M Grey post 154°-vis-162°

1485   **Harbour entrance E** Fl(2)G.8s9m3M Column

1486   **Harbour entrance W** Fl(2)R.8s8m5M Column

Río de Orio

1488.1   **Breakwater elbow** Fl.G.5s10m3M Green post

1488.21   **Breakwater head** Fl(4)G.11s18m5M Grey round tower

1488.2   **Breakwater head** Fl(4)R.11s12m3M Grey round tower

1488.3 and 32
    Bridge N & S sides Q.R.4m3M/Q.R.4m3M

1488.38   **No.9** Fl(4)G.8s.6m1M Green rectangular mast

1488.4   **No.10** Fl.G.5s6m1M Green rectangular mast

1488.44   **No.11** Fl(2)G.7s6m1M Green rectangular mast

1488.5   **Azipura head** Q.G.6m1M Green rectangular mast

Getaria

1489   **Isla de San Antón** Fl(4)15s91m21M White round tower and dwelling

1489.6   **Mole head** Fl(3)G.9s11m5M Masonry tower

1489.7   **Elbow** Q(3)5s14m3M E cardinal, black and yellow tower

1490   **N Pier head** Fl(4)G.11s10m1M Concrete mast

1490.5   **Breakwater head** Fl(3)R.9s11m3M Masonry tower.

1491   **S Pier head** Fl(4)R.11s10m1M Concrete mast

Zumaia

1493   **Zumaia light** Oc(1+3)12s39m12M White octagonal tower, blue cupola and building

1494   **W breakwater** Fl(2)G.7s18m5M Masonry tower

1494.2   **E breakwater** Fl(2)R.7s8m3M Masonry tower

1494.5   **Marina N head** Fl(3)R.9s6m1M White post on masonry tower

1494.6   **Marina pier** Fl(4)R.11s6m1M White post on masonry tower

1494.7   **Marina S head** Fl(2+1)G.10s6m1M White post on masonry tower

1494.7   **Esplanade corner** Q.R.8m1M Red post

Motrico

1494.9   **N Breakwater head** Fl.G.5s10m5M Grey rectangular mast

1495   **Inner breakwater** Fl(2)G.7s10m1M Post

1496   **Ldg lts 236.5°** *Front* Fl(2)R.7s10m3M Post

1496.1   *Rear* F.R.63m5M Clock tower of hermitage

Ondárroa

1498   **Breakwater head** Fl(3)G.8s13m12M Siren Mo(O)20s Green tripod

1499   **Mole head** Fl(2)R.6s7m6M White tower

1499.5   **Cargo wharf head** F.R.6m1M Grey tripod

1500   **Inner N mole** F.G.7m4M Grey tripod

1500.2   **S Mole head** F.R.7m4M White post

1502   **Cabo de Santa Catalina** Fl(1+3)20s44m17M Horn Mo(L)20s Grey truncated conical tower on octagonal base

Lequeitio

1504	**Amandarri** Fl.G.4s8m5M Grey tower
1505	**Aislado Rock** Fl(2)R.8s5m4M Grey conical tower
1506	**Tinglado head** F.G.5m2M Aluminium mast
1508	**Muelle Sur head** F.R.4m2M Red post

Elanchove

1510 **Dique Sur head** F.WR.7m8/5M Red metal tripod 000°-W-315°-R-000°

1510.4 **Dique Norte** Fl.G.3s8m4M Green metal tripod

Bermeo

1512 **Rosape** Fl(2)WR.10s36m7M White building 108°-R-204°-W-232°

1513 **Breakwater head** Fl.G.4.5s16m4M Grey truncated conical tower

1513.2 **Spur head** F.G.5m2M Green metal tripod

1513.4 **Breakwater head** Fl.R.3s6m3M Red metal tripod

1514 **N Pier head** F.G.5m3M Green tower

1515 **Muelle de Erosape** F.R.5m4M Red post

1520 **Cabo Machicaco** Fl.7s.120m24M Siren Mo(M)60s Masonry tower and building, aluminium lantern, DGPS projected

Arminza

1521 **Breakwater head** Fl(2)R.8s7m4M Grey masonry tower

1523 **Gorlitz (Cabo Villano)** Fl(1+2)16s163m22M White tower

Plencia

1523.5 **W breakwater** Fl(2)G.7s10m5M Green structure

1523.6 **E breakwater** Fl(2)R.7s6m5M Red structure

1523.7 **Inner basin W side** F.G.4m Green beacon

1523.75 **Inner basin E side** F.R.4m Red beacon

Bilbao

1524 **Punta Galea** Fl(3)8s82m19M 011°-vis- 227° Stone tower with dwelling, grey cupola

1524.01 **68m tower** Siren Mo(G)30s

1524.2 **E breakwater head** Fl.R.5s19m7M Red metal column

1524.4 **N jetty head end Ciervana** Fl(2)G.8s20m5M Green round tower

1524.45 **Wharf AZ-1 head** Fl.G.5s10m1M Green round column

1524.6 **Counter jetty head** Fl(2+1)G.10s13m3M Green round tower, red band.

1525 **Algorta (Getxo) jetty head** Fl.R.5s16m3M White tower

1525.1 **Algorta (Getxo) jetty** Oc.WR.4s9m3M Grey column 134°-W-149°-R-174°

1526.2 **Getxo marina head** Q.R.3m2M Red metal column

1526.3 **Las Arenas marina head** Oc.G.4s1m1M Round tower

1526.35 **Las Arenas marina head** Oc.R.4s2m1M Round tower

1526.4 **West breakwater head** Fl.G.5s21m10M Green tubular tripod Racon

1527.2 **Espignon 1 head (N)** Fl(4)G.12s14m1M Green tripod on hut

1527.22 **Espignon 1 head (S)** Fl.G.5s14m1M Green tripod on building

1527.4 **Espignon 2 head (N)** Fl(2+1)G.10s11m1M Green tower, red band, on dwelling

1527.42 **Espignon 2 head (S)** Fl(2)G.8s14m1M Green tripod on hut

1529 **Portugalete mole head** Fl(2+1)G.10s12m1M Green tower, red band

1531 **Churruca breakwater head** Fl(2)R.6s8m1M Red tripod on hut

There are many more lights in the commercial docks at Santurce, Portugalete, Zierbena and up the river to Bilbao of little interest to yachts going to Getxo or Las Arenas.

There are 3 red flashing buoys between Punta Galea and Getxo marking the E side of the main channel and one red flashing buoy off the end of Churruca breakwater at the entrance to the river.

Castro Urdiales

1536 **Castillo de Santa Ana** Fl(4)24s47m20M Siren Mo(C)60s Truncated conical tower on turret of castle

1537 **N breakwater head** Fl.G.3s12m6M Octagonal tower

1537.2 **Muelle Commerciale** Q(2)R.6s8m5M Grey pillar

1538 **Inner basin head** F.G.6m3M

1538.2 **Inner basin head** F.R.6m2M

Laredo

1540 **N breakwater head** Fl(4)R.11s9m5M Masonry column

1541 **Training wall** Fl.G.5s2M Green post

Santoña, Punta del Pasaje and Colindres

1542 **Punta Pescador** Fl(3+1)18s37m17M White truncated tower and building

1546 **Santoña Ldg lts 283.5°** *Front* Fl.2s5m8M Black triangle on metal framework

1546.1 *Rear* Oc(2)5s12m11M Disc on metal framework 279.5°-vis-287.5°

1547 **Basin N head** F.R.6m4M Red 3-sided tower

1547.1 **Basin corner** F.G.5m2M Concrete post

1547.2 **N head** F.G.6m4M

1548 **Basin S head** Fl(2)R.6s.6m4M White truncated tower, red band

1548.2 **New harbour S pier** Fl.G.5s6m3M White truncated tower, green band

Punta del Pasaje Four Fl.Y buoys mark the W extent of the moorings off the yacht club

Canal de Colindres The channel S to Colindres is marked on the W side by a number of Fl.G buoys and the entrance to the harbour by a Fl.R.2.5s on the N pier and a Fl.G.2.5s on the S pier

1552 **Cabo Ajo** Oc(3)16s.69m17M White round tower

Santander

1554 **Isla Mouro** Fl(3)21s37m7M White tower on dwelling

1556 **La Cerda** Fl(1+4)20s22m7M White square tower on dwelling Obscd when bearing less than 160°

1556.5 **Puntal ldg lts 236°** *Front* Q.7m6M Post on metal tower 231.8°-(intens)-239.8° Racon

1556.51 *Rear* Iso.R.4s10m6M Post on metal tower 231.8°-(intens)-239.8°

1557 **Peña Horadada** Fl(2)7s5m5M Black round tower, red band

1557.3 **Dir lt 259.5°** DirWRG18m6M Metal post

1557.4 **Punta del Rostro** Fl(2)G.7s5m3M Metal post

1557.5 **Canal de Pedreña** Fl(3)G.9s8m2M Green triangle on green post

1557.6 **Pedreña Marina** Q.G.7m2M Green post

1557.61 **Pedreña marina** Q.R.7m2M Red post

1558 **Dársena de Molnedo** Q.R.10m3M Red and white column

1558.2 **Dársena de Molnedo** Q.G.10m3M Green and white column

1559.95 **Marina del Cantabrico** Q.G.7m2M Grey metal column

1559.96 **Marina del Cantabrico** Q.R.7m2M Grey metal column

1559.97 **Ldg lts 235.6°** *Front* Iso.2s.9m2M Tall grey metal column

1559.98 *Rear* Oc.5s.10m2M White column, red bands

There are in addition a number of lit buoys marking the main channel up the Río Astillero and lights on the corners of docks and pier.

1561 **Cabo Mayor** Fl(2)10s89m21M Horn Mo(M)40s White tower

Comillas

1566 **Outer Ldg lt** 194° Iso.2s34m4M White conical tower, black band
1566.1 *Rear* Oc.4s38m4M White conical tower, black band
1568 **Inner Ldg lts** 245° Iso.2s14m3M White tower, black band
1568.1 *Rear* F.R.18m3M White tower, black band
1570 **Breakwater end** F.G.5m Green and white post
1571 **Contradique head** F.R.8M Red and white post

San Vicente de la Barquera

1574 **Punta de la Silla** Oc.3.5s41m13M 115°-vis-250° Horn Mo(V)30s Square white masonry tower and dwelling
1576 **W breakwater head** Fl.WG.2s6m7/6M Green truncated conical masonry tower 175°-G-235°-W-045°
1577 **E breakwater head** Fl(2)R.8s6m5M Red truncated conical masonry tower
1578 **Punta de la Espina** F.G.6m2M Green truncated conical masonry tower
1580 **Punta San Emeterio** Fl.5s66m20M Grey round tower on white dwelling

Llanes

1582 **Punta de San Anton** Fl(4)15s16m15M White octagonal tower, grey cupola and dwelling
1582 **Osa breakwater** Fl.G.5s13m5M Round green masonry tower
1585 **Dock breakwater head** Fl(2)G.7s.6m1M Round green masonry tower

Ribadesella

1586 **Somos** Fl(2+1)12s113m 25M Tower, grey cupola and dwelling
1587 **Wharf head** Fl(2)R.6s10m5M Round masonry tower 278.4°-vis-212.9°
1587.5 **Marina breakwater head** Q.3M NCM, yellow beacon, black top

Lastres

1589 **Breakwater head** Fl(3)G.9s13m4M Round concrete tower
1590 Fl(3)R.9s6m3M Round conical tower
1591 **Cabo Lastres** Fl(5)25s116m23M White round tower, green cupola

Tazones

1592 **Tazones** Fl.7.5s125m20M Octagonal masonry tower on white dwelling
1592.01 140m NNW Horn Mo(V)30s
1593 **Breakwater head** Fl.G.3s10m4M Masonry tower

Gijón (Muelles Locales)

1608 **Piedra Sacramento** Fl(2)G.6s9m5M Octagonal green masonry tower
1609 **Muelle Liquerica** Fl(2)R.6s7m3M Red post
1610 **Malecon de Fomento** Fl(3)G.10s6m1M Green post
1612 **Malecon E Poniente** Q.2m1M N cardinal

Puerto de Musel

1596 **Cabo de Torres** Fl(2)10s80m18M White octagonal tower and dwelling
1597 **Dique P de Asturias** Fl.G.4s22m7M Round grey tower
1597.4 **Contradique exterior** Fl(2)G.6s14m5M Green metal tower
1598 **Contra de la Osa** SW Fl(2)R.6s14m3M Red cabin
1598.1 **NE head** Fl.R.4s11m5M Red post
1598.3 **S corner** Fl(4)R.15s6m1M Red post
1598.4 **N corner** Fl(2+1)R.10s6m3M Red post, green band
1598.42 **NE corner** Q(3)10s11m4M E cardinal
1598.45 **SW corner** Fl(4)G.20s9m1M Green post
1598.5 **Dar de el Musel elbow** Fl.R.3s6m1M Red post

1598.7 **M del Rendienello NW** Fl(2)R.6s6m1M Red post
1598.8 **SE head** Fl(4)G.15s6m1M Green round post
1598.9 **W corner** Fl.G.3s6m1M Green post
1599 **Olano breakwater head** Fl(3)G.9s8m5M Green tower
1602 **Pier 2 head** Fl(2+1)R.12s4m1M Red post, green band.
1603 **Pier 1 NW corner** Fl(4)R.12s4m1M Red post
1603.2 **SE corner** Fl(2+1)G.10s6m1M Green post, red band
1606.5 **Fuel pier head** Fl.Y.3s8m1M Yellow X on yellow post

Candas

1614 **Punta del Cuerno** Oc(2)10s38m15M Horn Mo(C)60s Reddish tower, white dwelling
1616 **Canal de El Carrero Ldg lts** 290° *Front* F.R.8m3M White column
1616.1 *Rear* F.R.62m3M Window of house
1618 **Mole head** Fl(2)G.7s10m4M Grey truncated conical tower

Luanco

1622 **Mole head Ldg lts** 255° *Front* Fl.R.3s4m4M White patch on wall
1622.1 *Rear* Oc.R.8s8m4M White concrete tower
1624 **Juan de Melao breakwater** Fl.G.3s10m4M Round masonry tower
1628 **Cabo Peñas** Fl(3)15s115m35M Siren Mo(P)60s Grey octagonal tower with dwelling

Avilés

1630 **Punta del Castillo** Oc.WR.5s38m20/17M White square tower 091.5°-R(over Bajo El Péton)-113°-W-091.5°
1630.01 190m NW Siren Mo(A)30s
1630.4 **Punta de la Forcada** Fl.R.5s23m5M Red mast on white truncated tower
1631 **Entrance N side** Fl(2)R.7s8m3M Red truncated conical tower
1631.12 **Breakwater 1** Fl(3)R.9s9m1M Red mast on white truncated conical tower
1631.14 **Breakwater 2** Fl(4)R.11s9m1M Red mast on white truncated conical tower
From here there are a succession of red flashing lights and buoys leading up the NE and E sides of the channel
1631.28 **Breakwater W head** Fl.G.5s13m5M 106°-vis-280° Green round tower
1631.3 **S breakwater W end** Fl(2)G.7s12m5M 106°-vis-280° Green round tower, truncated conical base and top
From here there are a succession of flashing green lights and buoys leading up the S and W sides of the channel

San Esteban de Pravia

1634.2 **W breakwater** Fl(2)12s18m15M Siren Mo(N)30s White round tower
1634.5 **Entrance Ldg lts** 206.2° *Front* Q.7m1M White round tower, red bands
1534.6 *Rear* Iso.4s28m1M White metal structure, red bands
1636 **E training wall** Fl(4)G.11s9m3M Truncated pyramidal tower
1636.3 **Training wall No.3** Fl.G.5s8m3M Truncated pyramidal tower
1637 **Ldg lts** 202.5° *Front* Fl.2s7m3M Grey metal post
1637.1 *Rear* Oc.2s10m3M Grey metal post
1637.5 **Training wall No.4** Fl(2)G.7s8m3M Truncated pyramidal tower
1637.7 **Training wall No.5** Fl(3)G.9s7m3M Truncated pyramidal tower
1638 **Basin entrance N** Fl(4)G.11s5m3M Truncated pyramidal tower
1638.4 **Basin entrance S** Fl.R.5s5m3M Truncated pyramidal tower

Cudillero

1640   **Punta Rebollera** Oc(4)16s42m16M Siren Mo(D)30s Octagonal tower and dwelling

1640.2   **East breakwater** Fl(3)R.9s8m2M Red column

1640.4   **West breakwater** Fl(3)G.9s3m2M Green column

1641   **Cabo Vidio** Fl.5s99m25M Siren Mo(V)60s Round masonry tower and dwelling

1642   **Cabo Busto** Fl(4)20s84m25M White square tower

Luarca

1646   **Punta Blanca** Oc(3)15s63m14M Siren Mo(L)30s White square tower and dwelling

1647   **West breakwater** Fl(3)R.9s22m5M Round concrete tower

1649   **Ldg lts 170°** *Front* Fl.5s18m2M White masonry column red bands

1649.1   *Rear* Oc.4s25m2M White masonry column red bands

Vega

1652   **Punta Lama** Fl.R.5s13m3M Metal mast, concrete base

1653   **West breakwater** Fl.G.5s12m3M Metal mast

1654   **Ldg lts** *Front* F.Y.20m1M Triangular concrete structure

1654.1   *Rear* F.Y.27m1M Wooden mast

Navia

1657   **Cabo de San Augustín** Oc(2)12s70m25M White round tower, black bands

Viavélez

1657.5   **Outer breakwater** Fl(2)R.5s 8m4M Truncated conical masonry tower

1657.6   **Inner breakwater** Fl(2)G.5s8m4M Truncated conical masonry tower

Tapia

1658   **Isla Tapia** Fl(2+1)19s22m18M White square tower and dwelling

1659   **North mole** Fl(2)R.7s7m4M Truncated conical masonry tower

1659.2   **South mole** Fl.G.5s8m3M Truncated conical masonry tower

Ribadeo

1660   **Isla Pancha** Fl(3+1)20s26m21M Siren Mo(R)30s White round tower, black bands

1661   **Punta de la Cruz** Fl(4)R.11s16m7M Red round tower

1662   **Ldg lts140°** *Front* Iso.R.18m5M Red diamond on white tower

1662.1   *Rear* Oc.R.4s24m5M Red diamond on white tower

1664   **Ldg lts 205°** *Front* VQ.R.8m3M Red diamond on white concrete tower

1664.1   *Rear* Oc.R.2s18m3M White rectangular structure on house

1664.3   **Los Santos bridge** Fl(4)R.11s8m4M Red square on bridge pillar

1644.35   Fl(2)G.7s8m4M Green triangle on bridge pillar

1664.5   **Porcillan N side** Fl.G.5s9m3M Green post on green and white column

1664.7   **Porcillan S side** Fl.R.5s9m1M Red post on red and white column

1664.9   **Mirasol N side** Fl(2)G.7s9m1M Green post on green and white column

1666   **Mirasol S side** Fl(2)R.7s9m1M Red post on red and white column

1667   **Mirasol SE corner** Fl(3)G.9s9m1M Green post on green and white column

Rinlo

1667.5   **Breakwater** Q.G.12m3M Green round tower

Foz

1668.5   **Training wall head** Q.G.8m10M Post

Burela

1673   **Piedra Burela** Q(3)10s11m7M W cardinal tower

1675.2   **Breakwater head** Fl(2)RG.16m4M Green column 112°-R-162°-G-112°

1675.5   **T jetty head** Fl(3)G.9m3M Green tower

San Ciprián

1676   **Punta Atalaya** Fl(5)20s39m20M White round tower, black band

1676.4   **Islote La Anzuela** Fl.G.3s11m3M White masonry column green band

1677   **Quay SW corner** F.R.9m3M White masonry column

1678   **Dir lt 196°** DirQ.WR.9m5M Red triangle on white masonry tower 178°-R (over Los Farallones)-194°-W-198°

Puerto Alúmina Española

1678.2   **Ldg lts 204°** *Front* Fl(2)6s25m3M White round tower red bands

1678.21   *Rear* Oc.6s35m3M White round tower red bands

1678.3   **Ldg lts 273°** *Front* Fl(2)6s40m3M White round tower red bands

1678.31   *Rear* Oc.6s44m3M White round tower red bands

1678.4   **S Breakwater** Fl(3)R.8s25m4M Grey metal column

1678.6   **N Breakwater** Fl(2)WG.8s17m4M 110°-W-180°-G-110° Grey pyramid on octagonal tower

1678.8   **Punta Roncadoira** Fl.7.5s92m21M White round tower

Viveiro

1679   **Punta de Faro** Fl.R.5s18m7M White tower

1680   **Punta Socastro** Fl.G.5s18m7M Green tower

1681   **Cillero N mole** Fl(2)R.7s8m1M Red column

1682   **T jetty head** Fl(3)R.9s10m1M Column

1683   **S mole head** Fl(2+1)G.21s9m3M Green triangle on green structure

1683.2   **R Landrove channel** Fl(2)G.7s7m1M Green column

1683.5   **Viveiro breakwater** Fl(3)G.9s7m1M Green column

Ria del Barquero

1684   **Isla Colleira** Fl(4)24s87m7M Grey round stone tower on dwelling

1685   **Punta del Castro** Fl(2)7s14m5M White truncated conical tower

1685.11   **Vicedo N head** Fl(4)R.11s9m5M Red post on red and white round tower

1685.12   **Vicedo S head** Fl(4)G.11s9m3M Green post on green and white column

1685.2   **Punta de la Barra** Fl.WRG.3s15m5M White truncated conical tower 198°-G- 213°-W-240°-R-255°-G-070°

1686   **Punta Estaca de Bares** Fl(2)7.5s99m25M Octagonal tower and dwelling

1686.01   150m 345° Siren Mo(B)60s

Ensenada de Santa Marta

1686.1   **Espasante W mole** Fl.R.5s11m3M Red round tower

1686.2   **Espasante E mole** Fl.G.5s6m3M Green metal tower

1686.25   **Ortiguera Mole head** Fl(4)R.11s3M Round red tower

1686.26   **Ortiguera Mole head** Fl(4)G.11s5M Round green tower

1686.29   **Cariño mole head** Fl.G.2s12m3M Green and white round tower

1686.3   **Cabo Ortegal** Oc.8s122m18M White round tower, red band

1687   **Punta Candelaria** Fl(3+1)24s87m21M Octagonal tower and dwelling

Ria de Cedeira

1687.6   **Punta del Sarridal** Oc.WR.6s39m11M Red round tower Shore-R-145°-W-172°-R-shore

1688   **Punta Promontorio** Oc(4)10s24m11M White six sided tower

1689 **Breakwater head** Fl(2)R.7s10m4M Red round tower
1689.2 **Piedra de Media Mar** Fl(2)5s12m4M White truncated conical tower
1690 **P de la Frouseira** Fl(5)15s73m20M Pyramidal concrete tower, green cupola
1692 **Cabo Prior** Fl(1+2)15s105m22M Six sided stone tower on dwelling
1693 **Punta del Castro** Fl(2)7s42m8M White six sided tower

Ria de El Ferrol

1694 **Cabo Prioriño Chico** Fl.5s34m23M White octagonal tower on dwelling
1695 **San Cristobal** Oc(2)WR.10s19m7M 042°-W-053°-R-042° White truncated conical tower
1696 **San Martin Ldg lts 085.2°** *Front* Fl.1.5s10m5M White masonry tower
1696.1 *Rear* Oc.4s5M White masonry tower
1697 **C de la Palma** Oc(1+2)7s9m7M Round granite tower on house
1698.7 **Muelle Ladreda head** Fl.G.5s7m3M Green metal column
1698.84 **Curuxeiros head** Fl(4)R.11s.5m3M Red column
1698.96 **Dársena No.2 head** Fl(2+1)G.12s9m3M Green truncated conical tower, red band
There are many other lights in the harbour at jetty corners; only the major ones are shown above

Ares

1703 **Ares breakwater head** Fl(3)R.9s10m5M Red round tower

Sada Marina, Puerto de Fontán

1700 **Breakwater head** Fl(4)G.11s13m5M Green round tower
1700.15 **Muelle Pesquero NE** Fl(2)R.7s6m1M Red post
1700.2 **SW corner** Fl(3)G.11s6m1M Green post
1700.4 **Muelle end** Fl.G.5s6m1M Green post
1700.5 **Elbow** Fl(2)G.7s6m1M Green post
1702 **Pulgueira jetty head** Fl.R.5s6m1M Red post

Ria de Betanzos

1702.9 **Punta de San Pedro** Fl(2)WR.7s7m3M 350.5°-W-355.5°-R-350.5° Red post

La Coruña

1704 **Torre de Hércules** Fl(4)20s104m23M Square stone tower, octagonal top
1704.01 165m NW Siren Mo(L)30s
1706 **Punta Mera Ldg lts 108.5°** *Front* Oc.WR.4s54m8M White octagonal tower 000°-R-023° 100.5°-R-105.5°-W-114.5°-R-153° Racon
1708 *Rear* Fl.4s79m8M White octagonal tower
1710 **P Flateira Ldg lts 182°** *Front* Iso.WRG.2s27m10-7M Red and white chequered square tower 146°-G-180°-W-184°-R-218°
1710.1 *Rear* Oc.R.4s52m3M Red and white chequered square tower
1714 **Dique de Abrigo end** Fl.G.3s16m6M Truncated conical masonry tower
1716 **Castillo de San Antón** Fl(2)G.7s15m6M Six sided tower
1716.2 **Muelle del Centenario NW** Fl(3)R.9s9m3M Red post
1716.4 **NE** Fl(2)R.7s9m5M Red post
1716.6 **SE** Oc(2)G.5s9m4M Green post
1717 **Muelle del est head** Fl(4)R.11s10m1M Red round tower
1718 **Marina entrance E** Fl(4)G.11s9m1M Green post
1720 **Marina entrance W** Q.R.9m2M Red post
1723 **Oil pier** Fl(2+1)R.21s3M Red truncated conical tower, green band
There are other lights further S in the harbour and on jetty corners; only the ones between entrance and marina are shown

2. WAYPOINTS

There are clear direct tracks carrying at least 2m to a width of 400m between adjacent waypoints unless the space between is marked with -----. Nevertheless the waypoints and the tracks between them must be plotted and checked on an up-to-date chart before being used for navigation. Waypoints marked -- are in La Gironde river and are for planning purposes only.

The Atlantic coast of France

I Pointe de la Coubre to Cabo Higuer

⊕501	BXA Gironde	45°37′.50N	01°27′.57W
⊕502	Palmyre	45°39′.34N	01°10′.39W
⊕503	Bonne Anse	45°40′.34N	01°11′.49W

⊕504	Passe de Sud	45°30′.00N	01°15′.54W
⊕505	Cordouan	45°32′.63N	01°08′.25W

⊕506	Royan	45°36′.72N	01°02′.08W
⊕507	Port Bloc	45°34′.22N	01°03′.57W
⊕508	Port Médoc	45°33′.54N	01°03′.50W
⊕509	Meschers	45°33′.10N	00°56′.48W

⊕510	Mortagne	45°28′.20N	00°48′.99W

⊕511	Pauillac	45°11′.90N	00°44′.20W

⊕512	Blaye	45°07′.50N	00°40′.10W

⊕513--	Bourg	45°02′.19N	00°33′.50W

⊕514--	Cavernes	44°56′.20N	00°26′.50W

⊕515--	Bordeaux (Pont de Pierre)	44°50′.00N	00°34′.70W

⊕516	ATT Arcachon	44°34′.74N	01°18′.72W
⊕517	La Salle	44°30′.45N	01°17′.78W

No waypoints are given for ports inside the Bassin d'Arcachon.

⊕518	Capbreton	43°39′.25N	01°27′.48W
⊕519	Bayonne	43°31′.94N	01°32′.50W
⊕520	Biarritz	43°29′.00N	01°34′.00W

⊕521	St Jean-de-Luz	43°24′.23N	01°41′.82W

⊕522	Hendaye Fuenterrabía Gurutzeaundi	43°23′.44N	01°46′.54W
⊕523	Cabo Higuer	43°24′.24N	01°47′.50W

The north coast of Spain

II Cabo Higuer to Cabo Mayor

⊕524	P. Biosar	43°23′.00N	01°51,60W
⊕525	Pasajes	43°20′.75N	01°56′.60W
⊕526	P. Mompas	43°20′.90N	01°58′.30W
⊕527	S. Sebastián	43°19′.80N	01°59′.96W
⊕528	Orio	43°18′.40N	02°07′.80W
⊕529	Getaria Zarauz	43°18′.13N	02°11′.00W
⊕530	I. de San Anton	43°18′.94N	02°12′.00W
⊕531	Zumaia	43°18′.76N	02°14′.70W
⊕532	Deva	43°18′.80N	02°20′.70W
⊕533	Motrico	43°19′.03N	02°21′.75W
⊕534	Ondárroa	43°19′.70N	02°24′.70W
⊕535	Saustan	43°21′.34N	02°27′.08W
⊕536	Lequeitio	43°22′.20N	02°29′.75W
⊕537	C. de Catalina	43°22′.18N	02°30′.13W
⊕538	Río de Ea	43°24′.00N	02°34′.78W
⊕539	Elanchove	43°24′.43N	02°37′.28W
⊕540	C. Ogoño	43°25′.33N	02°38′.38W
⊕541	I. de Izaro	43°25′.83N	02°41′.30W

⊕542 Mundaca   43°25´.25N   02°41´.84W
       Bermeo
⊕543 C. Machicaco   43°28´.33N   02°45´.18W
⊕544 Bakio   43°27´.01N   02°48´.48W
⊕545 Arminza   43°27´.26N   02°53´.69W
⊕546 C. Villano   43°28´.71N   02°57´.00W
⊕547 Plencia   43°25´.23N   02°57´.58W
⊕548 Bilbao   43°23´.53N   03°04´.67W
⊕549 C. Urdiales   43°22´.70N   03°12´.00W
⊕550 P. del Rabanal   43°24´.13N   03°12´.82W
⊕551 Río de Oriñon   43°25´.27N   03°19´.88W
⊕552 Laredo   43°26´.10N   03°25´.60W
       Santoña
       P. del Pasaje
       Colindres

⊕553 P. Pescador   43°28´.73N   03°25´.57W
⊕554 Río Ajo   43°31´.24N   03°34´.28W
⊕555 Cabo Ajo   43°31´.53N   03°35´.08W
⊕556 Galizano   43°29´.54N   03°41´.37W
⊕557 Santander   43°28´.50N   03°44´.48W
⊕558 Cabo Mayor   43°29´.73N   03°47´.08W

III Cabo Mayor to Cabo Peñas
⊕559 S. Pedro del Mar   43°30´.00N   03°50´.40W
⊕560 Río de Mogro   43°27´.70N   03°58´.60W
⊕561 Suances   43°27´.10N   04°02´.75W
⊕562 Cabera   43°26´.40N   04°04´.65W
⊕563 Luaña   43°24´.60N   04°13´.20W
⊕564 Comillas   43°23´.80N   04°16´.98W
⊕565 Rabia   43°24´.40N   04°19´.16W
⊕566 C. Oriambre   43°25´.20N   04°20´.09W
⊕567 S. V. de la Barquera 43°23´.80N 04°22´.92W
⊕568 Tina Menor   43°24´.30N   04°28´.20W
⊕569 Tina Mayor   43°24´.50N   04°30´.70W
⊕570 Santiuste   43°24´.70N   04°34´.17W
⊕571 Llanes   43°25´.30N   04°44´.00W
⊕572 Póo   43°26´.55N   04°46´.81W
⊕573 Celorio   43°26´.75N   04°48´.55W
⊕574 Niembro   43°27´.10N   04°49´.50W
⊕575 S. Antonio de Mar 43°28´.40N   04°55´.30W
⊕576 Ribadesella   43°28´.51N   05°04´.00W
⊕577 P. de la Sierra   43°29´.50N   05°07´.09W
⊕578 Lastres   43°30´.85N   05°15´.20W
⊕579 Cabo Lastres   43°33´.00N   05°17´.70W
⊕580 Villaviciosa   43°33´.04N   05°23´.00W
       Tazones
⊕581 P. Olivo   43°33´.90N   05°24´.70W
⊕582 Gijón   43°33´.70N   05°40´.18W
⊕583 Musel   43°34´.00N   05°40´.00W
⊕584 Candas   43°36´.43N   05°44´.60W
⊕585 Luanco   43°37´.35N   05°45´.12W
⊕586 Lumeres   43°39´.43N   05°48´.50W
⊕587 Cabo Peñas   43°41´.07N   05°51´.25W
⊕588 Avilés   43°35´.83N   05°57´.30W

IV Cabo Peñas to Punta Runcadoira
⊕589 C. Vidrias   43°35´.08N   06°01´.75W
⊕590 San Esteban de
       Pravia   43°34´.60N   06°04´.50W
⊕591 Cudillero   43°34´.54N   06°06´.20W
⊕592 Ens de Artedo   43°35´.20N   06°11´.40W
⊕593 C. Vidio   43°36´.33N   06°14´.69W
⊕594 C. Busto   43°35´.15N   06°29´.10W

⊕595 Río Canero   43°33´.54N   06°29´.18W
⊕596 Luarca   43°33´.45N   06°32´.32W
⊕597 P. del Cuerno   43°34´.08N   06°35´.68W
⊕598 Romanellas   43°34´.93N   06°37´.79W
⊕599 Vega   43°34´.43N   06°39´.13W
⊕600 Navia   43°34´.14N   06°43´.42W
       San Augustin
⊕601 P. Engaramada   43°34´.94N   06°46´.09W
⊕602 Viavélez   43°34´.42N   06°51´.05W
⊕603 R. de Porcia   43°34´.25N   06°52´.90W

⊕604 San Sebastián   43°35´.00N   06°57´.08W
⊕605 Tapia   43°34´.35N   06°57´.39W
⊕606 Ribadeo   43°33´.76N   07°02´.27W
⊕607 Rinlo   43°34´.23N   07°06´.28W
⊕608 En de la Lousa   43°34´.23N   07°07´.59W
⊕609 Foz   43°34´.73N   07°14´.20W
⊕610 Río de Oro   43°35´.44N   07°16´.28W
⊕611 Burela   43°39´.24N   07°19´.08W
⊕612 Río Junco   43°42´.20N   07°24´.10W
⊕613 Los Farallones   43°42´.55N   07°23´.59W
⊕614 San Ciprián   43°42´.68N   07°26´.08W
⊕615 P. Alumina   43°42´.83N   07°27´.20W

V Punta Runcadoira to Torre de Hercules
⊕616 I. Amarón   43°44´.43N   07°28´.59W
⊕617 Portocelo   43°44´.43N   07°30´.60W
⊕618 I. Runcadoira   43°44´.60N   07°31´.34W
⊕619 Viveiro   43°43´.00N   07°35´.58W
⊕620 I. Coelleira   43°46´.25N   07°38´.00W
⊕621 Barquero   43°46´.34N   07°39´.00W
⊕622 Est de Bares   43°48´.04N   07°40´.15W
⊕623 Espasante   43°43´.38N   07°50´.05W
       E. Santa Marta
⊕624 Cariño   43°44´.24N   07°50´.68W
⊕625 C. Ortegal   43°47´.68N   07°51´.69W
⊕626 P. Candelaria   43°42´.74N   08°04´.09W
⊕627 Cedeira   43°40´.01N   08°04´.87W
⊕628 C. Frouseira   43°38´.54N   08°10´.79W
⊕629 C. Prior   43°33´.01N   08°20´.08W
⊕630 El Ferrol   43°26´.42N   08°21´.59W
⊕631 Ares   43°24´.60N   08°13´.88W
⊕632 Sada/Fontán   43°21´.63N   08°14´.39W

⊕633 La Coruña   43°22´.00N   08°22´.00W

3. CHARTS

CHARTS FOR PART I
British Admiralty Charts
1102 Bayonne to Santander (200)
1104 Bay of Biscay (1000)
1343 River L'Adour, Bayonne, Anglet. St Jean-de-Luz (10)
2664 La Coubre to Arcachon (200)
2750 Arcachon Basin (49)
3057 La Coubre to Négarde (50)
3058 Entrance to La Gironde (25)
3068 La Gironde (var)
3069 Garonne

SHOM charts
6557 Boucau, Bayonne (50)
6558 Bayonne to San Sebastián (50)
6766 Bassin d'Arcachon (49)
6786 Biscarosse to San Sebastián (130)
6991 La Gironde to Cabo Peñas (368)
7070 Oléron to Arcachon (167)
7425 Embouchure de La Gironde (25)
7426 La Coubre to Négarde (52)

Imray charts
C41   Les Sables d'Olonne to La Gironde (10.9)
       Plans: Jard-sur-Mer, Bourgenay, Ars-en-Ré,
       St-Martin-de-Ré, La Flotte-en-Ré, Rochefort, Douhet,
       St-Denis d'Oléron, Rade de Pallice, Boyardville,
       La Rochelle and Port des Minimes, Royan
C42   Embouchure de la Gironde to Bordeaux and
       Arcachon (12.7)
       Plans: Royan, Pauillac, Port Bloc, Bordeaux,
       Arcachon, La Garonne to Bordeaux, La Dordogne to
       Libourne

BRITISH ADMIRALTY AND IMRAY CHARTS
See list for large scale sheets

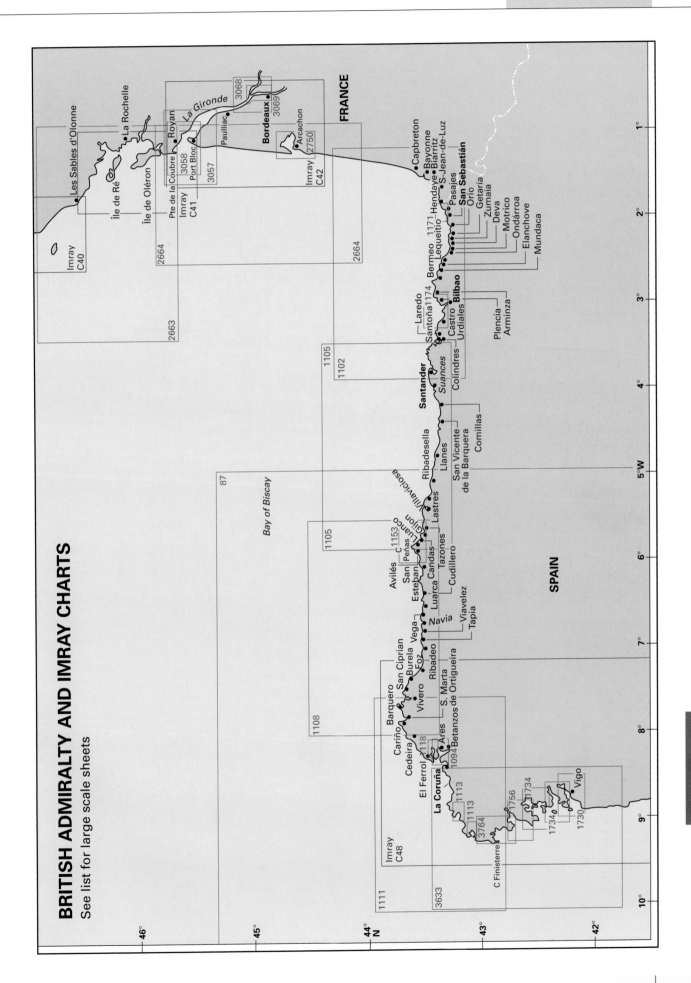

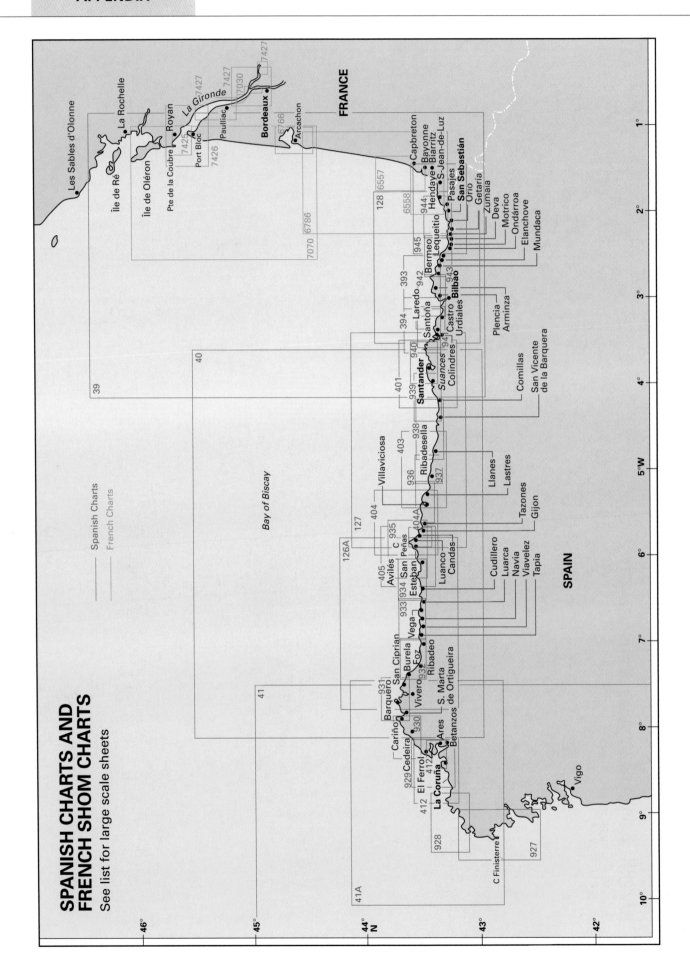

SPANISH CHARTS AND FRENCH SHOM CHARTS

See list for large scale sheets

Spanish Charts
French Charts

FRANCE

SPAIN

Bay of Biscay

Les Sables d'Olonne
La Rochelle
Île de Ré
Île de Oléron
Pte de la Coubre
Royan
La Gironde
Pauilliac
Port Bloc
Bordeaux
Arcachon
Capbreton
Bayonne
Biarritz
Hendaye
S-Jean-de-Luz
Pasajes
San Sebastián
Getaria
Orio
Zumaia
Deva
Motrico
Ondárroa
Elanchove
Mundaca
Bermeo
Lequeitio
Laredo
Santoña
Castro
Bilbao
Urdiales
Plencia
Arminza
Santander
Suances
Colindres
Comillas
San Vicente de la Barquera
Villaviciosa
Ribadesella
Llanes
Lastres
Tazones
Gijon
Cudillero
Luarca
Navia
Viavelez
Tapia
Luanco
Candas
San Peñas
Avilés
Esteban
San Ciprian
Burela
Foz
Ribadeo
S. Marta
de Ortigueira
Vivero
Barquero
Cariño
Cedeira
Ares
Betanzos
El Ferrol
La Coruña
Vigo
C Finisterre

7427
7030
7425
7426
6766
6786
7070
6557
6558
128
393
394
401
403
404
404A
405
40
39
41
41A
127
126A
945
944
943
942
941
940
939
938
937
936
935
934
933
932
931
930
929
928
927
412
C

46°
45°
44° N
43°
42°

1°
2°
3°
4°
5°W
6°
7°
8°
9°
10°

CHARTS FOR PART II, III, IV AND V

British Admiralty – North Coast of Spain
1094 Betanzos and La Coruña (25)
1096 North coast – Ribadeo (10)
1102 Bayonne to Santander (200)
1104 Bay of Biscay (1000)
1105 Cabo Ajo to Cabo Peñas (200)
1108 Gijón to Candelaria (200)
1110 La Coruña and approaches (10)
1111 Estaca de Bares to Cabo Finisterre (200)
1113 Plans on north coast (40)
1117 El Ferrol (10)
1118 Ria de El Ferrol (10)
1122 Harbours on north coast (25)
Cedeira, Barquero, Ribadeo, Carino, Viveiro, San Ciprián
1133 Ports on W of north coast of Spain (15)
Avilés, Luarca, Navia, San Esteban de Pravia
1142 Avilés (7.5)
1145 Santander (15)
1150 Ports on north coast of Spain (12.5)
Suances, S.V de la Barquera, Ribadesella, Lastres, Luanco
1153 Approaches to Gijón (10)
1154 Gijón (10)
1157 Pasajes (5)
1171 Ports on E of N coast of Spain (60)
Getaria, Ondárroa, Lequeitio, Bermeo, Elanchove, Santona, Castro Urdiales
1172 Bermeo and Mundaca (10)
1173 Bilbao (12.5)
1174 Approaches to Bilbao

Imray charts
C18 Western Approaches to the English Channel and Biscay (100)
C48 La Coruña to Porto (35)
Plans: Ria de Vivero, Ria de Cedeira, Rias de Ares and Betanzos, La Coruña, Ria de Camariñas, Ria de Muros, Ria de Arosa, Ria de Vigo, Viana do Castelo, Rias de Corme and Lage, Ria de Pontevedra, Póvoa de Varzim, Leixões

SPANISH CHARTS FOR PART II, III, IV AND V

North coast of Spain from E to W
39 De Isla de Ré a Cabo Mayor (35)
128 De Cabo Ajo a Cabo Higuer (15.6)
944 Del Río Bidasoa a Getaria (40.4)
3910 Ria de Hondarribia – Fuenterrabía (12.5)
Puerto de Donostia – San Sebastián (7.5)
3911 Ria y Puerto Pasaia-Pasajes (5.0)
943 De Getaria a Cabo Ogoño (40.5)
3921 Puertos de Getaria y Zumaia (10)
3922 Ens. de Deva y Puertos de Motrico y Ondárroa (10)
393 Del Puerto de Lequeitio al Puerto de Bilbao (50)
Lequeitio (7.5)
Elanchove (7.5)
3931 Puertos de Bermeo y Mundaca (10)
394 Del Cabo Villano al Cabo Ajo (50)
3941 Puerto de Bilbao (12.5)
Ria de Bilbao (25)
394A Aproches de Puerto de Bilbao (50)
Puerto de Castro Urdiales (10)
3942 Ria de Santoña (12.5)
40 De Cabo de Ajo a Cabo Ortegal (35)
127 De Cabo Peãs a Cabo Ajo (17.5)
401 Del Cabo de Ajo a la Punta Calderón (50)
4011 Puerto de Santander (15)
939 De la Virgen del Mar a Ria de Rabia (40.4)
4012 Ria de Suances (10)
938 De Comillas al Puerto de Llanes (40.4)
4021 Río y Puerto de San Vicente de la Barquera (10)
403 De la Punta Ballota a Cabo Lastres (50)
4031 Barra y Puerto de Ribadesella (10)
4041 Río y Puerto de Esteban de Pravia (10)
Puertos de El Puntal y Tazones (15)
Puerto de Lastres (15)
Puertos de Candas y Luanco (15)
404 Del Cabo Lastres al Cabo Peñas (50)
404A Aproches al Puerto de Gijón (25)
4042 Puerto de Gijón (10)
405 Del Cabo San Lorenzo al Cabo Vidio
126A Dela Estaca de Bares a Cabo Peñas (15.6)
405A Aproches a la Rioa de Avilés (25)
Puerto de Cudillero (10)
4052 Ria de Avilés (10)
934 De San Esteban de Pravia a Luarca (40.3)
4061 Puerto de Luarca (10)
933 De Luarca a Las Pantorgas (40.3)
Puerto de Viavélez (5)
932 De las Pantorgas a San Ciprián (40.3)
4071 Ria de Ribadeo (10)
931 De San Ciprián a Cabo Ortegal (40.2)
41 De Cabo de al Estaca de Bares a Río Lima (35)
41A La Estaca de Bares a Cabo Finisterre (20)
930 De Cabo Ortegal a Cabo Prior (40.3)
412 De la Punta Frouseira a las Islas Sisargas (50)
412A Rias de El Ferrol, Ares, Betanzos y La Coruña (50)

4. GLOSSARY OF SPANISH TERMS APPLICABLE TO THIS PILOT

A more complete glossary is given in the *Yachtsman's Ten Language Dictionary* compiled by Barbara Webb and Michael Manton with the Cruising Association (Adlard Coles Nautical). Terms related to meteorology and sea state follow at the end of each section.

General and chartwork terms

English	Spanish
anchor, to	fondear
anchorage	fondeadero, ancladero
basin, dock	dársena
bay	bahía, ensenada
beach	playa
beacon	baliza
beam	manga
berth	atracar
black	negro
blue	azul
boatbuilder	astillero
bottled gas	cilindro de gas, carga de gas
breakwater	rompeolas, muelle
buoy	boya
bus	autobús
cape	cabo
car hire	aquilar coche
chandlery (shop)	efectos navales, apetrachamento
channel	canal
charts	cartas náuticas
church	iglesia
crane	grua
creek	estero
Customs	Aduana
deep	profundo
depth	sonda, profundidad
diesel	gasoil
draught	calado
dredged	dragado
dyke, pier	dique
east	este
eastern	levante, oriental
electricity	electricidad
engineer, mechanic	ingeniero, mecánico
entrance	boca, entrada
factory	fábrica
foul, dirty	sucio
gravel	cascajo
green	verde
harbourmaster	diretor do porto
height, clearance	altura
high tide	pleamar, marea alta
high	alto/a
ice	hielo
inlet, cove	ensenada
island	isla
islet, skerry	islote
isthmus	istmo
jetty, pier	malecón
knots	nudos
lake	lago
laundry, launderette	lavandería, l. automática
leading line, transit	enfilación
leeward	sotavento
length overall	eslora total
lighthouse	faro
lock	esclusa
low tide	bajamar, marea baja
mailing address	dirección de correo

English	Spanish
marina, yacht harbour	puerto deportivo, dársena de yates
medical services	servicios médiocos
mud	fango
mussel rafts	viveros
narrows	estrecho
north	norte
orange	anaranjado
owner	propietario
paraffin	parafina
petrol	gasolina
pier, quay, dock	muelle
point	punta
pontoon	pantalán
port (side)	babor
Port of Registry	Puerto de Matrícula
port office	capitanía
post office	oficina de correos
quay	muelle
ramp	rampa
range (tidal)	repunte
red	rojo
reef	arrecife
reef, spit	restinga
registration number	ro registo
repairs	reparacións
rock, stone	roca, piedra
root (eg. of mole)	raíz
sailing boat	barca de vela
sailmaker, sail repairs	velero, reparacións velass
saltpans	salinas
sand	arena
sea	mar
seal, to	precintar
shoal, low	bajo
shops	tiendas, almacéns
shore, edge	orilla
showers (washing)	duchas
slab, flat rock	laja
slack water, tidal stand	repunte
slipway	varadero
small	pequeño
south	sur
southern	meridional
starboard	estribor
strait	estrecho
supermarket	supermercado
tower	torre
travel-lift	grua giratoria, pórtico elevador
water (drinking)	agua potable
weather forecast	previsión/boletin, metereológico
weed	alga
weight	peso
west	oeste
western	occidental
white	blanco
windward	barlovento
works (building)	obras
yacht (sailing)	barca de vela
yacht club	club náutico
yellow	amarillo

Meteorology and sea state

calm (Force 0, 0–1kts)	calma
light airs (Force 1, 1–3kts)	ventolina
light breeze (Force 2, 4–6kts)	flojitoa
gentle breeze (Force, 7–10kts)	flojo, brisa suave
moderate breeze (Force 4, 11–16kts)	bonancible
fresh breeze (Force 5, 17–21kts)	fresquito
strong breeze (Force 6, 22–27kts)	fresco, brisa forte
near gale (Force 7, 28–33kts)	frescachón
gale (Force 8, 34–40kts)	duro
severe gale (Force 9, 41–47kts)	muy duro
storm (Force 10, 48–55kts)	temporal

English	Spanish
violent storm (Force 11, 56–63kts)	borrasca, tempestad
hurricane (Force 12, 64+kts)	huracán
breakers	rompientes
cloudy	nubloso
depression (low)	depresión
fog	niebla
gust	racha
hail	granizada
mist	neblina
overfalls, tide race	escarceos
rain	lluvia
ridge (high)	dorsal
rough sea	mar gruesa
short, steep sea	mar corta
shower	aguacero
slight sea	marejadilla
squall	turbonada
swell	mar de leva
thunderstorm	tempestad

General and chartwork terms

Spanish	English
Aduana	Customs
agua potable	water (drinking)
alga	weed
almacéns	shops
alto/a	high
altura	height, clearance
amarillo	yellow
anaranjado	orange
ancladero	anchorage
apetrachamento	chandlery (shop)
aquilar coche	car hire
arena	sand
arrecife	reef
astillero	boatbuilder
atracar	berth
autobús	bus
azul	blue
babor	port (side)
bahía	bay
bajamar	low tide
bajo	shoal, low
baliza	beacon
barca de vela	sailing boat, yacht
barlovento	windward
blanco	white
boca	entrance
boya	buoy
cabo	cape
calado	draught
canal	channel
capitanía	port office
carga de gas	bottled gas
cartas náuticas	charts
cascajo	gravel
cilindro de gas	bottled gas
club náutico	yacht club
dársena de yates	marina, yacht harbour
dársena	basin, dock
dique	dyke, pier
dirección de correo	mailing address
diretor do porto	harbourmaster
dragado	dredged
duchas	showers (washing)
efectos navales	chandlery (shop)
electricidad	electricity
enfilación	leading line, transit
ensenada	bay, inlet, cove
entrada	entrance
esclusa	lock

Spanish	English
eslora total	length overall
este	east
estero	creek
estrecho	narrows, strait
estribor	starboard
fábrica	factory
fango	mud
faro	lighthouse
fondeadero	anchorage
fondear	anchor, to
gasoil	diesel
gasolina	petrol
grua giratoria	travel-lift
grua	crane
hielo	ice
iglesia	church
ingeniero, mecánico	engineer mechanic
isla	island
islote	islet, skerry
istmo	isthmus
lago	lake
laja	slab, flat rock
lavandería, l. automática	laundry, launderette
levante	eastern
malecón	jetty, pier
manga	beam
mar	sea
marea alta	high tide
marea baja	low tide
matricula	registration number
meridional	southern
muelle	breakwater, pier, quay, dock
negro	black
norte	north
nudos	knots
obras	works (building)
occidental	western
oeste	west
oficina de correos	post office
oriental	eastern
orilla	shore, edge
pantalán	pontoon
parafina	paraffin
pequeño	small
peso	weight
piedra	rock, stone
playa	beach
pleamar	high tide
pórtico elevador	travel-lift
precintar	seal, to
previsión/boletin metereológico	weather forecast
profundidad	depth
profundo	deep
propietario	owner
Puerto de Matrícula	Port of Registry
puerto deportivo	marina, yacht harbour
punta	point
raíz	root (eg. of mole)
rampa	ramp
reparacións	repairs
repunte	tidal range, stand, slack water
restinga	reef, spit
roca	rock
rojo	red
rompeolas	breakwater
salinas	saltpans
servicios médiocos	medical services
sonda	depth
sotavento	leeward
sucio	foul, dirty
supermercado	supermarket

Spanish	English
sur	south
tiendas	shops
torre	tower
varadero	slipway
velero	sailmaker,
reparacións velas	sail repairs
verde	green
viveros	mussel rafts

Meteorology and sea state

calma	calm (Force 0, 0–1kts)
ventolina	light airs (Force 1, 1–3kts)
flojito	light breeze (Force 2, 4–6kts)
flojo	gentle breeze (Force, 7–10kts)
bonancible	moderate breeze (Force 4, 11–16kts)
fresquito	fresh breeze (Force 5, 17–21kts)
fresco	strong breeze (Force 6, 22–27kts)
frescachón	near gale (Force 7, 28–33kts)
duro	gale (Force 8, 34–40kts)
muy duro	severe gale (Force 9, 41–47kts)
temporal	storm (Force 10, 48–55kts)
borrasca, tempestad	violent storm (Force 11, 56–63kts)
huracán	hurricane (Force 12, 64+kts)
aguacero	shower
depresión	depression (low)
dorsal	ridge (high)
escarceos	overfalls, tide race
granizada	hail
lluvia	rain
mar corta	short, steep sea
mar de leva	swell
mar gruesa	rough sea
marejadilla	slight sea
neblina	mist
niebla	fog
nubloso	cloudy
racha	gust
rompientes	breakers
tempestad	thunderstorm
turbonada	squall

Abbreviations used on Spanish charts

Lights

F.	Fixed
D.	Flashing
F.D.	Fixed and flashing
F.Gp.D.	Fixed and group flashing
Ct.	Quick flashing
Gp.Ct.	Interrupted quick flashing
Oc.	Occulting
Gp.Oc.	Group occulting
Iso	Isophase
Mo.	Morse

Colours

am.	Yellow
az.	Blue
b.	White
n.	Black
r.	Red
v.	Green

Seabed

A	Sand
Al	Weed
R.	Rock
F	Mud
Co.	Gravel

Useful phrases on arrival

Donde puedo amarrar?	Where can I moor?
A donde debo ir?	Where should I go?
Puedo amarrar al costado, por favor?	Can I moor alongside you, please?
Que es la profundidad?	What is the depth?
Para una noche	For one night
Donde es el capitanía?	Where is the harbour office?

5. SUGGESTED YACHT/CREW PARTICULARS LIST

Informacion de Yates
Nombre del yate (Name of Yacht)
Matricula (Flag)
Puerto asiento (Port of Registry)
Numero asiento (Registration number)
Tonelada asiento peso neto (Net registered tonnage)
Eslora (Length)
Manga (Beam)
Calado (Draught)
Propietario (Owner)
Nombre de Capitan del yate (Skipper's name) Passport number
Nombres de tripulantes (Crew names) Passport numbers
Puerto ultimo (Coming from)
Puerto proximo (Going to)
Llegarda el (Arrival date) *Hora* (Time)
Salido el (Departure date) *Hora* (Time)

Index

Ajo, Río, 97
Alúmina Española, Puerto, 163
Andernos-les-Bains, 32
Anglet Marina, 37–8
Arcachon, Bassin d', 28–34
Arcachon, Port d', 30
Ares, 180, 182–3
  Marina, 182
  Ria de, 183
Ares, Port d', 32
Arminza, 81–2
Artabro, Golfo, 180–9
Artedo, Ensenada de, 143
Audenge, Port d', 33–4
Avilés, 135–6

Baie de Chingoody, 45
Baie de Fontarrabie (Fuentarrabia),
  43–5
Bakio, Ensenada de, 81
Bares, 170
Barquero, 169, 171
Barquero, Ria del, 169–71
Barquero, Rìo, 170
Basques, 47
Bassin d'Arcachon, 28–34
Bayonne, 37–8
bearings
  France, 6
  Spain, 53
Bègles, 27
Bélisaire, 31
Bermeo, 76, 77, 79–80
Betanzos, Ria de, 183
Bétey, Port du, 32–3
Biarritz, 39
bibliography
  France, 7
  Spain, 54
Bidasoa, Río, 43, 45
Bilbao, 85–8
Blaye, 20
Bloc, Port, 22
Bonne Anse, 15
Bordeaux, 25, 26–7
Bourg, 21
buoyage, 6, 54
Burela, 160–1

Cabera, Ensenada de, 108
Cabo Higuer, 44, 55
Cabo Machicaco, 55, 77
Cabo Peñas, 134, 135, 137
Cabo Prior, 179
Cabo de San Augustin, 148
Cala Bursa, Ensenada de, 58
Cala de Ortiguera, 148
Callognes, Port des, 22
Canal Latéral de la Garonne, 15, 27
Candas, 132
Canero, Ensenada y Río de, 143

Cantabrico, Marina del (Parayas), 100
Capbreton, 35–6
Cariño, 174
Cassy, Port de, 33
Castets, 27
Castro Urdiales, 89–90
Castro Vilela, Playa, 170
Castropol, 154, 156
Cavernes, 22
Cedeira, 177–9
Celorio, Ensenada de, 119
certificates
  France, 3
  Spain, 51
chart datum
  France, 5
  Spain, 53
charts
  France, 6, 196, 197, 198
  Spain, 54, 196, 197, 198
Chingoody, Baie de, 45
Ciboure, 40–2
Cillero, 167–8
Claouey, 32
Colindres, 96–7
Colleira, Isla, 169
Comillas, 109–10
Compelo, Playa, 170
Conac, Port de, 22
COSPAS/SARSAT, 5
CROSS Etel, 5
Cudillero, 141–2
Cuerno, Punta del, 145
currents
  France, 1–2
  Spain, 48
customs and excise
  France, 3
  Spain, 51

Deva, 68
documentation
  France, 3
  Spain, 51
Donostia (San Sebastin), 59–61

Ea, Río de, 73
El Ferrol, 180, 181
El Puntal, 127
Elanchove, 74–5
emergency services
  France, 5
  Spain, 52
Ensenada de Artedo, 143
Ensenada de Bakio, 81
Ensenada de Cabera, 108
Ensenada de Cala Bursa, 58
Ensenada de Canero, 143
Ensenada de Celorio, 119
Ensenada de la Lousa, 158
Ensenada de Luaña, 108

Ensenada de Lumeres, 134
Ensenada de Mera, 187
Ensenada de Póo, 118–19
Ensenada de Porcia, 151
Ensenada de Rabia, 110
Ensenada de Santa Marta, 173
Ensenada de Saustan, 72
Espasante, 172
Estaca de Bares, Punta, 172
European Union (EU), 3–4, 51, 52

ferries, Spain, 53
fiestas, Spain, 50
Figueras, 154, 155, 156
firing ranges, France, 7
fishing and fishing boats
  France, 4
  Spain, 51–2
fog
  France, 1
  Spain, 48
Fontainevieille, Port de, 33
Fontan, 184–5
Fontarrabie, Baie de (Fuentarrabia), 43–5
formalities
  France, 3
  Spain, 51
Foz, 158–9
Freneau, Port de, 22
Frouseira, Punta del, 179
fuel
  France, 2–3
  Spain, 50
Fuentarrabia (Baie de Fontarrabie),
  43–5

Gernika, 77
Getaria, 64–5
Getxo (Bilbao), 85, 87
Gijón, 129–31
glossary, 199–201
Golfo Artabro, 180–9
Grand Piquey, Port de la, 32
Gujan, Port de, 34
Gurutzeaundi, Puerto, 43–5

harbour dues, Spain, 52
health, Spain, 52–3
heights
  France, 6
  Spain, 53
Hendaye, Port, 43–4
Higuer, Cabo, 44, 55
Higuer, Rada de, 43–5
holidays, Spain, 50
Hondarribia Marina, 43–5
Hume, Port de la, 34

Ile aux Oiseaux, 31
inland waterways, France, 4
Isla Colleira, 169

Junco, Río, 161

La Coruña, 180, 186–9
La Gironde estuary, 9–27
La Graña (El Ferrol), 181
La Roquejada, 107
La Vigne, Port de, 32
Lanton, 33
Laredo, 92–3
Larraldénia, 40–2
Larros, Port de, 34
Las Arenas (Bilbao), 85, 86–7
Lastres, 124–5
laying-up
  France, 4
  Spain, 52
Lège, Port de, 32
Lequeitio, 72–3
  passage to Bermeo, 76–80
lifeboats, Spain, 52
lights
  France, 6, 190–1
  Spain, 54, 191–4
Llanes, 116–18
Lousa, Ensenada de la, 158
Luaña, Ensenada de, 108
Luanco, 133
Luarca, 143–4
Lumeres, Ensenada de, 134

Machicaco, Cabo, 55, 77
Marina del Cantabrico (Parayas), 100
maritime rescue
  France, 5
  Spain, 52
Maubert, Port, 22
medical advice, France, 5
Médoc, Port, 23
Mera, Ensenada de, 187
Meschers, 18
Mestras, Port de, 34
Meyran, Port de, 34
Mogro, Río de, 105
Monards, Port des, 22
Mondeo, Río, 183
Mortagne, 19
Motrico, 69–70
Mundaca, 77, 78
Mundaca, Río, 77
Musel, Puerto de, 131

Navia, 147–8
navigational information
  France, 5
  Spain, 53
Niembro, Ria de, 120–1

Oiseaux, Ile aux, 31
Ondárroa, 71
Oriñon, Río de, 91
Orio, Río de, 62–3
Oro, Río de, 159
Ortiguera, 175–6
Ortiguera, Cala de, 148

Parayas (Marina del Cantabrico), 100
Pasaje, Punta del, 96, 97
Pasajes, 57–8
Pauillac, 24–5

Pedreña Marina (Santander), 100–1
Peñas, Cabo, 134, 135, 137
Petit Vitrezay, Port de, 22
Picos de Europa, 46, 103, 113
Piraillan, Port de, 32
Playa Castro Vilela, 170
Playa Compelo, 170
Playa de San Antonio del Mar, 122
Playa de Xilloy, 170
Plencia, 83–4
Póo, Ensenada de, 118–19
Porcia, Ensenada y Río de, 151
Porcillan, 154, 155
Port d'Arcachon, 30
Port d'Ares, 32
Port d'Audenge, 33–4
Port du Bétey, 32–3
Port Bloc, 22
Port des Callognes, 22
Port de Cassy, 33
Port de Conac, 22
Port de Fontainevieille, 33
Port de Freneau, 22
Port de la Grand Piquey, 32
Port de Gujan, 34
Port Hendaye, 43–4
Port de la Hume, 34
Port de Larros, 34
Port de Lège, 32
Port Maubert, 22
Port Médoc, 23
Port de Mestras, 34
Port de Meyran, 34
Port des Monards, 22
Port de Petit Vitrezay, 22
Port de Piraillan, 32
Port des Portes Neuves, 22
Port St Georges de Didonne, 22
Port de St Sevrin d'Uzet, 22
Port de Talmont, 22
Port de Tassaut, 33
Port du Teich, 34
Port de la Teste, 34
Port de la Vigne, 32
Port de Vitrezay, 22
port radio stations, France, 7
Portes Neuves, Port de, 22
Portocelo, 166
Prior, Cabo, 179
provisions
  France, 2
  Spain, 49–50
Puentedueme, 183
Puerto Alumina Española, 163
Puerto Gurutzeaundi, 43–5
Puerto de Musel, 131
Punta del Cuerno, 145
Punta Estaca de Bares, 172
Punta del Frouseira, 179
Punta del Pasaje, 96, 97
Punta de Santa Catalina, 77

Rabia, Ria y Ensenada de, 110
Rada de Higuer, 43–5
radio services
  France, 5, 7
  Spain, 54
Red Cross, 5

rescue services
  France, 5
  Spain, 52
Ria de Ares, 183
Ria del Barquero, 169–71
Ria de Betanzos, 183
Ria de Canero, 143
Ria de Niembro, 120–1
Ria de Rabia, 110
Ria de San Pedro del Mar, 105
Ria de Santiuste, 116
Ria de Tina Mayor, 115
Ria de Tina Menor, 114
Ria de Villaviciosa, 126–7
Ribadeo, 155–6
Ribadesella, 122, 123
Rinlo, 157
Río Ajo, 97
Río Bidasoa, 43, 45
Río de Ea, 73
Río Junco, 161
Río de Mogro, 105
Río Mondeo, 183
Río Mundaca, 77
Río de Oriñon, 91
Río de Orio, 62–3
Río de Oro, 159
Río de Porcia, 151
Río Urumea, 59
Rodiles, 127
Royan, 16–17

Sada, 180, 184–5
  Marina, 184–5
St Georges de Didonne, Port, 22
St Jean-de-Luz, 40–2
St Sevrin d'Uzet, Port de, 22
Salinas, 136
San Antonio del Mar, Playa de, 122
San Augustin, Cabo de, 148
San Ciprián, 162–3
San Esteban de Pravia, 139–41
San Juan, 139, 140–1
San Pedro del Mar, Rìa de, 105
San Sebastián (Donostia), 59–61
San Vicente de la Barquera, 111–13
Santa Catalina, Punta de, 77
Santa Marta, Ensenada de, 173
Santa Marta de Ortiguera, 175–6
Santander, 98–102
Santiago de Compostela, 188
Santiuste, Ria de, 116
Santoña, 94–5, 97
Saustan, Ensenada de, 72
search and rescue
  France, 5
  Spain, 5
shopping
  France, 2
  Spain, 50
Socoa, 40–2
Socoburu Marina, 43–5
Spanish language, 199–201
Suances, 106–8
swell
  France, 2
  Spain, 48–9

Talmont, Port de, 22
Tapia, 151–2
Tassaut, Port de, 33
Tazones, 128
Teich, Port du, 34
telephones
  France, 3
  Spain, 50
Teste, Port de la, 34
tidal streams
  France, 1–2
  Spain, 48
Tina Mayor, Ria de, 115
Tina Menor, Ria de, 114
travel ashore, Spain, 53
Trompeloup, 24

Unquera, 115
Urumea, Río, 59

VAT, 4, 51
Vega, 145–6
Vegadeo, 154
Verdon, 23
Viavélez, 149–50
Vicedo, 169, 170, 171
Vigne, Port de la, 32
Villaviciosa, Ria de, 126–7
visibility
  France, 1
  Spain, 48
Vitrezay, Port de, 22
Viveiro, 167–8

water
  France, 2
  Spain, 50
waypoints
  France, 6, 195
  Spain, 53, 195–6

weather and safety broadcasts
  France, 5
  Spain, 54
winds
  France, 1
  Spain, 48

Xilloy, Playa de, 170

yacht clubs
  France, 4
  Spain, 51
yacht and equipment
  France, 2
  Spain, 49

Zarauz, 64
Zumaia, 65, 66–7